POSTWAR ARTILLERY
1945–PRESENT

THE ESSENTIAL
WEAPONS IDENTIFICATION GUIDE

POSTWAR ARTILLERY
1945–PRESENT

MICHAEL E. HASKEW

amber
BOOKS

This edition published in 2011 by
Amber Books Ltd
Bradley's Close
74–77 White Lion Street
London N1 9PF
United Kingdom
www.amberbooks.co.uk

A catalogue record for this book is available from the British Library.

ISBN: 978-1-907446-60-3

Project Editor: Michael Spilling
Design: Hawes Design
Picture Research: Terry Forshaw

Printed in China

PICTURE CREDITS
Art-Tech/Aerospace: 8, 12, 30, 41, 61, 94–97, 113, 149, 153
Art-Tech/MARS: 112
Cody Images: 10, 13, 58, 71
Corbis: 110 (Sygma/Christian Simonpietri), 126 (Reuters/Gil Cohen Morgan)
Press Association Images: 161 (Valery Levitin)
Rex Features: 165 (Sipa)
U.S. Department of Defense: endpapers, 6, 9, 68, 80, 83, 142–146, 159, 172

All artworks courtesy of Art-Tech/Aerospace except for the following which are
© Amber Books: 16(b), 73(b), 75(b), 77, 79(t), 86, 92(b), 101(b), 102–105(all),
114, 116(both), 119(b), 123, 125, 126, 129, 132, 137(t), 148, 153, 164(b),
166(both), 173, 175, 176(t), 179, 180(t), 181, 184–185(all)

Contents

Introduction

For centuries, artillery has demonstrated the
capability to change the course of history. Its
evolution through modern times has maintained
the potential to dominate the battlefield in a
tactical sense and to bring nations to the brink
of destruction or the negotiating table as an
instrument of strategic diplomacy. Conventional,
nuclear, biological and chemical weapons,
guided munitions and smart systems continue to
keep artillery relevant during the conflicts of the
twenty-first century. Although some have
theorized that the days are over when artillery
will dominate the battlefield landscape, a
student of recent history need only observe the
nature of combat since the end of World War II.
Artillery has not only exerted influence on
the ground; it has stretched into the sky and
beyond the horizon.

◀ **Infantry support**
Gunners with the US 31st Regimental Combat Team fire a 75mm (2.95in) recoilless rifle in support of
infantry units directly across the valley, somewhere in Korea, June 1951.

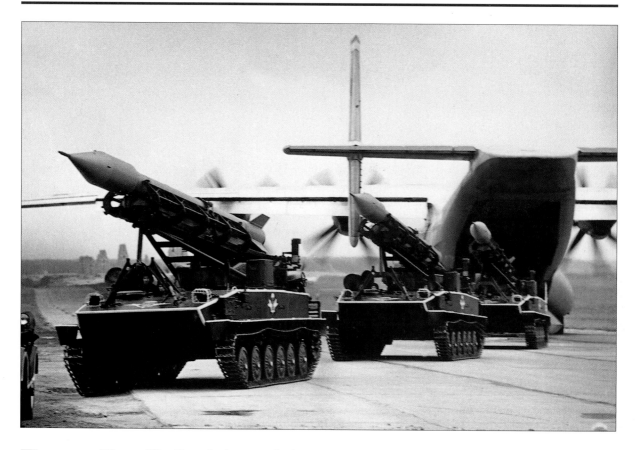

THE END OF WORLD WAR II marked a watershed in modern history. Weapons systems were modernized, upgraded and invented with astonishing rapidity. While the repercussions of the war itself are still being felt on a global scale, these advances in arms and armament have themselves become influencers during the last half-century and will continue as such in the future. The idea and application of artillery was altered perhaps more than any other weapon type as a result of the massive conflict of 1939–45.

Flash and fire

With a flash and a detonation of unprecedented destructive power, the nuclear age was born. With a cloud of smoke and flame, hurtling towards the stratosphere, the ballistic missile came into being. These awesome events have shaped the development and influence of artillery on the course of political and military events far beyond the ability of most to comprehend. Artillery, therefore, is at centre stage in modern military thinking. Civilian leaders and

▲ **Mobile nuclear threat**
Mounted on top of light tracked launchers, Soviet FROG-5 missiles are unloaded from a massive transport aircraft. Precursor of the more numerous FROG-7, the FROG-5 strategic missile was first deployed in the early 1960s. Its 503kg (1100lb) nuclear warhead had a range of 32km (20 miles).

military commanders must consider its potential impact on the outcome of battle more so than ever before. The introduction of artillery shells tipped with nuclear warheads; air defence missiles which control the skies for hundreds of kilometres around them; anti-tank projectiles capable of defeating the most advanced armoured vehicles; and intercontinental ballistic missiles packing such devastating power that they could destroy civilization as we know it in a matter of minutes – all give reason for analysts and observers to pause.

The prospect of devastating chemical and biological weapons has been sufficient to send troops to war around the world, while such capabilities at the disposal of terrorist organizations could place the lives of millions in peril.

Power and potential

'An artillery barrage is a terrifying thing,' wrote author Erich Maria Remarque in his classic *All Quiet on the Western Front*. While the image of a soldier huddled in a shell crater in the midst of the no man's land moonscape during World War I is familiar enough, such a scene has often been repeated. As General George S. Patton Jr noted at the end of World War II, there was no question in anyone's mind as to how the war was won. It was the artillery which made the difference.

During the modern era, technology and ingenuity – and indeed the flow of armed conflict itself – have not altered the conclusion that artillery is a deciding factor in the course of a fight. Prolonged air bombardment may well soften the resolve of an enemy to resist; however, the 1991 Gulf War and Operation Iraqi Freedom which followed a decade later were prosecuted to final victory by troops advancing on the ground, preceded by sustained artillery bombardment and accompanied by towed, self-propelled, air-defence and anti-tank artillery

▼ **Big gun raid**

A column of M109A2 155mm (6.1in) self-propelled howitzers of the US 29th Field Artillery Regiment drive through the town of Donje Caparde, Bosnia and Herzegovina, in the Zone of Separation, during a patrol in support of Operation Joint Endeavour, April 1996.

capable of engaging and defeating a mechanized and determined enemy.

While the complexity of artillery has increased substantially since 1945, the capabilities of artillery have grown exponentially. Not only is its destructive capacity unequalled in military history but artillery is also able to go more places, engage a greater variety of targets and displace more quickly than ever before. The introduction of lighter materials facilitates airlift and rapid deployment. The refinement of the laser, sophisticated radar and integrated fire-control systems results in astonishing accuracy. The well-trained and motivated soldier manipulates an offensive and defensive system of awesome complexity and immense destructive force. The future of the entire planet is placed in the hands of a relative few.

Considering a forward focus, the future of artillery as a tactical weapon seems assured, while its strategic implications are unlikely to diminish. From high-tech futuristic engagements between modern armies to the suppression of terrorist guerrillas ensconced in mountainous hideaways, artillery exerts its force today and will do so tomorrow with saturation and precision. In truth, modern artillery has assumed an authoritative role in both peace and war. Today, for those who are aware of its capabilities, the silence of artillery is as deafening as its roar.

Chapter 1

Cold War Europe, 1945–91

With the end of World War II, the map of Europe
was redrawn. Spheres of influence and differing world views
resulted in a face-off between two armed camps along a
closed border between East and West – and the drama was
to last half a century. For the armed forces of each, the
organization and firepower of modern artillery would shape
combat doctrine and serve to heighten the tension of the
Cold War. A new generation of technologically advanced
conventional artillery – towed, self-propelled, airmobile or
specifically designed for air defence – outfitted the ranks
of modern armies, while strategic and tactical artillery
capable of delivering nuclear warheads raised the
stakes in a global contest of wills.

◀ Show of strength
Red Army 2S3 (M1973) self-propelled guns take part in a parade in Moscow's Red Square, sometime
during the 1980s. Developed as a response the US Army's M109, the 2S3 provided highly mobile fire
support for motorized rifle and tank divisions.

Introduction

The Cold War in Europe presented specific offensive and defensive requirements for both NATO and Warsaw Pact forces, resulting in the refinement of strategic and tactical doctrines.

WHILE ARTILLERY is theoretically utilized in coordination with air assets and manoeuvring ground troops to gain victory on the battlefield, one US Army field manual states that aggressive employment of artillery may in itself serve as the decisive element in the defeat of enemy ground forces in certain circumstances, particularly when an aggressor assumes the offensive.

'Artillery theory employs the concept of fire strike, which is a severe and intense bombardment by all artillery weapons to defeat the enemy without the use of ground troops,' it reads. 'Artillery fires are laid down with such weight, volume, and accuracy that the artillery fire itself is an offensive.'

At the outset of the Cold War, it was apparent to Western military strategists that the potential to be on the receiving end of such a devastating utilization of offensive firepower was very real. The Soviet Red Army was by far the most capable military force on the European continent. Should the word be given, the tremendous artillery capability of the Red Army might devastate US and other troop concentrations in Western Europe, resulting in catastrophically high casualties and a loss of combat efficiency from which the defenders could not recover.

For a relatively brief period, the trump card for the West was the exclusive nuclear capability of the United States. Demonstrated with telling effect

▲ **Towed tank killers**
East German MT-LB tracked prime movers tow T12 (2A19) anti-tank guns on manoeuvres somewhere in Eastern Europe.

◄ **Popular model**
The Czech-built DANA 152mm (6in) self-propelled gun was cheap to manufacture and easy to maintain. First entering service in 1981, by 1994 over 750 units had been produced.

The armed force which achieved the upper hand more swiftly on the European battlefield might at least dictate the future of the continent, or what was left of it. Therefore, the development of tactical nuclear weapons became a priority for the armies of both NATO and the Warsaw Pact, which was formed by the Soviet Union and its satellite states of Eastern Europe in the spring of 1955.

against the Japanese cities of Hiroshima and Nagasaki in World War II, the nuclear edge was a perceived advantage for the US even though the number of atomic bombs available was either limited or zero and their delivery against Soviet targets would certainly be problematic. By the summer of 1949, even this perceived advantage for the US military had evaporated. Although the North Atlantic Treaty Organization (NATO) had been formed in the West for collective defence against Soviet aggression, that August the Soviets successfully detonated a plutonium bomb. The nuclear arms race was on.

While the superpowers expended billions of dollars and roubles to gain the upper hand with strategic nuclear arms, developing successive generations of intercontinental ballistic missiles (ICBMs) with multiple warheads, varied methods of delivery and destructive capabilities many times that of the bombs which had brought Japan to its knees in 1945, the issue of armies facing one another across hostile borders in Western Europe remained. Tension had heightened to a dangerous level even before 1950, with the Soviet blockade of Berlin and the subsequent airlift. The former allies had reached the brink of a shooting war less than three years after their defeat of Nazi Germany.

Tactical nuclear weapons

For both the United States and the Soviet Union it seemed likely that a strategic nuclear exchange would follow the initiation of ground combat in Europe.

While some military planners envisioned a war in Europe which would rival the scope of World War II in terms of troops and materiel involved, there was no doubt that both conventional artillery and tactical nuclear weapons delivered by means of artillery would be employed. The prospect for victory would be determined by the effectiveness of the first nuclear strikes and the capability of the manoeuvring ground troops to exploit the advantage gained.

Without doubt, the most logical strategy for NATO forces in Europe was that of tactical nuclear defence. In such a scenario, the artillery and the air forces of the NATO powers would serve as the delivery system for these nuclear weapons. Conventional weapons, such as tanks along with self-propelled guns and mechanized infantry, would subsequently assume the mobile offensive or maintain a strong defensive line to block the westward advance of Warsaw Pact forces.

During World War II, the Soviets had already demonstrated that their doctrine of massed conventional artillery could serve as an effective precursor to offensive operations. Tactical nuclear weapons would serve only to enhance the power of the Red Army to strike first, while the defensive capabilities of Red Army artillery were also well known. For both NATO and the Warsaw Pact one conclusion was inescapable. On the tactical level, artillery would serve as the weapon of decision on the ground. On the strategic plane, ICBMs might render the entire exercise moot.

Early Soviet artillery
1945–70

The Red Army possessed tremendous artillery assets at the close of World War II and began to modernize with missiles, radar-directed weapons and heavier guns in the coming years.

THE SPECTACULAR SOVIET COUNTERATTACK at Stalingrad, which eventually surrounded and annihilated the German Sixth Army, was preceded by a devastating artillery barrage. Massed cannon and howitzers wreaked havoc on German positions and enabled a rapid advance by Red Army ground troops.

This established success continued to dictate the offensive doctrine of Soviet military planners during the early years of the Cold War as they employed the proven Model 1942 76.2mm (3in) field gun in both an anti-tank and infantry support role and the 152mm (6in) gun-howitzer variants, which were capable of firing a 43.5kg (96lb) shell more than 17,000m (19,000 yards), among their standard field artillery weapons.

By 1955, the Red Army had deployed its first nuclear-capable artillery piece, the 152mm (6in) D-20 gun-howitzer, which eventually replaced the Model 1937 152mm (6in) weapon and could fire rocket-assisted ammunition up to 29,992m (32,800 yards). Developed by the F. Petrov Design Bureau, the D-20 could fire conventional shells at a rate of up to six per minute in a burst mode or one per minute at a sustained rate. It remains in use around the world today and has been built under licence as the Type 66 in the People's Republic of China.

As nuclear field artillery gained in importance, the development of missiles followed suit, and in the mid-1950s the Soviet Union took the lead in surface-to-air missile (SAM) deployment with the S-25 Berkut, or Golden Eagle, which was known to NATO as the SA-1 Guild. The first operational guided-missile system in the world, the SA-1's development was authorized in the summer of 1950. Besides the SAMs, the system included early-warning and targeting radar, fighter aircraft and Tupolev early-warning planes. As such, the coordination of the system was truly groundbreaking in modern warfare.

By the spring of 1955, batteries of SA-1 missiles were deployed in defensive positions around Moscow, while a companion, the mobile SA-2 Guideline missile, was also in the field. In the early 1960s, a supply of SA-1s was shipped to North Korea. Subsequent Soviet surface-to-air missiles were to gain notoriety defending the cities of Hanoi and Haiphong during the Vietnam War and in the

▲ **S-25 Berkut (SA-1 Guild)**

Soviet Air Defence Force, 1957

The S-25 Berkut, or SA-1 Guild in NATO nomenclature, was the first surface-to-air missile in the world to become operational. The SA-1 combined target-acquisition and early-warning radar and was based on a German design of World War II. The system was primarily deployed in defence of the Soviet capital of Moscow.

Specifications

Configuration: single, liquid-fuel rocket motor	Launch weight: 3500kg (7716lb)
Deployment: launch site	Range: 40km (24.8 miles)
Length: 12m (39ft 4in)	Launch preparation time: 5 minutes
Diameter: 700mm (27.5in)	

arsenals of Egypt and other Arab nations during the wars with Israel in 1967 and 1973.

Coordinated firepower

In the support of offensive operations, Soviet military doctrine stressed the importance of coordinated artillery action involving several tenets. These included continuous reconnaissance by ground, air and instrument capabilities; concentrated artillery support in the direction of the main attack; coordination of massed conventional artillery fires, nuclear missile attacks and air strikes; acquisition of targets for artillery, tactical air support and nuclear fire means; strong anti-tank reserves at regiment and higher levels; and continuous close coordination between all combat levels.

The Soviets stressed continuous fire support from artillery, and necessarily this meant that mobility was

a key component of the offensive. Artillery supporting the initial advance was expected to displace and follow the front-line battalions and regiments on a pre-planned basis. Theoretically, the ability of substantial artillery to keep pace with infantry posed problems which were solved at the lowest operational level with man-portable mortars or light towed weapons such as the 82mm (3.2in) PM-37 and PM-41 mortars. The PM-37 was capable of firing up to 30 rounds of high explosive per minute. Its 11.5kg (25.3lb) shell had a maximum range of 3040m (3325 yards), and due to its success on the battlefield, the PM-41, which was easier to manufacture, was introduced.

The heavier towed infantry mortar which was prevalent with the Red Army of the early Cold War was the 160mm (6.3in) M1943, which had been the heaviest weapon of its type utilized by the Red Army

▶ 85mm M1939 anti-aircraft gun

Soviet Army / 20th Air Defence Regiment, 1960

The longevity of the 85mm (3.3in) M1939 anti-aircraft gun was remarkable, spanning four decades from 1939 into the 1970s. The weapon was adept in both anti-aircraft and anti-tank roles and was utilized in later versions of the T-34 medium tank and the SU-85 self-propelled gun. It was widely exported and equipped units of the Egyptian and North Vietnamese armies.

Specifications	
Crew: 4	Weight: 3057kg (6000lb)
Calibre: 85mm (3.3in)	Range: 7620m (25,000ft)
Elevation: - 2 degrees to + 82 degrees	Muzzle velocity: 800m/sec (2625ft/sec)

◀ 160mm M1943 mortar

Soviet Army / 27th Guards Motorized Rifle Division, 1970

A heavy, breechloading mortar which was towed by a light truck or personnel carrier, the 160mm (6.3in) M1943 was deployed in brigades of 32 mortars, each brigade consisting of four battalions with eight weapons apiece. The heavy recoil of the weapon was absorbed by an internal system and a substantial baseplate.

Specifications	
Crew: 4	Weight: 1170kg (2580lb)
Calibre: 160mm (6.3in)	Range: 5150m (5630 yards)
Elevation: + 45 degrees to + 80 degrees	Muzzle velocity: 245m/sec (804ft/sec)

▲ BM-24 multiple rocket launcher

Soviet Army / 54th Artillery Regiment, 1955

Introduced in the early 1950s, the BM-24 introduced slight improvements over the BM-13 multiple-launch rocket system, which gained fame as the 'Stalin Organ' during World War II. Artillery and motorized infantry regiments of the Red Army fielded the BM-24, which was mounted atop a 6X6 truck and was later replaced by the BM-21.

Specifications

Crew: 6
Calibre: 240mm (9.45in)
Rocket length: 1.18m (46.45in)
Rocket weight: 112.5kg (248lb)
Range: 10,300m (11,265 yards)
Rate of fire: 2 rds/sec
System combat weight: 9200kg (10.14 tons)

Specifications

Crew: 3
Weight: 3300kg (7260lb)
Length: 4.995m (16ft 4.7in)
Width: 2.086m (6ft 10in)
Height: 1.18m (3ft 10.5in)
Engine: M-20E 41.25kW (55hp) 4-cylinder
   gasoline
Speed: 45km/h (28mph)
Road range: 250km (155 miles)
Armament: 1 x 57mm (2.2in) gun

▲ ASU-57 SP gun

Soviet Army / 78th Guards Airborne Division, 1969

Designed to be parachuted with a rocket-assisted apparatus into combat in order to support Red Army airborne divisions, the ASU-57 was an excellent design which remained in service with Soviet forces for more than 20 years. Although the weapon was light, using the engine of an automobile and with a welded aluminium hull construction, its firepower augmented the ability of airborne troops to sustain combat operations.

Specifications

Crew: 7
Weight: 50,167kg (110,600lb)
Engine: V-12-5 525kW (700hp) diesel
Armament: 1 x 420mm (16.5in) mortar

▲ 2B1 Oka self-propelled mortar

Soviet Army, not deployed, 1957

The Oka self-propelled mortar was an experimental 420mm (16.5in) mortar which was found to have numerous shortcomings, including a recoil which damaged drive sprockets, gears and mountings, a low rate of fire and continuing maintenance issues. Its development was abandoned by 1960 as resources were diverted to the production of tactical ballistic missiles.

during World War II. The M1943 was originally an upgunned version of the 120mm (4.7in) mortar; however, it was quickly determined that a breechloading weapon would be necessary since the weight of the projectile at 40.8kg (90lb) was too great for infantrymen to lift and load from the muzzle at a reasonable rate. As a breechloader, the M1943 could fire up to ten rounds per minute with a range of 5150m (5630 yards).

Even with advances in the mobility of surface-to-air missiles, the Soviets depended on anti-aircraft guns to provide the necessary defence against enemy planes. Among their finest guns of this type was the 85mm (3.3in) M1939, developed on the eve of World War II but unavailable in large numbers until 1942. The M1939 proved a versatile weapon and also equipped

later versions of the famed T-34 medium tank and the SU-85 self-propelled assault gun. M1939 crews were issued both anti-aircraft and anti-tank ammunition, and the weapon had an effective range against enemy planes of 7620m (25,000ft) while its muzzle velocity of 800 metres per second (2625 feet per second) was a key element in its effectiveness against armour. The M1939 remained in service with numerous armed forces into the 1970s.

The largest towed artillery piece fielded by the Red Army during the Cold War was the 180mm (7.1in) S-23 gun, which made its debut in 1954. Capable of firing nuclear ammunition, the S-23 had a range of 30,000m (32,808 yards) with conventional shells and up to 43,000m (47,025 yards) with rocket-assisted ammunition.

Soviet Mortar Battery (part of Motorized Infantry Battalion), 1968

The Soviet motorized infantry battalion deployed in Eastern Europe at the height of the Cold War included a battery of 120mm (4.7in) mortars composed of three sections of two weapons each. The 120mm (4.7in) mortar was indicative of the Soviet philosophy of treating mortars as artillery weapons for close infantry support. The 120mm (4.7in) mortar could be fired by dropping the round down the muzzle or by trip wire. Additional equipment included reconnaissance armoured personnel carriers and trucks to transport infantry and communications gear and personnel.

Battery HQ (1 x field car, 1 x APC)   **Reconnaissance (1 x APC)**   **Communications (1 x truck)**

Section (2 x 120mm/4.7in mortar, 2 x truck)

Section (2 x 120mm/4.7in mortar, 2 x truck)

Section (2 x 120mm/4.7in mortar, 2 x truck)

Soviet ICBMs
1950–89

Soviet tactical nuclear missiles comprised potentially the most damaging threat to NATO forces in Western Europe, and were sometimes deployed on mobile launchers. By the mid-1960s, the Soviet Union had deployed intercontinental ballistic missiles (ICBMs) and developed a series of intermediate-range missiles which could degrade NATO nuclear capabilities in Europe.

MEDIUM-RANGE NUCLEAR MISSILES deployed by the Soviets during the Cold War were capable of striking vital NATO installations and population centres throughout Western Europe. Prior to the implementation of treaties limiting such missiles, the Soviet arsenal contained as many as 550 weapons of this type, and they provided the primary offensive nuclear threat to NATO and the West in Europe. Medium-range ballistic missiles (MRBMs) typically included weapons with ranges of 300km (190 miles) to 3500km (2175 miles) and were classified between intermediate-range ballistic missiles (IRBMs) and tactical missiles, with strategic ICBMs right at the top.

Soviet research into medium-range ballistic missiles began in earnest in the early 1950s, and by the end of the decade the R-12 Dvina, known to NATO as the SS-4 Sandal, had been deployed in the Eastern Bloc. Although early design efforts had been centred around shorter-range engines and overall aerodynamics and in-flight stability, the liquid oxygen which powered these earlier engines was replaced by a nitric acid oxidizer in combination with kerosene as a fuel source. The SS-4 played a significant role in the early years of the Cold War, with the capability of delivering warheads up to 2.3 megatons with devastating results.

▲ R-12 Dvina (SS-4 Sandal)
Soviet Army / 24th Guards Division, 1960

The SS-4 Sandal medium-range ballistic missile entered service with Soviet forces on 4 March 1959 and constituted the bulk of the Soviet nuclear threat to Western Europe. The SS-4 was powered by a single-stage liquid-fuelled rocket engine and was manufactured by the Yuzhmash factory in the Ukraine. The deployment of the SS-4 precipitated the Cuban Missile Crisis of October 1962.

Specifications

Configuration: single-stage, liquid fuel	Launch weight: 27,000kg (59,536lb)
Deployment: launch pad or silo	Range: 2000km (1250 miles)
Length: 22.4m (73ft 6in)	Launch preparation time: 1-3 hours
Diameter: 1.65m (5ft 5in)	

Specifications

Configuration: single-stage, liquid fuel	Launch weight: 60,000kg (118,100lb)
Deployment: mobile, launch pad or silo	Range: 3500km (2175 miles)
Length: 25m (82ft)	Launch preparation time: 2 hours
Diameter: 2.44m (8ft)	

▲ R-14 Chusovaya (SS-5 Skean)
Soviet Army / 24th Guards Division, 1961

The R-14 intermediate-range ballistic missile increased the range of the SS-4 substantially and was the first Soviet ballistic missile to have implications of near worldwide range. First observed by the West in 1964, it was estimated that the SS-5 had been in service for several years. The SS-5 is believed to have entered production in the spring of 1961, and it was launch-capable from hardened silos, pads or mobile systems.

According to Soviet sources, the SS-4 was deployed in March 1959, and it was first seen by Western observers during the autumn of the following year. In October 1962, it was the deployment of the SS-4 to Cuba which precipitated the Cuban Missile Crisis. The range of the SS-4, which was estimated at 2000km (1250 miles), placed numerous major American cities within range of Soviet-built nuclear warheads. President John F. Kennedy imposed a naval blockade of the island, and negotiations were eventually successful in defusing the confrontation. However, it may be reasonably concluded that the crisis brought the superpowers closer to a nuclear exchange than at any other time in the history of the Cold War.

By the mid-1960s, the longer-range R-14 Chusovaya, or SS-5 Skean, had been deployed by the Soviet strategic rocket forces. Its hydrazine and nitrogen tetroxide propellant boosted its range to 3500km (2175 miles), while the blast yield remained sizeable at up to two megatons. Production of the SS-5 commenced in April 1961, and continued for nearly a decade.

ICBM research was very successful, and some estimates stated that the Soviets had deployed significant numbers of these weapons in hardened silos by 1960. In fact, the US Central Intelligence Agency (CIA) once asserted that up to 500 Soviet ICBMs would be operational by 1963. In the spring of 1961, the construction of at least two sites which would facilitate the development and testing of Soviet ICBMs was detected following the authorization of a solid-fuel missile with a range of up to 12,000km (7456 miles) in the autumn of 1959.

Arms race

A nuclear arms race which was to last more than 30 years ensued, with the destructive capabilities of such weapons steadily increasing. Numerous systems were developed, deployed, and then dismantled by treaty. Even so, the Russian Federation maintains a substantial nuclear arsenal today, and in retrospect

▶ UR-100 (SS-11 Sego)

Soviet Army / 28th Missile Division, 1967

More than 1400 variants of the UR-100 intercontinental ballistic missile were deployed by the Soviet Union from 1966 to 1976. The UR-100 was a single-stage liquid-fuelled missile which made up the majority of the Soviet nuclear inventory for more than 20 years; however, it was rarely seen in public. The UR-100 was improved on several occasions, with variants produced with decoy warheads to ward off anti-missile defences and with multiple re-entry vehicles.

Specifications

Configuration: single-stage, liquid fuel	Launch weight: 48,000kg (47.24 tons)
Deployment: silo	Range: 10,600km (6650 miles)
Length: 19m (62ft 4in)	Launch preparation time: 3 minutes
Diameter: 2.4m (7ft 10in)	

▲ RT-2 (SS-13 Savage)

Soviet Army / 7th Guards Missile Division, 1969

Seen in public for the first time in 1965 and deployed in 1969, the RT-2, known to NATO as the SS-13 Savage, joined the SS-16 system as the first solid-propellant ICBMs in the Soviet inventory. Development of the SS-13 had begun in 1959, and testing was conducted from 1966 to 1968. The missile was modified several times, and its most common warhead yield was 600 kilotons. The SS-13 remained in service for two decades and was eventually replaced by the SS-25 Topol.

Specifications

Configuration: three-stage, solid fuel	Launch weight: 34,000kg (33.46 tons)
Deployment: silo	Range: 8000km (4970 miles)
Length: 20m (65ft 7in)	Launch preparation time: 3-5 minutes
Diameter: 1.7m (5ft 7in)	

there is little doubt that the tremendous expense of ICBM and intermediate-range missile development and maintenance adversely affected the economy of the Soviet Union and hastened its downfall.

Among the first operational Soviet ICBMs to be deployed in significant numbers was the RT-2, or SS-13 Savage in NATO nomenclature. The design of the SS-13 was completed in 1963, the missile was successfully test-fired in late 1966 and the system was deployed by the end of 1968. Modified several times, the basic SS-13 was capable of delivering a single warhead with a yield of up to one megaton, although Western sources placed the yield somewhat higher. The SS-13 remained in service for 20 years, the last of the missiles being dismantled and replaced by the SS-25 Topol in the mid-1990s.

In the West, the greatest threat was without doubt the development of the R-36 series of ICBMs. These

missiles were also utilized in the Soviet space programme, and their continuing improvement, culminating in the R-36M, labelled the SS-18 Satan by NATO, was cause for alarm among Western analysts due to a perceived first-strike capability. The first missile of the R-36 series, the SS-9 Scarp, appeared in the mid-1960s, while the SS-18 was tested in the early 1970s with more than 50 deployed by 1977.

SS-18 Satan

The SS-18 was capable of delivering a single warhead of up to 20 megatons, and SS-18 variants were also configured for MIRV (multiple independent re-entry vehicles). It was these variants which caused such consternation in the West, as the estimated MIRV capacity of the SS-18 was up to ten warheads of 550 to 750 kilotons. Theoretically, the MIRV-equipped

▲ R-36 (SS-9 Scarp)

Soviet Army / 28th Guards Missile Division, 1970

The comparatively massive Soviet R-36 intercontinental ballistic missile fairly startled Western observers. Designated the SS-9 Scarp, the missile entered service in underground silos in the mid-1960s and displayed tremendous range and accuracy, while its nuclear payload and number of warheads increased steadily with successive versions. Some NATO analysts believed the SS-9 provided the Soviets with first-strike capability.

Specifications

Configuration: three-stage, liquid fuel
Deployment: silo
Length: 36m (118ft)
Diameter: 3.1m (10ft 2in)

Launch weight: 190,000kg (87 tons)
Range: 12,000km (7456 miles)
Launch preparation time: 5 minutes

▲ R-36M (SS-18 Satan)

Soviet Army / 62nd Rocket Division, 1975

The MIRV-capable SS-18 Satan caused great concern in the West with its potential first-strike capability. The heaviest ICBM in the world, the SS-18 was one of several missiles in the R-36 series which originated in the 1960s. Capable of carrying a conventional 20-megaton warhead, the SS-18 was modified several times, with the MIRV variant appearing in 1970. The R-36M, which was deployed in late 1975, was theoretically capable of destroying Western missiles in their silos. In the early 1990s, more than 300 R-36M launch sites were known to NATO. The SS-18 was transported in a launch container and loaded into the silo.

Specifications

Configuration: two-stage, liquid fuel
Deployment: silo
Length: 37m (121ft 3in)
Diameter: 3.2m (10ft 4in)
Launch weight: 220,000kg (216.5 tons)
Range: 16,000km (10,000 miles)
Launch preparation time: unknown

SS-18 could destroy contemporary US missiles before they could be readied to launch.

Treaty reductions

By the late 1980s, the United States and the Soviet Union had conducted negotiations intended to reduce the number and types of nuclear missiles in their respective arsenals. The Intermediate-Range Nuclear Forces Treaty was concluded in 1987 and banned most cruise missiles and ground-launched intermediate ballistic missiles with ranges of 500km (310 miles) to 5500km (3418 miles). With the signing of the treaty, the SS-4 and SS-5 components of the Soviet nuclear complement were disarmed at the Lesnaya Missile Elimination Facility. The last of the SS-4s, 149 missiles, were disassembled in May 1990.

▲ MR-UR-100 Sotka (SS-17 Spanker)

Soviet Army / 28th Missile Division, 1983

The SS-17 Spanker, designated by the Soviets as the MR-UR-100 Sotka, was a MIRV-capable ICBM which was intended as a replacement for the outdated SS-11 missile. The SS-17 was a cold-launch system, which ignited the liquid propellant of the first stage once the missile had been launched from its silo by a gas generator. More than 260 SS-17s had been deployed by the early 1980s. By the early 1990s these missiles were dismantled under treaty.

Specifications

Configuration: two-stage, liquid fuel
Deployment: silo
Length: 24.4m (80ft)
Diameter: 2.5m (8ft 3in)
Launch weight: 65,000kg (63.97 tons)
Range: 11,000km (6835 miles)
Launch preparation time: unknown

▲ UR-100N (SS-19 Stiletto)

Soviet Army / 60th Missile Division, 1985

Intended as a replacement for the earlier silo-launched SS-11 ICBM, the SS-19 utilized an onboard computer to improve accuracy. It was also larger than the SS-11 and was transported in a launch cylinder which was then inserted into the silo. Research on the SS-19 was begun in 1974, and by the early 1980s more than 350 were in service. Contrary to previous treaty terms, the missiles may be rearmed with MIRV warheads. More than 130 SS-19 missiles remain active with the armed forces of the Russian Federation.

Specifications

Configuration: two-stage, liquid fuel
Deployment: silo
Length: 27.3m (85ft 6in)
Diameter: 2.5m (8ft 3in)
Launch weight: 78,000kg (76.78 tons)
Range: 10,000km (6200 miles)
Launch preparation time: unknown

▲ RSD-10 Pioneer (SS-20 Saber)

Soviet Army / 60th Missile Division, 1985

Known to NATO as the SS-20 Saber, this mobile intermediate-range ballistic missile was in service from 1976 to 1988 and could target and destroy most major NATO bases or cities in Western Europe, complementing strategic SS-18 missiles with a first-strike capability of their own. In 1979, at least 14 operational SS-20 launchers had been identified, and nearly 700 missiles were eventually constructed to replace the SS-4 and SS-5 systems. These were dismantled in the early 1990s as a result of treaty agreements.

Specifications

Configuration: two-stage, solid fuel
Deployment: mobile
Length: 16.4m (53ft 9in)
Diameter: 1.4m (55in)
Launch weight: 13,000kg (12.8 tons)
Range: 5000km (3100 miles)
Launch preparation time: continual readiness

Early NATO artillery
1947–70

NATO forces depended largely on artillery of World War II-vintage during the early years of the Cold War in Europe; however, some light weapons were developed along with nuclear-capable systems.

WITH THE DEVELOPMENT of the Cold War, the NATO troops opposing the Red Army were at a distinct disadvantage in terms of numbers, including troops, tanks and artillery. During the brief period of the US nuclear monopoly, such a deficiency seemed less significant to a degree; however, when the Soviet Union became a nuclear power in 1949 it was readily apparent to military planners in the West that tactical, intermediate and long-range nuclear capability was of the utmost importance to ensure the balance of power and provide not only defensive capabilities to forces in Western Europe but also sufficient strength to act as a deterrent to possible Soviet aggression.

Such a necessity was acutely realized with the Berlin crisis of the late 1940s and the outbreak of the Korean War in 1950. Throughout the course of the Cold War, the United States deployed 15 infantry and armoured divisions and five armoured cavalry regiments to Western Europe. Each of these was equipped with a variety of conventional artillery weapons suited for specific purposes. Along with the forces of other NATO countries, the US Army relied on the 105mm (4.1in) M2A1 howitzer, the M114 155mm (6.1in) howitzer, the M1 240mm (9.45in) howitzer, the M2 Long Tom 155mm (6.1in) gun and the M115 203mm (8in) howitzer for primary firepower during the early years of the Cold War.

Classic Light Gun

By the late 1960s, the British Army was developing its own L118 105mm (4.1in) gun, which was commonly referred to as the 'Light Gun'. Designed to replace various types in service with the British Army since World War II, the Light Gun was designed by the Royal Armament Research and Development Establishment at Fort Halstead, Kent, and was capable of firing up to eight rounds per minute to a range of 17,200m (18,810 yards). As the Light Gun began to appear in greater numbers, older models such as the venerable 25-pounder, the Italian OTO Melara Mod 56 pack howitzer, the 105mm (4.1in) L5 pack howitzer, and a number of aging 75mm (2.95in) weapons were retired.

▲ **3.7in RCL Gun**

British Army / 1st Battalion, Green Howards, 1958

The 3.7in (94mm) RCL Gun had its origins during World War II but did not see service during that conflict. A later variant of 120mm (4.7in) was also issued to NATO troops in Europe. The recoilless rifle used a system of jets to the rear which counterbalanced its recoil, allowing the carriage to be relatively lightweight.

Specifications

Crew: 3-5	Weight: 170kg (375lb)
Calibre: 94mm (3.7in)	Range: 2000m (2185 yards)
Elevation: - 5 degrees to + 10 degrees	Muzzle velocity: 1000m/sec (3280ft/sec)

The 155mm (6.1in) FH-70 towed artillery piece, which was developed in the 1960s and reached front-line units in Western Europe more than a decade later, was the result of collaborative efforts between British, West German and, later, Italian engineers. Intended as a replacement for the M114, the FH-70 was served by a crew of eight, fired at a sustained rate of three to six rounds per minute and reached an

Specifications

Crew: 3-4	Weight: 5150kg (5.06 tons)
Calibre: 40mm (1.57in)	Range: 3500m (3834 yards)
Elevation: - 4 degrees to + 90 degrees	Muzzle velocity: 1005m/sec (3300ft/sec)

▲ **40mm Bofors L/70 anti-aircraft gun**

British Army / 16th Light Air Defence Regiment Royal Artillery, 1963

The Swedish Bofors 40mm L/70 anti-aircraft gun was an improvement over the previous 40mm (1.57in) weapon with a longer barrel which increased the weapon's rate of fire. Introduced in the 1950s, the gun was transported aboard a similar carriage to that of its predecessor and was sold widely.

29 Commando Light Regiment Royal Artillery, 1962

The typical organization of light artillery regiments of the British Army during the early 1960s included three batteries of four 105mm (4.1in) pack howitzers. The most prevalent pack howitzer then in service with the British Army was the Italian OTO Melara Mod 56, which was originally designed for use by mountain troops. For ease of transport, the Mod 56 could be broken down into a dozen components and loaded aboard pack animals.

8 'Alma' Battery (4 x 105mm/4.1in pack howitzers)

79 'Kirkee' Battery (4 x 105mm/4.1in pack howitzers)

145 'Maiwand' Battery (4 x 105mm/4.1in pack howitzers)

effective range of 30,000m (32,808 yards) depending on the type of ammunition used.

While a new generation of conventional artillery had taken on added importance, older weapons such as the 3.7in (94mm) RCL Gun maintained an important role with infantry units of the British Army in Europe. The weapon had been developed in Britain by the Broadway Trust and dated to World War II but did not enter service during that conflict.

The original version, which fired a 'wallbuster' shell containing plastic explosive, was later supplanted by a 120mm (4.7in) gun which was issued during the Cold War. The Swedish 40mm (1.57in) Bofors L/70 was also delivered to armed forces around the world during the 1950s and equipped NATO anti-aircraft units. An improved version of the famed World War II anti-aircraft weapon, this variant included a longer barrel which effectively doubled the weapon's rate of fire and accommodated a larger round.

Early nuclear weapons

Among the early nuclear weapons deployed with NATO forces to Western Europe was the MGR-1 Honest John, which was tested in 1951 and entered service two years later. The Honest John was used in conjunction with several launchers and delivered conventional high-explosive rounds, chemical weapons such as Sarin nerve gas and tactical nuclear warheads up to 30 kilotons. Although the Honest John rocket was fin-stabilized, its accuracy was suspect when firing chemical or high-explosive rounds. As precision guided systems were introduced, production ceased in 1965. More than 7000 were manufactured, and the Honest John continued in service with the armed forces of numerous countries until the mid-1980s.

The Davy Crockett recoilless rifle was developed during the late 1950s to fire the M388 tactical nuclear weapon. The Davy Crockett is perhaps more accurately described as two weapons systems, one which utilized the M28 102mm (4in) and a second which used the M29 155mm (6.1in) gun. The weapon's rather ungainly appearance belied its potential destructive power: the M29, for example, could project the M388 out to a distance of four kilometres (2.5 miles).

The warhead itself weighed 23kg (51lb) and delivered a blast equivalent to around 20.3 tonnes (20 tons) of TNT. Originally intended as a stopgap weapon, the Davy Crockett was deployed with detachments of infantrymen who would target Soviet tanks and infantry and destroy them while contaminating the surrounding area with radiation for up to two days, during which NATO forces could deploy and react to an attack in strength.

▲ MGR-1 Honest John

US Army / Eighth Army Field Artillery Detachment, 1961

The MGR-1 Honest John was the first surface-to-surface missile in the US arsenal capable of firing a nuclear warhead. Tested in 1951 and deployed to Western Europe in 1953, the Honest John could also deliver conventional or chemical weapons. The MGR-1 was transported in three sections which were rapidly assembled just prior to firing.

Specifications

Calibre: 762mm (30in)
Rocket length: 7.57m (24ft 10in)
Rocket weight: 1950kg (4300lb)
Range: 36.8km (23 miles)

◀ **M29 Davy Crockett**

US Army / 55th Infantry Platoon, 82nd Airborne Division, 1964

The M29 Davy Crockett recoilless rifle weapon system was one of two which fired the nuclear M388 projectile. Whereas the M28 utilized a 102mm (4in) gun to project the weapon, the M29 used a 155mm (6.1in) rifle. One of the smallest nuclear weapons of the Cold War, the Davy Crockett was deployed to infantry units and was to be used in delaying actions against Soviet formations.

Specifications

Crew: 3	Weight: 34.5kg (76lb)
Diameter: 280mm (11in)	Range: 4km (2.5 miles)
Length: 787mm (31in)	

Western self-propelled guns
1947–90

Countering the firepower and mobility of the Warsaw Pact forces, self-propelled guns were designed to accompany NATO infantry across the rolling countryside of Northern Europe during combat.

A VARIETY OF SELF-PROPELLED GUNS supported NATO ground capabilities during the Cold War in Europe, providing mobile firepower in opposition to the early SU-76 and SU-85 weapons which appeared in the Warsaw Pact order of battle along with heavier guns such as the ISU-152, which was prominent in the suppression of the 1956 uprising against the communist government of Hungary.

Under the US Army ROAD (Reorganization Objective Army Division) structure, infantry, armoured and mechanized divisions might each include attached or organic self-propelled artillery units, while the role of the self-propelled artillery was not only to provide fire support for infantry formations but also to add punch to the armoured cavalry regiments which were tasked with reconnaissance and combat roles.

Early NATO self-propelled guns included the 105mm (4.1in) M7 Priest, which initially appeared with US forces in the spring of 1942, and the M41 Gorilla, which debuted in 1945. The M41 mounted the 155mm (6.1in) M1 howitzer atop the chassis of the M24 Chaffee light tank. Powered by twin

Cadillac 44T24 V8 gasoline engines generating a combined 165kW (220hp), the M41 had a maximum range of 160km (100 miles). Fewer than 300 were built. The M7 was powered by the nine-cylinder Continental R-975 412.5kW (550hp) gasoline engine and served into the late 1950s, seeing action during the Korean War.

One of the longest-lived basic designs of the Cold War era is the US M109, which was developed from the early 1950s as a replacement for the M44, which was active from 1953 until about 1962. The M109 entered service in the 1960s and was equipped with a 155mm (6.1in) main weapon capable of firing tactical nuclear ammunition. At the time of writing, more than 4000 variants of the M109 remain in service with the armed forces of more than 30 countries. The M109 had also replaced the M108 105mm (4.1in) howitzer, which was developed during the early 1960s and withdrawn from service by the middle of the decade. Sharing some common components with the M109 and the M113 armoured personnel carrier, the M108 was served by a crew of five with an operational range of 360km (224 miles).

The M110 203mm (8in) howitzer was the largest Cold War weapon of its kind in the US arsenal. Its heavy firepower was often assigned to the divisional level in battalion strength and also in battalions at the higher corps and army levels. Powered by a General Motors 8V71T supercharged diesel engine which generated 304kW (405hp), the vehicle had an impressive range of 523km (325 miles).

Specifications

Crew: 4

Weight: 16,494kg (36,288lb)

Length: 5.84m (19ft 2in)

Width: 2.641m (8ft 8in)

Height: 2.489m (8ft 2in)

Engine: 179kW (240hp) Rolls-Royce 6-cylinder

Speed: 47.5km/h (30mph)

Road range: 390km (240 miles)

Armament: 1 x 105mm (4.1in) gun, plus

1 x 7.62mm (0.3in) anti-aircraft MG and

3 x smoke dischargers

▲ **Abbot SP howitzer gun**

British Army of the Rhine / 6th Armoured Division, Germany, 1969

Beginning in the late 1960s, the Abbot self-propelled howitzer was deployed to units of the Royal Artillery serving with NATO. Mounting a 105mm (4.1in) L13A1 gun, the Abbot featured an enclosed, fully rotating turret atop the modified chassis of the FV430 armoured fighting vehicle.

1st Regiment Royal Horse Artillery, British Army of the Rhine (BAOR), 1989

As the Cold War began, the 1st Regiment of the Royal Horse Artillery served in Palestine supporting anti-terrorist operations. Amid the growing threat from the Soviet Red Army, the regiment redeployed to Germany during the early 1950s with the 20th Armoured Brigade, 6th Armoured Division. During the 1950s, the regiment had been armed with the M44 155mm (6.1in) self-propelled howitzer, a US design which was later supplanted by the M109. In 1989, prior to being refitted with the AS-90 self-propelled gun, the regiment was equipped with the durable and long-serving Abbot 105mm (4.1in) self-propelled howitzer.

Regiment (24 x Abbot 105mm/4.1in SP howitzers)

▲ MK61 SP howitzer

French Army / II Corps, Germany, 1957

The 105mm (4.1in) MK61 self-propelled howitzer was a variant of the AMX-13 light tank, constructed with its enclosed turret atop the AMX-13 chassis. Developed concurrently with the AMX-13, it was eventually supplanted by the 155mm (6.1in) GCT self-propelled gun.

Specifications

Crew: 5

Weight (approx): 16,500kg (36,382lb)

Length: 6.4m (30ft)

Width: 2.65m (8ft 3.3in)

Height: 2.7m (8ft 10.3in)

Engine: 186.4kW (250hp) SOFAM 8Gxb

 8-cylinder petrol

Speed: 60km/h (37.3mph)

Road range: 350km (217.5 miles)

Armament: 1 x 105mm (4.1in) gun, plus

 2 x 7.5mm (0.295in) MGs

▲ Canon de 155mm Mk F3 Automoteur

French Army / II Corps, Germany, 1964

Constructed on a modified AMX-13 light tank chassis, the Mk F3 155mm (6.1in) self-propelled gun is the smallest of its kind ever produced. Designed in the early 1950s as a replacement for older US-made M41 self-propelled guns, the Mk F3 entered service with the French Army a decade later.

Specifications

Crew: 2	Engine: 186kW (250hp) SOFAM 8Gxb 8-cylinder
Weight: 17,410kg (38,304lb)	petrol
Length: 6.22m (20ft 5in)	Speed: 60km/h (37mph)
Width: 2.72m (8ft 11in)	Road range: 300km (185 miles)
Height: 2.085m (6ft 10in)	Armament: 1 x 155mm (6.1in) gun

In response to the NATO requirement for a standard 105mm (4.1in) weapon, the British Abbot was developed by Vickers in the early 1950s. The Abbot mounted the 105mm (4.1in) gun atop a modified FV430 chassis which accommodated the fully rotating turret and the rear housing of the main weapon. The Abbot entered service in 1965 and was replaced more than 20 years later by the M109 and another Vickers system, the AS-90. With a crew of six, an operational range of 390km (240 miles) and a top speed of 47.5km/h (30mph), the Abbot was well suited for close infantry support.

The MK61, an early French self-propelled howitzer, was a variant of the AMX-13 light tank constructed with an enclosed turret and mounting a 105mm (4.1in) main weapon. The MK61 was intended to be airmobile and possibly used in support of airborne troops. By the 1970s, it had been replaced by the GCT 155mm (6.1in) gun, which was also sold to the armed forces of Saudi Arabia and Iraq.

Western ICBMs
1946–90

The development of tactical, intermediate-range and intercontinental ballistic missiles in the West was undertaken as a deterrent to Soviet military aggression and to maintain some balance of power in Europe.

SOON AFTER THE END OF WORLD WAR II, it was apparent in the West that a nuclear arsenal capable of defending the member countries of the NATO alliance was essential to the strategic defence doctrine which was employed to deter Soviet territorial expansion around the globe and to counter the numerical superiority of Warsaw Pact conventional forces poised to strike Western Europe.

Incorporating the research and development of rocket engines which had resulted in the successful launch of the V-2 rocket by the Germans during World War II, the United States advanced its early research into long-range ballistic missiles under the auspices of Project Paperclip. The country's defence establishment committed to the deployment of long-range nuclear missiles which could target cities in the Soviet Union from the continental United States while also continuing to research tactical missile systems and heavy bombers capable of delivering nuclear weapons. In time, these systems would include long-range ICBMs which could reach targets thousands of kilometres away.

Strategic nuclear umbrella

For the half-century of the Cold War, the nuclear doctrine of the United States – and as a follow-on

that of NATO – rested upon the 'triad' of land-based ICBMs, long-range heavy bombers such as the B-52 Stratofortress which could deliver nuclear weapons, and submarine-launched ICBMs. This strategic doctrine was developed in the early 1950s, and the first operational US ICBM, the Atlas D, was placed in service at Vandenberg Air Force Base, California, in the autumn of 1959. Within two years, the US Air Force could report three squadrons of an updated Atlas E missile located in a least four sites across the country.

In 1955, the Titan programme was undertaken as a successor to the Atlas ICBM. The resulting Titan I missile was rapidly improved with the Titan II, a mainstay of the US ICBM complement into the 1980s. The Titan II was test-fired in December 1961 and placed in service two years later. It initially carried one nine-megaton W-53 nuclear warhead with a range of 15,000km (9300 miles). At any given time, more than 50 were stationed in silos and could be launched within 60 seconds.

By the mid-1960s, the US had deployed at least 1000 Atlas, Titan and Minuteman I and Minuteman II missiles with a like number of warheads. Meanwhile, the British government, in cooperation with the United States, briefly pursued the

▲ **Titan II ICBM**

US Air Force / 308th Strategic Missile Wing, 1962

The Titan missile programme was undertaken in the mid-1950s and rapidly developed the Titan I ICBM. The Titan II, which was more accurate over a greater distance with a heavier nuclear payload, was tested in 1961 and became operational in 1963. Dozens were placed in silos in the Midwestern United States, fuelled and ready for launch, for the next 20 years. The Titan II also served as a launcher for the NASA (National Aeronautics and Space Administration) manned space flight programme.

Specifications

Configuration: two-stage, liquid fuel
Deployment: silo
Length: 29.9m (98ft)
Diameter: 3.05m (10ft)
Launch weight: 99,792kg (98.21 tons)
Range: 15,000km (9300 miles)
Launch preparation time: 60 seconds

Blue Streak missile, a medium-range weapon which could complement the ongoing US ICBM programme. This endeavour was undertaken in 1955 and abandoned five years later. The US attempted to develop an air-launched nuclear missile, named Skybolt, but this project was rendered impractical with the advent of submarine-launched ballistic missiles.

The early Titan and Minuteman missile systems were operational simultaneously during the early 1960s and were placed on alert during the Cuban Missile Crisis of October 1962. At the end of that year, the US strategic ICBM arsenal totalled over 200 warheads; however, most of these were configured with the Atlas missile system, which was rapidly being outclassed by both US technology and rising Soviet capabilities.

Indicative of US missile development at the height of the Cold War was the Minuteman programme, which was undertaken in the late 1950s. Even as the Minuteman I reached operational status, the upgrade to Minuteman II was in progress. Under the Minuteman Force Modernization Program, the upgrade included an improved guidance system, heavier second stage, longer range and greater

survivability in the event of a Soviet first strike. The payload of the MIRV-capable Minuteman II was increased to the 1.2-megaton W-56 nuclear warhead, while the missile could reach targets as far away as 13,000km (8100 miles).

The modern US strategic nuclear arsenal consists solely of the Minuteman III missile, following the retirement of the Peacekeeper missile, popularly known as the MX, of which only about 50 were built. The LGM-30G Minuteman III reached deployment in 1970, and plans to decrease the maximum load of three warhead re-entry vehicles to one have been considered during the post-Cold War era. The total US strategic ICBM force is estimated at 500 Minuteman III missiles today.

The SSBS S3 missile marked a second generation of French intermediate-range ballistic missiles. Its development was undertaken in 1973 to replace the aging S2, and deployment began during the early 1980s. By 1984, a total of 18 hardened sites were in service to complement the concurrent MSBS submarine-launched missile programme. Each SSBS S3 carried a 1.2-megaton nuclear warhead with a range of 3500km (2175 miles).

▲ SSBS S3

French Army / 1st Strategic Missile Group, 1980

With a more powerful second stage engine and advanced re-entry vehicle, the SSBS S3 missile improved on the S2 design and entered service with the French armed forces in 1980. The weapon carried a 1.2-megaton nuclear warhead and was launched from hardened silos located in the Plateau d'Albion region of France. By the mid-1990s, the French government had announced that it would dismantle all land-based nuclear missiles, relying on submarines and bombers for nuclear deterrence.

Specifications

Configuration: two-stage, solid fuel
Deployment: silo
Length: 13.7m (44ft 11in)
Diameter: 1.5m (60in)
Launch weight: 25,800kg (25.39 tons)
Range: 3500km (2175 miles)
Launch preparation time: unknown

▲ LGM-30F Minuteman II

US Air Force / 447th Strategic Missile Squadron, 1965

Improving on the navigation system, range and nuclear payload of the Minuteman I missile, the Minuteman II was the result of the Minuteman Force Modernization Program of the early 1960s. Better accuracy was provided by an onboard computer which could provide data for multiple targets. The Minuteman II was supplanted by the design's third generation, the Minuteman III, in the 1980s.

Specifications

Configuration: three-stage, solid fuel	
Deployment: silo	Launch weight: 31,746kg (31.24 tons)
Length: 18.2m (69ft 8in)	Range: 12,500km (7770 miles)
Diameter: 1.84m (6ft)	Launch preparation time: 30 seconds

Early Western air defence missiles
1947–70

The threat of Soviet air interdiction on the battlefield and long-range Soviet bombers carrying nuclear payloads led NATO to develop missile systems with the latest technology.

WITH THEIR AIR DEFENCE missile programmes in their infancy, both the United States and the Soviet Union leveraged their own technology while appropriating advances by German scientists who had previously worked under the Nazi regime. The missile systems themselves might potentially be utilized as replacements for heavy air defence artillery, which was often inaccurate and difficult to transport. By the time NATO was formed in 1949, the US and Great Britain were well on their way to the deployment of operational air defence missiles.

Evolving NATO doctrine included the deployment of missile systems to protect major cities in Western Europe and North America, while air defence in depth theorized that attacking Warsaw Pact aircraft would be required to run a gauntlet of fire. Coordinated NATO air defence included fighter aircraft, surface-to-air missiles and anti-aircraft guns. Attacking aircraft would first be located by early-warning radar and then engaged by fighter planes and long-range missiles. In response to the radar, enemy pilots would be required to fly low to avoid detection, making them vulnerable to shorter-range missiles fired from both mobile and hard sites, as well as effective anti-aircraft guns which would engage the aircraft at lower altitude.

NATO air defence planners believed strongly that somewhat redundant systems and defence in depth would take a toll on any Warsaw Pact pilot's ability to execute his mission. If the enemy plane was not destroyed outright, the pilot would be required to maintain readiness to take evasive action throughout his mission. Further, action taken to avoid or exploit the weaknesses of one defensive system would likely expose the enemy aircraft to another.

Intercontinental cordon

In the case of the strategic-bombing threat, missiles were deployed as a last line of defence around major cities. As early as 1944, the United States had

▲ **Test fire**
A Thunderbird missile is launched somewhere from British soil. The Thunderbird was design for medium-range air defence.

Specifications

Configuration: two-stage, solid then liquid fuel

Deployment: site-launched

Length: 10.62m (34ft 10in)

Diameter: 305mm (12in)

Launch weight: 1114kg (2455lb)

Range: 40km (25 miles)

Launch preparation time: immediate

▲ Nike Ajax

US Army / 3rd Battalion, 71st Air Defense Artillery, 1959

The first surface-to-air guided missile in service with an active army, the Nike Ajax was controlled by a computer which directed and detonated the missile based on data from two radar systems, one with a guiding beam and another which tracked the target. The Ajax was relatively short-ranged at 40km (25 miles).

▲ MIM-14 Nike Hercules

US Army / 2nd Battalion, 52nd Air Defense Artillery, 1965

Used for a time in concert with the Ajax and sharing a number of the same components, the MIM-14 Hercules was a distinct improvement, with an increased speed of Mach 3.5 and a much greater range than the first-generation Ajax. The Hercules, which was also nuclear-capable, entered service in 1958 and was deployed to several NATO countries as an upgrade to the Ajax.

Specifications

Configuration: two-stage, solid fuel

Deployment: site-launched

Length: 12.5m (41ft)

Diameter: 800mm (31.5in)

Launch weight: 4720kg (10,405lb)

Range: 155km (96 miles)

Launch preparation time: immediate

undertaken the Nike project, and by the end of 1953 the Nike Ajax became the first weapon of its kind to enter service with an active military force. In December of that year, Nike Ajax units were positioned around Washington DC, replacing hundreds of anti-aircraft guns. The missile delivered warheads of up to 81kg (179lb) with a maximum range of 40km (25 miles). The first successful test-firing of the Ajax occurred in 1951 when a Boeing B-17 Flying Fortress bomber drone was destroyed. The Ajax remained in service with air defence units until the mid-1960s.

Components of the Ajax system were expensive to manufacture and were also utilized in the next generation of Nike project missiles, designated the MIM-14 Hercules, which was deployed beginning in the spring of 1958. Aside from positions protecting US cities and intercontinental ballistic missile sites, the Hercules was also posted to Western Europe and the Far East. Its effective range was more than double

that of the Ajax at 155km (96 miles), while the system was also capable of delivering a nuclear warhead of up to 20 kilotons. The Hercules often worked in tandem with the MIM-23 HAWK system, which was developed in the early 1950s and has remained in use for decades.

British air defence missile development was active during the 1940s with the English Electric Thunderbird, which was under development as a high-altitude interceptor system as early as 1949. The first missile designed and produced for the British Army, the Thunderbird entered service in 1959 and equipped heavy air defence regiments of the Royal Artillery or designated squadrons of the Royal Air Force. It delivered a high-explosive warhead to a maximum range of 75km (46 miles). Another primary air defence missile of British and NATO forces was the Bristol Bloodhound, which had a range of 80km (50 miles). It entered service in 1958 and remained active into the 1990s.

▲ Bristol Bloodhound Mark 1

Royal Air Force / No. 242 Squadron, 1959

Entering service in 1958, the Bristol Bloodhound was fired from fixed positions and intended initially to protect squadrons of Royal Air Force V Bombers deployed at eight sites in Britain. The Bloodhound was improved several times and easily recognized with its distinctive quartet of external boosters. The missile carried a high-explosive warhead with a proximity fuse. The last battery in British service was retired in 1991.

Specifications

Configuration: external booster
Deployment: site-launched
Length: 8.46m (27ft 9in)
Diameter: 546mm (27.5in)

Launch weight: 2270kg (5000lb)
Range: 80km (50 miles)
Launch preparation time: immediate

▲ English Electric Thunderbird

British Army / 457th Heavy Air Defence Regiment, Royal Artillery, 1963

Development of the Thunderbird surface-to-air missile was undertaken by English Electric Corporation in 1949, and the system entered service with the Royal Artillery in 1959. The Thunderbird was intended to replace heavy anti-aircraft guns such as the 94mm (3.7in) weapons which were prevalent among British units during World War II. Large tail fins and short wings stabilized the missile, which could be detonated with a proximity fuse or on command.

Specifications

Configuration: external booster
Deployment: site-launched
Length: 6.35m (20ft 10in)
Diameter: 527mm (20.75in)

Launch weight: unknown
Range: 75km (46 miles)
Launch preparation time: immediate

Specifications

Configuration: two-stage, solid fuel
Deployment: site launched
Length: 6m (19ft 8in)
Diameter: 400mm (15.75in)
Launch weight: 400kg (882lb)
Range: 30km (19 miles)
Launch preparation time: unknown

▲ RSD 58 SAM

Swiss Air Force / Ground Based Air Defence, 1961

An early surface-to-air missile developed in 1947 by the Oerlikon and Contraves companies, the RSD 58 entered service with the Swiss, Italian and Japanese armed forces following the conclusion of testing in 1952. Sliding rear fins stabilized the missile in flight and corrected its path along a radar beam which guided it to within lethal distance of the target. A radio-triggered proximity fuse detonated the warhead.

Late Warsaw Pact artillery
1970–89

The need for direct fire support for ground troops in Europe led to the development of Soviet artillery capable of keeping pace with advancing infantry and concentrating decisive firepower, while Soviet client states produced their own variants of some Red Army weapons.

THE PRINCIPLES OF SOVIET combined-arms doctrine as understood by Western analysts during the 1970s included several interdependent concepts such as mobility and high rates of combat operations; concentration of main efforts and creation of superiority in forces and means over the enemy at the decisive place and at the decisive time; surprise and security; combat activeness; preservation of the combat effectiveness of friendly forces; conformity of the goal; and coordination. Particularly in the cases of mobility and coordination, modern artillery would be a key element in any Red Army or Warsaw Pact combat operation in Western Europe.

During World War II, the Red Army had demonstrated its ability to coordinate self-propelled, field and heavy artillery with offensive movement, concentrating where necessary. As the Cold War dragged on, heavy guns such as the 122mm (4.8in) D-30 were deployed during the 1960s and widely exported. Older weapons, including the 152mm (6in) D-1 howitzer, remained in service into the 1980s. Heavy mortars of 120mm (4.7in) and 160mm (6.3in) were deployed with smaller infantry units, their plunging fire expected to eliminate fixed targets or disrupt infantry assaults. Mobile rocket launchers such as the BM-21 system, which was mounted atop a 6X6 truck, were continually improved during the 1960s as well. With the advent of tactical nuclear weapons, the artillery took on the additional responsibility of a delivery system for these, and missiles such as the FROG (Free Rocket Over Ground) series were deployed.

Wielding the hammer

At the height of the Cold War, Soviet Marshal of Artillery G.E. Peredelsky wrote, '... artillery has become the basis of firepower of the ground forces. It has the decisive role of creating the preponderance of power over the enemy which frequently determines the outcome of the battle.'

▲ **2S3 (M1973) 152mm SP gun-howitzer**

Soviet Army / 6th Guards Separate Motor Rifle Brigade, 1981

Introduced to the Red Army in 1973, the 2S3 (M1973) 152mm (6in) self-propelled gun-howitzer replaced the older D-20 system in artillery regiments of Soviet and Warsaw Pact forces to provide fire support for tank and motorized rifle regiments.

Specifications

Crew: 6	Speed: 55km/h (34mph)
Weight: 24,945kg (54,880lb)	Road range: 300km (186 miles)
Length: 8.4m (27ft 6.7in)	Armament: 1 x 152mm (6in) gun, plus
Width: 3.2m (10ft 6in)	1 x 7.62mm (0.3in) anti-aircraft MG
Height: 2.8m (9ft 2.25in)	Radio: n/k
Engine: 388kW (520hp) V12 diesel	

To that end, the development of a new generation of Soviet weapons, with a late emphasis on self-propelled artillery, was undertaken in earnest during the mid-1960s. The 152mm (6in) 2S3 Akatsiya, or Acacia, known in the West as the M1973, had been designed largely in response to the appearance of the US-made M109 self-propelled howitzer.

The main weapon of the 2S3 was mounted atop a modified chassis similar to that of the SA-4 surface-to-air missile. Its development was authorized in 1967, and it entered service six years later. By the 1980s, Western intelligence sources estimated that front-line Soviet armoured and mechanized infantry divisions stationed in East Germany included a battalion of 2S3s, usually totalling 18 vehicles, in their organic artillery regiments. Near the end of the decade, this number had increased to as many as three battalions and up to 54 of the self-propelled guns.

The 2S4 Tyulpan, or Tulip, was first identified by Western observers in 1975 and mounts a 240mm (9.45in) mortar designed to be particularly effective against fortified and fixed targets. Deployed with Red Army troops to Afghanistan, the 2S4 remains the

▲ **2S4 (M1975) self-propelled mortar**

Soviet Army / 5th High Powered Artillery Brigade, 1979

Derived from the chassis of the GMZ minelaying combat vehicle, the 2S4 Tyulpan, or Tulip, mounts a 240mm (9.45in) breechloading mortar, the largest weapon of its kind currently in service. The Tyulpan was first identified by NATO observers in 1975 and is capable of firing laser-guided or nuclear ammunition.

Specifications

Crew: 9	Engine: 390kW (520hp) V-59 diesel
Weight: 30,481kg (30 tons)	Speed: 62km/h (38.53mph)
Length: 8.5m (27ft 10in)	Road range: 420km (261 miles)
Width: 3.2m (10ft 6in)	Armament: 1 x 240mm (9.45in) mortar
Height: 3.2m (10ft 6in)	

Specifications

Crew: 4

Weight: 13,800kg (13.58 tons)

Speed: 63km/h (39.15mph)

Road range: 550km (342 miles)

Armament: 1 x 120mm (4.7in) mortar

Rate of fire: 8 rounds per minute

▲ **SPM-85 PRAM 120mm self-propelled mortar**

Czech People's Army / 7th Artillery Division, 1983

Adapted from the chassis of the versatile Soviet-designed BMP-1 amphibious tank, the SPM-85 PRAM was deployed with the Czech People's Army in the early 1980s. Its 120mm (4.7in) mortar is capable of firing up to 40 rounds in five minutes or a maximum of 70 rounds in ten minutes. The weapon has also been reported as highly mobile. It may also be equipped with anti-tank guided missiles.

largest self-propelled mortar in service in the world. Although its rate of fire is extremely low at one round per minute, it has proven to be an effective weapon.

In the early 1980s, the Czechoslovak armed forces deployed the self-propelled SPM-85 PRAM 120mm (4.7in) self-propelled mortar, mounted on the adapted chassis of the Soviet-designed BMP-1 amphibious tank. With an impressive rate of fire, 18 to 20 rounds per minute, the highly mobile SPM-85 was allocated to mechanized infantry units to provide accurate fire against targets at a distance of up to 8000m (8750 yards).

172nd Artillery Regiment, Red Army, Rudelstadt, German Democratic Republic, 1989

The composition of the 172nd Artillery Regiment of the Soviet Red Army is indicative of the emphasis placed on firepower and mobility during the later years of the Cold War. The combination of the BM-21 rocket launcher and 2S3 Akatsiya with its 152mm (6in) D-22 howitzer L/27 provided the ability to saturate enemy positions with area fire and follow up with self-propelled artillery which could provide direct support. In both cases, the weapons systems were mobile and able to displace in a relatively short period of time in order to accompany mechanized infantry during an advance.

Regiment (48 x 2S3 SP artillery, 18 x BM-21 rocket launchers)

Soviet theatre missiles
1950–89

Western intelligence sources observed the development of Soviet missile technology from the late 1940s and correctly judged that the progress achieved was largely based upon the work of German scientists relocated to the Soviet Union following World War II.

THE SOVIETS ACTIVELY pursued cruise-missile capabilities based on the German V-1 design. During the mid-1950s, it was believed that the majority of Soviet nuclear delivery would be by heavy bombers flying one-way missions. However, at the same time no less than four separate programmes for the development of what came to be known as the Scud family of intermediate-range missiles was detected.

Scud squad

Smaller nuclear weapons were often mounted on the tracked ISU-152 chassis, which was a variant of the heavy JS-3 tank chassis produced late in World War II. The initial mobile-launched nuclear-capable missiles produced in the Soviet Union were designated R-11 through R-17 and known to NATO as the Scud series. The R-17 Elbrus, or SS-1C Scud B, was representative of Soviet capabilities during the 1950s and 1960s. The R-17 programme was undertaken in 1958 as an improvement to the R-11 and utilizing a more powerful kerosene and nitric acid single-stage liquid-propellant rocket. The first successful launch of the R-17 occurred in 1961, and the missile had entered service by 1964. It was capable of delivering high-explosive, chemical or nuclear warheads exceeding 50 kilotons.

Scud technology has been exported to numerous countries, and the system has also been copied and produced under licence. Modified Iraqi Scud missiles were fired on Israel and inflicted the highest number of Coalition casualties during the Gulf War of 1991. The Scud threat was taken so seriously by Coalition commanders that special forces units were dropped in enemy territory to seek out and destroy the mobile launchers.

Tactical leap

Among the unguided rocket systems which were widely deployed by Warsaw Pact forces was what NATO designated the FROG (Free Rocket Over Ground) series of mobile launchers. The last of these, the Luna M, or FROG-7, was mounted atop the

▲ **R-17 Elbrus (SS-1C Scud B)**

Soviet Army / 8th Guards Artillery Brigade, 1970

The best known of the Soviet tactical ballistic missiles, the R-17 Elbrus, a member of the Scud family to NATO observers, has served as a component of the Soviet arsenal since the 1960s and has been exported to more than 30 countries. An improvement over the R-11 missile, the R-17 was larger and included an improved guidance system.

Specifications	
Configuration: single-stage, liquid fuel	Launch weight: 6300kg (13,888lb)
Deployment: mobile	Range: 280km (173 miles)
Length: 11.25m (36ft 11in)	Launch preparation time: 1 hour
Diameter: 850mm (33.5in)	

▼ TR-1 Temp (SS-12 Scaleboard)
Soviet Army / 3rd Shock Army Surface-to-Surface Missile Brigade, 1982

The TR-1 Temp, known to NATO as the SS-12 Scaleboard, was a mobile intermediate ballistic missile originally intended to replace the Scud. The SS-12 entered service in 1969 and was rarely seen by Western observers due to the fact that it was mobile and deployed from a container which opened only when the weapon was to be fired. The weapon remained with the Red Army during its service life and was never sold to other countries.

modified ZIL-135 8X8 truck which included a transporter, erector and launcher apparatus, and made its operational debut in 1965. The FROG-7 rocket warhead weighed 550kg (1200lb) and could reach targets as far away as 70km (43 miles). Its mobility was a decided advantage on the battlefield, allowing for displacement following firing and providing a greater chance of survivability by avoiding retaliatory action.

The FROG-7 could be made ready to launch within 30 minutes and was capable of delivering high-explosive, chemical or tactical nuclear weapons. It has been exported to numerous countries, some of which have modified the system to extend its range and payload.

Specifications

Configuration: single-stage, liquid fuel

Deployment: mobile

Length: 12m (39ft 4in)

Diameter: 1m (39in 4in)

Launch weight: 9700kg (9.55 tons)

Range: 900km (555 miles)

Launch preparation time: 15 minutes

▲ OTR-23 Oka (SS-23 Spider)
Soviet Army / 6th Motorized Rifle Brigade, 1981

By the end of the 1970s, the aging SS-1C Scud-B mobile missile had become obsolete and was replaced by the OTR-23 Oka, or SS-23 as it was known to NATO. The SS-23 was intended to suppress NATO tactical nuclear weapons, which Soviet analysts assumed would be employed early in a military confrontation in Western Europe to neutralize Warsaw Pact superiority in conventional arms and personnel. The OTR-23 was transported on a wheeled launcher and capable of firing within approximately five minutes.

Specifications

Configuration: single-stage, solid fuel

Deployment: mobile

Length: 7.5m (24ft 7in)

Diameter: 900mm (2ft 11in)

Launch weight: 29,465kg (29 tons)

Range: 400km (250 miles)

Launch preparation time: 5 minutes

▼ Luna M (FROG-7)

Soviet Army / 11th Surface-to-Surface Missile Battalion, 1980

Although the Soviet FROG (Free Rocket Over Ground) system was first deployed during the late 1950s, the FROG-7 appeared in 1965 and was still in active service with the Red Army a quarter-century later. The FROG-7 is carried atop an 8X8 transporter-erector-launcher vehicle. Its single-stage solid-fuel rockets are unguided and may carry nuclear, chemical or high-explosive weapons.

Specifications

Crew: 4

Diameter: 550mm (21.65in)

Rocket length: 9.11m (29ft 10in)

Rocket weight: 2500kg (5512lb)

System combat weight: 23,000kg (22.63 tons)

Range: 70km (43 miles)

Road range: 500km (310 miles)

Launch preparation time: 15-30 minutes

4th SSM Battalion, Red Army, Erfurt, German Democratic Republic, 1989

The typical Red Army FROG-7 battery of the late Cold War era was equipped with a headquarters battery and a pair of firing batteries, each equipped with two transporter-erector-launcher vehicles and long-range meteorological radar. The FROG-7b was an improved version capable of carrying cargo ordnance which could distribute bomblets or anti-personnel mines. The unguided nature of the FROG series resulted in a fairly inaccurate result; however, its longevity is testament to its filling a significant tactical role on the battlefield.

**Battalion
(4 x FROG-7)**

SSM Brigade, Red Army (Western Group of Forces (WGF), Western TVD, Neubrandenburg, German Democratic Republic, 1989

The Red Army intermediate-range ballistic-missile brigade of the 1980s consisted of a complement of 18 mobile OTR-23 Oka missile launchers. The Oka included an 8X8 truck with an operational range of 500km (310 miles). Each Oka was capable of firing conventional high-explosive fragmentation, chemical or nuclear warheads. The Oka, which could be readied to fire in five minutes or less, was designed to neutralize NATO command-and-control centres, and other high-priority theatre targets.

Brigade (18 x SS-23)

Warsaw Pact air defence
1965–90

Soviet and Warsaw Pact air defence stressed a cooperative effort between aircraft, surface-to-air missiles and anti-aircraft guns to provide comprehensive defence in depth against enemy attack.

SATURATING THE SURROUNDING air space from low to high altitude was the objective of Soviet ground air defence during the Cold War. Heavy reliance was placed on surface-to-air missiles, mobile and capable of reacting to any threat within minutes. At greater range, fighter aircraft would engage enemy planes, while effective mobile anti-aircraft guns would provide a short-range layer of fire, theoretically building a wall of defence for Red Army and Warsaw Pact ground forces against air attack. Military planners further equipped infantry units with shoulder-fired missiles, such as the SA-7 Grail, for use against low-flying fixed-wing aircraft and helicopters.

Curtain of steel

Early warning and rapid intervention by air defences were considered essential to maintaining control of the air. At the height of the Cold War, large Warsaw Pact Army or Front (Army Group) formations were protected against air attack by the SA-2 Guideline and SA-4 Ganef missile systems, which could engage enemy aircraft at long range.

Each tank or motorized infantry division of the Red Army included an organic air defence regiment equipped with either anti-aircraft guns or surface-to-air missiles. Rarely, if ever, were these systems intermingled. Therefore, a typical air defence regiment might deploy four batteries of six S-60 57mm (2.2in) guns for a complement of 24; five batteries of four mobile 2K12 Kub surface-to-air missiles, known to NATO as the SA-6 Gainful, for a total of 20 launchers; or five batteries of four mobile 9K33 Osa surface-to-air missiles, designated as the SA-8 Gecko by NATO command, for a total of 20 launchers. The SA-6 entered service in 1970 and was intended for low- to medium-altitude air defence with a range of up to 24km (15 miles). The SA-8 provided low-altitude and short-range missile

▲ **9K33 Osa (SA-8 Gecko)**

Soviet Army / 21st Motorized Rifle Division, 1983

Initially identified in the West in 1976, the SA-8 Gecko mobile anti-aircraft missile was the first weapon of its kind to mount its own engagement radar on the same vehicle which transported the missile, the 6X6 9K33 transporter-erector-launcher. The SA-8 delivers a 19kg (42lb) high-explosive fragmentation or proximity-fused warhead. By 1980, an improved SA-8B Mod 1 carried up to six missiles.

Specifications

Configuration: single-stage, solid fuel	Launch weight: 130kg (287lb)
Deployment: mobile	Range: 15km (9.3 miles)
Length: 3.15m (19ft 4in)	Launch preparation time: 5-minute reload
Diameter: 210mm (8.26in)	

▲ **2K12 Kub (SA-6 Gainful)**

Soviet Army / 30th Guards Motorized Rifle Division, 1988

Designed to protect Warsaw Pact ground forces from air attack, the SA-6 Gainful utilizes a solid-fuel rocket booster to achieve speeds in excess of Mach 1.5. Its high-explosive proximity-fused warhead claimed an alarmingly high number of Israeli aircraft during the 1973 Yom Kippur War, and the SA-6 has become one of the most widely used systems of its type in the world. To date, at least 20 countries have fielded the system.

Specifications	
Configuration: single-stage, solid fuel	
Deployment: mobile	
Length: 5.7m (18ft 9in)	
Diameter: 335mm (13.2in)	
Launch weight: 600kg (1323lb)	
Range: 20km (13 miles)	
Launch preparation time: 15 minutes	

7th Air Defence Regiment, Red Army, Zeithan, German Democratic Republic, 1989

Stationed in East Germany near the end of the Cold War, the Red Army's 7th Air Defence Regiment was equipped with the SA-6 Gainful mobile air defence missile system. Regiments such as the 7th, equipped with missiles, were further complemented by units which employed anti-aircraft guns. Together these constituted an in-depth air defence system. Each carrier transported four missiles in firing position. The vehicle acquisition radar was effective at a distance of 20km (12.5 miles).

Regiment (20 x SA-6)

defence. The Gecko was deployed in 1972, and its maximum missile range was estimated at 15km (9.3 miles). Both the SA-6 and SA-8 systems remain widely used.

Each air defence regiment was further augmented by an additional platoon of ZSU-23-4 anti-aircraft guns. The ZSU-23-4 was proved effective during the Vietnam War and the Arab–Israeli wars of 1967 and 1973. The system mounted four 23mm (0.9in) guns,

each with an effective rate of fire of 1000 rounds per minute. These were often deployed in defence of the SA-6 and SA-8 launchers. In addition, the SA-9 Gaskin close-support anti-aircraft system was utilized as a last echelon of defence. The SA-9 mounted four infrared homing missiles atop an amphibious scout car. Airborne units utilized the SA-7 Grail and the light, airmobile ZSU-23-2 organized in batteries of six with up to 36 vehicles per division.

Late Western artillery
1970–91

Artillery components of NATO forces in Western Europe were counted on to resist the advance of Warsaw Pact forces during a ground offensive, buying time for deliberation on the use of nuclear weapons.

ACKNOWLEDGING THE NUMERICAL superiority of Soviet and Warsaw Pact forces in Europe, NATO nevertheless devised a cooperative defensive programme to resist the advance of enemy forces in the event of a ground war. There is little doubt that a decisive outcome in favour of NATO forces on the ground would have required the use of nuclear weapons at least on a tactical scale. To that end, the early Cold War saw the deployment of low-level weapons such as the M28/29 Davy Crockett system, which utilized a 102mm (4in) gun or 155mm (6.1in) recoilless rifle to discharge a shell armed with a 23kg (51lb) nuclear warhead.

While the nuclear alternative was difficult even to contemplate since Soviet retaliation was virtually assured, it remained a reality. In addition, the improvement of conventional artillery was undertaken with vigour by the 1970s, resulting in several improved systems which were deployed with NATO armed forces in Western Europe and indeed with armies around the world.

Organizational changes among the various armies which made up the NATO forces also occurred. The typical structure of a US Army Division during the early to mid-Cold War period included a divisional artillery component comprising four artillery battalions. Three of these usually contained up to three batteries of 105mm (4.1in) howitzers, each containing four guns for a complement of 36; the

fourth battalion had three batteries of four 155mm (6.1in) howitzers, totalling 12.

Shoot and scoot
By the 1990s, the US Army had reorganized several times, with the motorized and light divisional concepts arranged for rapid deployment but with sufficient firepower to defeat enemy formations which included substantial armoured assets. Modern US divisions maintain an organic divisional artillery component together with a separate air defence

▲ **LARS training**
West German troops man a LARS multiple rocket launcher during winter manoeuvres. Armed with 36 rockets, the weapon was designed for rapid concentration of fire on designated targets.

▲ Flugabwehrkanonenpanzer (Flakpanzer) Gepard

German Army / 11th Flak Regiment, 1988

Deployed primarily to provide air defence for armoured formations, the Gepard utilizes high-explosive and armour-piercing ammunition fired from a pair of 35mm (1.38in) autocannon mounted externally from the crew compartment to avoid the introduction of gases into a confined space. The Gepard employs both acquisition and tracking radar which feed data to an onboard computer system to control the guns.

Specifications

Crew: 4	Engine: 623kW (830hp) 10-cylinder MTU MB 838
Weight: 47,300kg (104,060lb)	Ca M500 multi-fuel
Length: 7.68m (25ft 2in)	Speed: 65km/h (40mph)
Width: 3.27m (10ft 9in)	Road range: 550km (342 miles)
Height: 3.01m (9ft 10in)	Armament: 2 x 35mm (1.38in) autocannon

▲ SIDAM-25 self-propelled anti-aircraft gun

Italian Army / 4th Air Defence Regiment, 1987

The SIDAM-25, developed by the Italian firm of OTO Melara, mounts four 25mm (0.98in) Oerlikon cannon guided by laser rangefinding equipment and a fire-control computer. The SIDAM-25 includes a complete turret system mounted atop the chassis of the M113 armoured personnel carrier. It has also been modified to fire the French Mistral surface-to-air missile.

Specifications

Crew: 3	Engine: 161kW (215hp) 6-cylinder Detroit Diesel
Weight: 14,500kg (14.27 tons)	Speed: 65km/h (40mph)
Length: 4.86m (20ft)	Road range: 500km (310 miles)
Width: 2.69m (8ft 10in)	Armament: 4 x 25mm (1in) Oerlikon cannon
Height: 1.83m (6ft)	

artillery battalion. As the exigencies of combat demanded greater mobility, the development of light, airmobile field artillery and self-propelled systems for both ground support and anti-aircraft defence became priorities. Among the prerequisites for modern mobile fire-support systems is the 'shoot and scoot' capability, which allows the weapon to deploy, acquire targets, fire its ordnance, displace and then assume a favourable firing location before enemy

counterbattery fire or any other response can be brought to bear.

By the 1990s, the principal weapons deployed with a direct fire support battalion of the US Army, particularly one working within a brigade combat team, would often include the M119 105mm (4.1in) howitzer, a towed weapon which was actually designed by Royal Ordnance Factories of Great Britain as the L118/L119 Light Gun. With a

1st Flak Regiment, German Army, Federal Republic of Germany, 1989

Flak regiments of the German Army were often detailed to provide close anti-aircraft defence against enemy fixed-wing aircraft and helicopters. Coordinating with missile defences and other guns, the Gepard SP anti-aircraft gun was capable of firing a combined 1100 rounds per minute from its radar-directed 35mm (1.38in) autocannons. The turret is mounted on the chassis of the Leopard 1 main battle tank. Although the Gepard has been upgraded several times, it is scheduled for replacement by a new system in the coming years.

Regiment (36 x Flakpanzer Gepard)

Specifications

Crew: 5

Weight: 20,000kg (19.7 tons)

Length: 4.86m (15ft 11in)

Width: 2.69m (8ft 10in)

Height: 2.16m (7ft 1in)

Engine: 159kW (212hp) 6-cylinder Detroit Diesel

Speed: 66km/h (41mph)

Road range: 483km (300 miles)

Armament: 1 x 120mm (4.72in) mortar; 1 x 7.62mm (0.3in) MG

▲ M113A1G PzMrs (Panzermörser)

German Army / 7th Panzer Artillery Regiment, 1988

Utilized by the German Army as a light reconnaissance vehicle, the M113A1G is a converted version of the US M113 armoured personnel carrier, designed to carry a 120mm (4.72in) mortar in the troop compartment. The mortar is fired directly out of an open space in the rear of the hull roof. Specialized versions are often used for forward air control or artillery observation.

▲ LARS II MLRS

German Army / 11th Rocket Artillery Battalion, 1988

Entering service with the German Army in 1970, the LARS (Light Artillery Rocket System) has been largely replaced by the MLRS and MARS (Mittleres Artillerie Raketen System) systems more common in NATO usage. The LARS II entered service in 1980 and is capable of firing high-explosive fragmentation ammunition as well as a cargo warhead which distributes anti-tank mines. The system is fired from inside the cab of the transporter.

Specifications

Crew: 3

Rocket diameter: 110mm (4.33in)

Rocket length: 2.263m (7ft 5in)

Rocket weight: 35kg (77.16lb)

System combat weight: 17,480kg (17.2 tons)

Range: 14,000m (15,310 yards)

Rate of fire: 36 rounds in 18 seconds

12th Rocket Artillery Battalion, German Army, Federal Republic of Germany, 1989

The LARS II multiple launch rocket system was portable atop a wheeled 6X6 MAN high-mobility-truck chassis and was designed to deliver heavy fire support to NATO ground troops. It was capable of delivering 36 rockets in 18 seconds or firing a cluster warhead which distributed anti-tank mines. Rocket artillery battalions of the German Army each had 16 LARS II systems, all 209 LARS IIs in service having been upgraded from an earlier configuration. Retired from the Germany Army by 1998, the system is still in use with numerous countries.

Battalion (16 x LARS II)

maximum rate of fire of eight rounds per minute for three minutes, the M119 is capable of a sustained rate of fire of three rounds per minute for up to 30 minutes. Its light weight makes the weapon ideal for transport by air and for operations in company with fast-moving infantry formations. Light formations such as airborne units have fielded the L118/L119 in batteries of six guns.

The M198 155mm (6.1in) gun-howitzer is a primary weapon of general support artillery battalions. Introduced in the late 1970s as a replacement for the M114 of World War II vintage, the M198 is capable of firing at a maximum range

of more than 29,992m (32,800 yards) with ammunition assisted by rocket propulsion, and 17,800m (19,685 yards) with conventional high-explosive ammunition. Further, the M198 is nuclear-capable and was intended to provide NATO forces with the modern tactical nuclear punch which had become a priority with the onset of the Cold War a generation earlier. The M198 has a sustained rate of fire of two rounds per minute and can reach up to four rounds per minute during maximum exertion. It is served by a crew of nine.

Early in the 1990s, the British firm of BAE Land Systems began research on yet another improved

▲ **155mm SB-155/39 towed howitzer**

Spanish Army / 17th Artillery Regiment, 1983

The Spanish government's armament factory, known as Empresa Nacional Santa Barbara, developed the 155mm (6.1in) SB-155/39 towed howitzer during the late 1970s and equipped some artillery units with the weapon during the following decade. The SB-155 is a split-trail howitzer, which, with its disengagement of the wheels and use of a firing pedestal in action, provides more stability when firing.

Specifications

Crew: 8	Weight: 9500kg (9.35 tons)
Calibre: 155mm (6.1in)	Range: 24,700m (27,010 yards)
Elevation: - 3 degrees to + 70 degrees	Muzzle velocity: 800m/sec (2625ft/sec)

C Battery, 94th Field Artillery Battalion, US Army, Europe, 1989

The typical field artillery battalion of the US Army in NATO service in Western Europe included a complement of eight M109A3 self-propelled guns. The M109A3 was one in a series of upgrades to the original M109 series originated in the 1950s and included as many as 27 improvements such as an upgraded rammer and recoil system for the main weapon, a redesigned bustle to carry an additional 22 rounds of ammunition, redesigned hatches and an improved hydraulic system.

Battery (8 x M109A3 SP guns)

155mm (6.1in) howitzer. Designated the M777, it has equipped numerous units of the British armed forces and is slated to replace the M198 batteries of the US Army and Marine Corps. Weighing 4082kg (9000lb), it has components of lightweight titanium, which contributed to its original name – the Ultralightweight Field Howitzer (UFH). The M777 is easily moved by truck or helicopter and delivers heavy firepower at a rate of five rounds per minute. Its rocket-assisted ammunition can reach out to 30km (18.6 miles).

The primary self-propelled artillery component of NATO forces has long been the US-produced M109

Specifications

Configuration: single-stage, liquid fuel

Deployment: mobile

Length: 6.1m (20ft)

Diameter: 560mm (22in)

Launch weight: 1290kg (2850lb)

Range: 120km (75 miles)

Launch preparation time: unknown

▲ M548 with MGM-52 Lance missile

US Army / 44th Air Defense Battalion, 1970

The US Army utilized a modified M548 cargo carrier, designated the M752, as a platform both for the transport and firing of the MGM-52 Lance missile. The Lance missile was capable of firing conventional and nuclear warheads with a yield of up to 100 kilotons. A chemical delivery option was considered but abandoned by 1970. The system was withdrawn from Western Europe following the Intermediate-Range Nuclear Forces Treaty of 1987.

Specifications

Crew: 3

Weight: 54,430kg (119,746lb)

Length: 7.674m (25ft 2in)

Width: 3.632m (11ft 11in)

Height: 4.611m (15ft 2in)

Engine: 563kW (750hp) Continental
    AVDS-1790-2D diesel

Speed: 48 km/h (30mph)

Road range: 500km (311 miles)

Armament: 2 x 40mm (1.57in) L/70 Bofors guns

▲ M247 Sergeant York SPAAG

US Army / Prototype

In response to the successes of Soviet self-propelled anti-aircraft guns, the US Army embarked on the development of a replacement for its M42 Duster and MIM-72 Chaparral air defence systems in the mid 1970s. The M247 Sergeant York self-propelled anti-aircraft gun mounted a pair of 40mm (1.57in) Bofors L/70 guns atop the chassis of the M48 main battle tank. The M247 was plagued with problems, and only 50 were built. Most of these were used as targets on ordnance ranges. The programme was scrapped in 1985.

155mm (6.1in) howitzer, which was originally designed in the 1950s and upgraded on numerous occasions. The latest variant of the M109, the M109A6 Paladin, is the product of a lengthy improvement programme for the venerable system and includes improved Kevlar-based armour protection, greater range and accuracy for its main weapon and an upgraded powerplant. By the end of the 1990s, more than 1000 of the M109A6 were in the hands of US forces or pending delivery.

Both British and German designers, however, embarked on their own development programmes while fielding M109 variants. A series of joint efforts undertaken in the 1970s between the British, Germans and Italians to produce a mutually acceptable self-propelled gun, designated the SP70, had collapsed for various reasons. Therefore, the British Ministry of Defence authorized the development of a self-propelled weapon during the mid-1980s to replace the M109 system, the ageing

Field Artillery Regiment, British Army, 1989

The standard field artillery regiment of the British Army of the Rhine deployed in Western Europe consisted of three batteries of towed FH-70 155mm (6.1in) howitzers, each with three guns. Transportation was provided by the Land Rover reconnaissance vehicle. The FH-70 was a joint design undertaken by Britain, Germany and Italy, and the weapon was eventually assigned as a direct infantry support gun after original plans to equip medium artillery regiments were changed.

Battery (1 x Land Rover [Recon], 3 x FH-70 155mm/6.1in Howitzers)

Battery (1 x Land Rover [Recon], 3 x FH-70 155mm/6.1in Howitzers)

Battery (1 x Land Rover [Recon], 3 x FH-70 155mm/6.1in Howitzers)

Specifications

Crew: 8

Calibre: 155mm (6.1in)

Elevation: - 4.5 degrees to + 70 degrees

Weight: 9300kg (9.15 tons)

Range: 24,700m (27,010 yards)

Muzzle velocity: 827m/sec (2713ft/sec)

▲ **FH-70 towed howitzer**

British Army / 101st Northumbrian Regiment Royal Artillery, 1991

During the late 1960s, Britain, Germany and Italy embarked on a cooperative effort to design a close infantry support towed artillery piece. The split-trail carriage of the FH-70 provides a stable platform in action, while the gun is capable of firing a variety of high-explosive and rocket-assisted ordnance. The gun entered service in 1978 and utilizes an auxiliary power unit to relocate short distances. Its sustained rate of fire is three to six rounds per minute.

FV433 Abbot and in some cases the towed FH-70 155mm (6.1in) gun in regiments of the Royal Artillery and the Royal Horse Artillery. The result was the AS-90, mounting a 155mm (6.1in) L31 gun and powered by a 495kW (660hp), eight-cylinder Cummins diesel engine. Entering service in 1993, the AS-90 was designed as a complete vehicle, rather than the marriage of a turret and gun which could be mounted atop an existing tank hull, and utilizes the latest in Chobham anti-missile armour protection.

Meanwhile, German engineers worked to develop the PzH 2000, which mounted the Rheinmetall 155mm (6.1in) L52 gun atop a chassis based on that

of the Leopard 1 main battle tank and built by Krauss-Maffei Wegmann. The PzH 2000 is capable of firing up to 60 shells in 12 minutes, and its operational range is 420km (261 miles). The PzH 2000 design placed the engine and transmission forward of the crew compartment to provide greater protection against penetrating projectiles and boasts the latest in composite armour.

An integral component of NATO artillery, particularly in heavy field artillery brigades at corps level within the US Army, is the M270 Multiple Launch Rocket System (MLRS). The M270 entered service in 1983 and is capable of delivering up to 12

▲ GDF-CO3

Swiss Army / Artillery Battalion 54, 1992

The Oerlikon-Bührle company produced the GDF-CO3 as a mobile air defence system to protect rear areas, including production facilities, marshalling yards, and command and control centres. The system mounts twin 35mm (1.38in) Oerlikon cannon and is either tracked or wheeled. The tracked version is based on a modified M113 armoured personnel carrier chassis, while the wheeled variant employs the HYKA 4X4 vehicle.

Specifications

Crew: 3	Engine: 161kW (215hp) 6-cylinder
Weight: 18,000kg (39,600lb)	GMC 6V-53T diesel
Length: 6.7m (22ft)	Speed: 45km/h (28mph)
Width: 2.813m (9ft 3in)	Road range: 480km (297 miles)
Height: 4m (13ft 2in)	Armament: 2 x 35mm (1.38in) Oerlikon cannon

▶ Oerlikon GAI-BO1

Swiss Army / Mechanized Infantry Battalion 29, 1995

Mounted on a tripod-shaped platform, the GAI-BO1 20mm (0.79in) anti-aircraft gun includes the Oerlikon 20mm (0.79in) cannon. It is also a capable ground-defence weapon. Simple to deploy and operate, the GAI-BO1 uses no hydraulic power. Elevation is cranked with a hand wheel, and traverse is controlled by the feet of the gunner. The weapon may be transported easily aboard a truck or trailer and is in use by armed forces around the world.

Specifications

Crew: 3	Weight: 405kg (892lb)
Calibre: 20mm (0.79in)	Range: 1500m (4920ft)
Elevation: - 5 degrees to + 85 degrees	Muzzle velocity: 1100m/sec (3609ft/sec)

rockets in less than one minute. The German Army has operated a rocket system called MARS, which is based on MLRS. Development of an improved US battlefield rocket system, HIMARS (High Mobility Artillery Rocket System), was begun in 1996.

Air defence was a further priority with NATO forces, and during the 1960s the US marked off air defence artillery as a separate command from the field artillery. A variety of self-propelled anti-aircraft guns provided close air defence for NATO armour, troops and command-and-control centres. Among the most widely used of these is the German Flakpanzer Gepard (Cheetah), which was developed in the 1960s and deployed by 1970. The Gepard mounts a pair of 35mm

(1.38in) autocannon atop the chassis of the Leopard 1 main battle tank. Its radar-controlled guns work in tandem with teams of infantrymen using the shoulder-fired Stinger anti-aircraft missile, designed to shoot down low-flying fixed-wing aircraft and helicopters.

The Italian firm of OTO Melara produced another effective close air defence weapon in the SIDAM-25, which incorporates four Oerlikon 25mm (0.98in) guns, each capable of firing up to 570 rounds per minute, atop the adapted chassis of the ubiquitous M113 armoured personnel carrier. The effectiveness of the SIDAM-25, however, is limited due to its lack of radar. Its laser rangefinding equipment is efficient during periods of good weather.

▲ **Bandkanon**

Swedish Army / Södra Skånska Regiment, Sweden, 1981

The 155mm (6.1in) Bandkanon self-propelled artillery vehicle was developed by Bofors in the early 1960s and combined the chassis of the Stridsvagn 103 with the heavy cannon. The system entered service with the Swedish Army in 1967.

Specifications

Crew: 5	Engine: 1 x 179kW (240hp) Rolls-Royce diesel;
Weight: 53,000kg (116,600lb)	1 x 224kW (300hp) Boeing gas turbine
Length: 11m (36ft 1in)	Speed: 28km/h (17.4mph)
Width: 3.37m (11ft 0.7in)	Road range: 230km (143 miles)
Height: 3.85m (12ft 7.5in)	Armament: 1 x 155mm (6.1in) gun, plus
	1 x 7.62mm (0.3in) anti-aircraft MG

Self-propelled artillery battalion, Sweden, 1985

Organized in two battalions of 12 vehicles originally, the basic Swedish self-propelled artillery formation later changed to three battalions of eight vehicles. The Bandkanon was at one time one of the heaviest self-propelled artillery vehicles in the world; however, only 26 were built. Its development was undertaken in 1960, and the vehicle entered service in the middle of the decade. The Bandkanon is noteworthy as the world's first fully automatic self-propelled artillery weapon. Its ammunition was stored in clips of 14 rounds.

Battalion (8 x Bandkanons SP artillery)

Western theatre missiles
1970–90

Among the most prominent of the theatre nuclear missiles in the Western inventory is the BGM-109 Tomahawk cruise missile.

THE MOBILE, NUCLEAR-CAPABLE Tomahawk eventually was configured for launch by land, sea and air; however, only the submarine-launched version remains active today. The ground-launched nuclear Tomahawk and its launch apparatus were scheduled to be dismantled due to treaty agreements between the US and the Soviet Union during the late 1980s, and this was accomplished with the removal of all 200-kiloton W-80 nuclear warheads by 1992.

The Tomahawk armed with a conventional 454kg (1000lb) warhead has been utilized during recent conflicts and has proved a remarkably versatile and accurate weapon.

The MGM-31 Pershing intermediate-range ballistic missile was also a factor in the move towards nuclear disarmament during the Cold War. Developed during the late 1950s and deployed to Western Europe and the Korean peninsula soon after,

56th Pershing II Brigade, US Army, Schwäbisch-Gmünd, Federal Republic of Germany, 1989

Typical of the field artillery formations under the control of the US Army Missile Command in Western Europe was the 56th Pershing II Brigade with a complement of more than 100 mobile Pershing II intermediate-range ballistic missiles. The Pershing II utilized the HEMTT prime mover for launching, which included a crane for assembly and a generator to provide power to the erector and launcher. It carried a nuclear warhead of up to 400 kilotons.

1–9th Field Artillery Battalion (36 x Pershing II)

2–9th Field Artillery Battalion (36 x Pershing II)

4–9th Field Artillery Battalion (36 x Pershing II)

the Pershing I was mounted atop the tracked M474 transporter-erector-launcher vehicle. Its warhead was either conventional or the nuclear W-50 with a yield of up to 400 kilotons.

Following an upgrade to the original Pershing, designated the Pershing IA, specifications were issued in 1973 for yet another improved missile. The Pershing II was intended, along with nuclear-capable Tomahawk cruise missiles, to counter the Soviet deployment of the SS-20 Saber intermediate-range ballistic missile. The Pershing II was mounted aboard the HEMTT prime mover, which included a crane to

facilitate assembly. The terms of the Intermediate-Range Nuclear Forces Treaty of 1987 resulted in the dismantling of the Pershing series and the SS-20 by the early 1990s.

▲ BGM-109 Tomahawk

US Air Force / 11th Bomb Squadron, 1982

Originally designed for the US Navy, the BGM-109G Gryphon variant of the Tomahawk cruise missile, known as a GLCM (Ground-Launched Cruise Missile), became a primary ground-launched nuclear weapon of NATO forces in Western Europe before treaty limitations ended its nuclear capability with the removal of its 200-kiloton W-80 warheads by 1992. The Tomahawk has been deployed with a 454kg (1000lb) conventional warhead since and remains a notably successful sea-launched system. Onboard guidance capability has enhanced the accuracy of the Tomahawk.

Specifications

Configuration: solid-fuel booster, turbofan
Deployment: mobile
Length: 6.4m (21ft)
Diameter: 530mm (20in)
Launch weight: 1443kg (3181lb)
Range: 2500km (1555 miles)
Launch preparation time: 20 minutes

Specifications

Configuration: two-stage, solid fuel
Deployment: mobile
Length: 10.61m (34ft 10in)
Diameter: 1m (39.5in)
Launch weight: 4600kg (10,141lb)
Range: 1800km (1118 miles)
Launch preparation time: 15 minutes

▲ MGM-31 Pershing II

US Army / 41st Field Artillery Regiment, 1983

Reaching operational status in Western Europe in 1983, the Pershing II intermediate-range ballistic missile carried a nuclear warhead of five to 50 kilotons and was intended to engage military targets in the event of armed conflict with Warsaw Pact forces, although its improved range theoretically brought the Soviet capital of Moscow within striking distance of highly mobile launchers located in West Germany. Preceded by the Pershing I and IA, the third-generation Pershing II missiles were dismantled along with Soviet SS-20 intermediate-range missiles as a result of the Intermediate-Range Nuclear Forces Treaty of 1987.

French missile development concentrated on short- and intermediate-range systems such as the SSBS and Pluton. The Pluton, a mobile-launch system mounted atop the chassis of the AMX-30 tank, was capable of carrying conventional warheads and nuclear payloads of up to 25 kilotons. It was a short-range weapon and its operational reach of 120 km (75 miles) was meant for targets inside France or West Germany. Conceived as a replacement for the US Honest John system, the Pluton was lightweight and highly mobile. It entered service in 1974 and was operational for nearly 20 years before it left service in the mid-1990s, scheduled to be replaced by the Hadès system.

▲ **Pluton**

French Army / 3rd Artillery Regiment, 1976

Mounted atop the chassis of the AMX-30 tank, the Pluton tactical nuclear missile entered service with the French Army in 1974, and a total of 42 launchers were produced and fielded in artillery regiments of six launchers each. A 15-kiloton warhead was to be used on the battlefield, while a 25-kiloton warhead was meant for more distant targets. Targeting assistance was provided by an airborne drone.

Specifications

Configuration: two-stage, solid fuel	Launch weight: 2423kg (5342lb)
Deployment: mobile	Range: 120km (75 miles)
Length: 7.64m (26ft 1in)	Launch preparation time: unknown
Diameter: 650mm (25.6in)	

Western air defence missiles
1970–90

Coordinated air defences presented a challenge for NATO military planners as cooperation among member nations was achieved with advancing technology and systems.

A S WESTERN NATIONS independently pursued modern air defence systems based on the deployment of anti-aircraft guns, missiles and aircraft, it became apparent to NATO leaders that without coordination such endeavours would be more costly and would, in time, result in a more vulnerable military posture in Western Europe. When the alliance was formed in 1949, research had been ongoing to develop surface-to-air-missile defence capabilities; however, these efforts sometimes produced redundant systems or missile command-and-control structures which were unable to communicate with one another.

By the 1970s, NATO member nations had determined that should such conditions continue control of vital air space would be in peril in the event of an attack by Warsaw Pact forces. Therefore, an integrated air defence system was initiated and ultimately placed under the control of the NATO Air Defence Committee, which would assume responsibilities for promoting cooperation among member nations.

While missile technology continued to advance, the alliance established the NATO Air Defence Ground Environment as a component of a comprehensive system with sites stretching from

Turkey in the eastern Mediterranean to Scandinavia. Early-warning and tracking would enable coordinated interception of hostile planes by aircraft, surface-to-air missiles and anti-aircraft guns. Such a scenario is based on the rapid exchange of intelligence and the ability to bring assets to bear across national boundaries and great distances unhindered by communications difficulties or incompatible equipment.

Mobility, quick reaction, range and reliability have figured prominently in the development of air

Specifications

Configuration: two-stage, solid fuel
Deployment: mobile
Length: 5.12m (16ft 9in)
Diameter: 356mm (14in)
Launch weight: 626kg (1380lb)
Range: 40km (25 miles)
Launch preparation time: 5 minutes

▲ **M727 HAWK**

US Army / Test Platoon, Fort Bliss, Texas, 1969

The M727 HAWK (Homing All the Way Killer) was the short-lived self-propelled version of the system which combined the modified M548 tracked vehicle with the MIM-23 HAWK surface-to-air missile. Although the 'SP HAWK', as it was commonly called, was discontinued by August 1971, the missile itself was not phased out of service with the US Army and Marine Corps until 2002. The HAWK, which underwent several operational upgrades, was primarily transported and fired from the M192 triple missile launcher. HAWK batteries remain in service with the armed forces of numerous nations.

Specifications

Configuration: single-stage, solid fuel
Deployment: mobile
Length: 2.87m (113in)
Diameter: 127mm (5in)
Launch weight: 88.5kg (195lb)
Range: 4000m (4375 yards)
Launch preparation time: 5 minutes

▲ **M48 Chaparral FAADS**

US Army / 44th Air Defense Battalion, 1988

The M48 self-propelled Chaparral surface-to-air missile combined the M548 tracked launch vehicle with a variant of the AIM-9 Sidewinder air-to-air missile. With the failure of the Mauler programme, a joint effort with Great Britain, the US developed the Chaparral, which was deployed in 1969 and was in service for the next 30 years. Several upgrades kept the Chaparral in service, and one of these was target-acquisition equipment borrowed from the FIM-92 Stinger missile. Originally, the Chaparral launcher was simply pointed towards the target to allow the missile to lock on. Later, it was capable of all-weather operation.

defence missiles deployed by NATO countries. Among the most common of these during the Cold War years were the US-built MIM-23 HAWK and MIM-72 Chaparral missiles.

Development of the HAWK began in 1952 as the US Army considered options for a medium-range surface-to-air missile. Within five years, test-firing and evaluation had been completed, and the system was deployed by the end of the decade. The mobile HAWK is transported, positioned and launched with the M192 towed launcher, and a self-propelled version, the M727, was configured utilizing a modified M548 tracked vehicle. This variant was tested in 1969 but proved impractical and was abandoned in the summer of 1971.

The HAWK has undergone numerous upgrades over the years, including improved navigation, targeting and all-weather capabilities. Its basic 54kg (119lb) high-explosive warhead has been

proved effective against Soviet-manufactured aircraft, particularly during the Arab–Israeli wars of 1967 and 1973, while heavier warheads have been successfully installed. The fragmentation warheads have been improved for use against incoming ballistic missiles as well.

Although the HAWK was retired from active service with the US Army and Marine Corps by 2002, it remains a primary air defence weapon with the armed forces of more than 20 nations, and its adaptability and service life of nearly half a century are truly remarkable. More than 40,000 are believed to have been manufactured.

The MIM-72 Chaparral entered service with the US Army in 1969 as an adaptation of the successful AIM-9 Sidewinder air-to-air missile. The self-propelled Chaparral utilizes the M730 transport vehicle, which is a modification of the M548 and a direct descendant of the M113 armoured personnel

▶ Roland surface-to-air missile

German Army / 54th Artillery Regiment, 1978

Developed jointly by France and Germany, the Roland surface-to-air missile series included the Roland I, which operated during favourable weather conditions, the all-weather Roland II, and the Roland III with improved thermal sighting and laser rangefinding. The Roland variants were mounted either on the chassis of the French AMX-30 main battle tank or the German Marder infantry fighting vehicle and also on wheeled vehicles. The Roland entered service with the French Army in 1977 and with the German Army in 1978.

Specifications

Configuration: two-stage, solid fuel

Deployment: mobile

Length: 2.4m (94.5in)

Diameter: 1160mm (6.3in)

Launch weight: 63kg (139lb)

Range: 6.2km (3.9 miles)

Launch preparation time: unknown

▲ Bofors RBS-70 MANPADS

Swedish Army / Life Grenadier Regiment, 1979

Developed as a low-cost short-range man-portable air defence missile, the Bofors RBS-70 MANPADS entered service with the Swedish military in 1977 and remains deployed today. The RBS-70 launch system includes a seat for the soldier operating the weapon, and instructions on target acquisition are received through radar signals, which are then processed by a combat control terminal computer. The RBS-70 employs a laser-activated proximity fuse to destroy its target.

Specifications

Configuration: two-stage, solid fuel	Launch weight: 15kg (33lb)
Deployment: man-portable	Range: 5km (3 miles)
Length: 1.32m (52in)	Launch preparation time: immediate
Diameter: 106mm (4.17in)	

carrier. The entire system was designated the M48. Intended to work in tandem with the M163 Vulcan anti-aircraft gun, the original Chaparral was fired manually and required an interval for the missiles to lock onto their targets by identifying exhaust heat.

Two significant upgrades to the missile occurred in the late 1970s with the addition of FLIR camera technology for improved capability in adverse weather conditions; a smokeless motor which allowed better visibility after firing and helped to conceal the launcher location; and an improved target-acquisition apparatus borrowed from the shoulder-fired FIM-92 Stinger anti-aircraft missile. The service life of the Chaparral extended into the late 1990s.

The British Rapier system, which is fired from fixed launch sites or the tracked M548, is one of the longest-serving weapons of its kind in the world. The Rapier entered service in 1971 and was considered a

viable air defence system in 2010. The primary air defence weapon of the British Army, it has essentially replaced other missiles and most anti-aircraft guns in the British arsenal.

A joint effort between France and Germany in the early 1960s produced the Roland surface-to-air missile, which was later improved with all-weather capabilities but endured a lengthy testing period and was not deployed by either nation's armed forces until 1977. Although the Roland and the improved Roland II were never produced in large numbers due to delays during evaluation and rising costs, the US did make a notable purchase of the system in 1975. This attempt to deploy a modified Roland in front-line air defence artillery units, however, met with failure due to difficulties in technology transfer and increasing expense. Fewer than 30 modified Roland missiles were produced.

Specifications

Configuration: single-stage, solid fuel
Deployment: mobile
Length: 2.93m (9ft 7in)
Diameter: 156mm (6.14in)
Launch weight: 85kg (187lb)
Range: 8.5km (5.3 miles)
Launch preparation time: 5 minutes

▲ **Crotale EDIR**

French Army / 3rd Air Defence Squadron, 1991

Originally designed during the 1950s in France for the armed forces of South Africa where it was named 'Cactus', the Crotale EDIR (Infrared Differential Ecartometry) short-range air defence missile has been mounted on a wheeled chassis as well as that of the AMX-30 main battle tank. The Crotale launcher holds up to eight missiles which utilize radar, electro-optical and infrared equipment for target acquisition and tracking. Production of the modernized Crotale NG began in 1990, incorporating the launcher and radar in one vehicle.

Light Air Defence Battery (Tracked Rapier), British Army, 1989

The British Army light air defence battery was composed of an FV432 command vehicle, a variant of the FV430 infantry fighting vehicle, and a complement of six tracked Rapier surface-to-air-missile launchers. The development of the Rapier was subsequent to the failure of the Mauler programme, a joint effort with the United States. The Rapier entered service in 1971 and remains active today. Its longevity is due in large part to its rapid response time and versatility as a radar- and laser-guided missile which is deployed atop mobile M548 launchers or from fixed positions. It has essentially replaced all other missiles and guns in air defence roles with the British Army.

Battery (1 x FV432 command APC, 6 x Tracked Rapier SAM)

Soviet–Afghan War
1979–89

The firepower of Soviet artillery was often negated by rugged terrain and the persistent, low-technology campaign waged by the guerrilla forces in Afghanistan.

FOR A DECADE, the Soviet Union waged a costly, unsuccessful war against the Muslim Mujahideen in Afghanistan. The mechanized might and heavy weaponry of the Red Army were often frustrated by the hit-and-run tactics of guerrilla fighters who struck at convoys and military installations swiftly and then melted away into the rugged countryside. Mountainous terrain, inhospitable desert, and tactics which proved ineffective in counter-insurgency warfare made pursuit and decisive action problematic for Soviet forces. However, when the guerrillas appeared in significant numbers or were caught in the open, the superior firepower and modern technology of the Red Army was telling.

Stinging the Hind

One of the most effective weapons deployed by the Soviets in Afghanistan was the large, yet agile, Mil Mi-24 Hind helicopter gunship, which was in country from the very start. The Mi-24 was heavily armed with a combination of rockets and machine guns and capable of carrying up to eight fully equipped combat infantrymen. Swift airmobile operations supported by the Mi-24 took their toll on the Mujahideen until the United States government intervened with a programme to arm the guerrillas.

The most significant weapon appropriated for the Afghan guerrillas was the shoulder-fired FIM-92 Stinger air defence missile. The Mujahideen possessed few effective anti-aircraft guns, and it was the Stinger which mounted an appreciable challenge to Soviet mastery of the air. With an effective ceiling of approximately 3000m (10,000ft), the Stinger could be fired from distances as great as five kilometres (three miles) from its target, utilizing heat-seeking sensors to lock on. Perhaps one of the greatest advantages of the weapon was its ease of transport and the fact that little or no training was needed to operate it. One defence analyst commented, 'The missile's complexity can be accommodated by almost any potential user nation or group.'

The first shipment of 300 Stinger missiles arrived in Afghanistan in 1986, and this was followed by another 700 the next year. During their first action, the Stingers were reported to have shot down three Mi-24s. They are credited with destroying at least 275 Soviet fixed-wing aircraft and helicopters before the Red Army withdrawal in 1989.

While such a turn of events appears remarkable, it must be noted that the improved air defence capability of the guerrillas made the war effort more costly for the Soviets and was probably the primary

Specifications

Configuration: two-stage, solid fuel

Deployment: man-portable

Length: 1.52m (60in)

Diameter: 70mm (2.75in)

Launch weight: 10.1kg (22.25lb)

Range: 5000m (3.1 miles)

Launch preparation time: 8 seconds

▲ **FIM-92 Stinger**

Mujahideen guerrilla forces, 1986

Years of research and development were committed to the FIM-92 Stinger shoulder-fired surface-to-air missile, which replaced the US Army's first such weapon, the Redeye. The Stinger continues to utilize infrared homing equipment which locks onto a target's heat source; however, its capability is enhanced by ultraviolet detection as well. The Stinger is armed with an impact-fused high-explosive fragmentation warhead which weighs three kilograms (6.6lb). Supply of the weapon to the Mujahideen in Afghanistan hastened the Soviet withdrawal in 1989.

reason for the decision to abandon the effort to prop up a weak Marxist government in Kabul.

Heavy Red Army hardware

When the Soviet Red Army invaded Afghanistan in 1979, its operational doctrine had been formulated to fight a war against a traditional NATO foe on the rolling terrain of Western Europe. Therefore, military planners maintained a tradition of dependence on massed artillery and close ground support by aircraft.

Traditionally, the Red Army considered artillery a primary weapon of decision on the battlefield; however, the acquisition of targets of high value was difficult due to the nature of counter-insurgency warfare.

The missions of the artillery were nevertheless those of direct and indirect support for manoeuvre elements but also to block escape routes of guerrillas during search-and-destroy missions and to cover the withdrawal of Soviet forces when the decision had been made to disengage. During such withdrawal

▲ **122mm D-30 2A18 howitzer**

Soviet Army / 108th Motorized Rifle Division, 1980

Developed in the early 1960s as a replacement for the aging M1938 howitzer, the 122mm (4.8in) D-30 was a common element of the Soviet units engaged in Afghanistan and deployed in Europe during the Cold War. The D-30 mounts the 2A18 howitzer, which is the same weapon used on several self-propelled assault guns. Its wide, three-piece trail separates when the weapon is deployed to provide a stable firing platform. The weapon is capable of firing a variety of ordnance, including high-explosive fragmentation and laser-guided shells.

Specifications

Crew: 7

Calibre: 122mm (4.8in)

Elevation: - 7 degrees to + 70 degrees

Weight: 3150kg (6945lb)

Range: 15,400m (16,840 yards)

Muzzle velocity: 690m/sec (2264ft/sec)

Specifications

Crew: 6

Calibre: 23mm (0.9in)

Elevation: - 10 degrees to + 90 degrees

Weight: 950kg (2094lb)

Range: 2000m (6560ft)

Muzzle velocity: 970m/sec (3182ft/sec)

▲ **ZU-23-2 towed anti-aircraft cannon**

Soviet Army / 56th Separate Airborne Assault Brigade, 1983

Mounting twin 23mm (0.9in) 2A14 autocannon, the ZU-23-2 was developed in the late 1950s to replace the 14.5mm (0.57in) heavy machine gun in an air defence role and remains in service with the armed forces of more than 20 nations today. Intended for use against low-flying aircraft, it is also effective against light armoured vehicles. When the weapon is deployed, its wheeled carriage folds rapidly underneath, allowing it to get into action quickly.

▲ **Firing range**

Red Army soldiers practice firing the D-30 122mm (4.8in) howitzer. First entering service in the early 1960s, the D-30 became the mainstay of many armies during the Cold War period, proving superior to the US-produced 155mm (6.1in) M114 as well as virtually every piece in the 105mm (4.1in) class. The gun is still used today in some developing countries, and has been deployed in the war in Afghanistan by the Afghan National Army.

movements, the Soviets learned to direct fire well beyond the suspected positions of the Mujahideen and walk the fire backwards towards their own troops until it was judged that sufficient covering fire had been laid to suppress the small arms of the guerrillas. Artillery officers maintained control of their weapons most of the time; however, on rare occasions the officers of infantry units were given the authority to order fire support in critical situations.

While the firepower of artillery may indeed have a telling and decisive effect on a stationary enemy which maintains a defined, continuing front, the Mujahideen guerrillas did not oblige. Analysts have noted that the lack of ground manoeuvre and close

combat actions taken by the Soviets facilitated the longevity and eventual victory of the guerrilla forces.

Throughout the course of the war, Soviet commanders in Afghanistan recognized the flaw in this policy and attempted to compensate. One tactic employed by the Red Army was the artillery ambush. Motion detectors were distributed to pick up the sounds of passing insurgent groups or vehicles, and contacts were often followed by heavy fire from 122mm (4.8in) D-30 field howitzers. The self-propelled 2S1 122mm (4.8in) and 2S9 120mm (4.7in) howitzers were often deployed in support of short-duration operations, while truck-mounted rocket launchers such as the BM-21 and BM-27 were frequently used to saturate fixed enemy positions. Still, a lack of light infantry and the difficulties inherent in the manoeuvrability of mechanized infantry hampered ground operations. In turn, the reliance on artillery continued, and by the end of the war more than 400 artillery pieces and mortars had been lost.

Workhorse

The 122mm (4.8in) D-30 howitzer proved to be a workhorse among towed artillery weapons used by the Red Army in Afghanistan. The D-30 entered service in the mid-1960s as a replacement for the M1938 howitzer, which had been in production until 1955. The weapon is similar in design to an earlier howitzer produced during World War II for the German Army by Czechoslovakia's Skoda works. An interesting feature is its split trail, which divides into three stabilizing legs to assist with the absorption of recoil in action.

The Soviets considered mortars and anti-tank weapons to be artillery and as a matter of course integrated artillery personnel into mechanized infantry units to operate them. When engaged with Mujahideen in mountainous terrain, Soviet commanders often found that the 82mm (3.2in) Vasilek mortar, with its high trajectory and plunging fire, was more effective than the howitzer. This was particularly true when engaging enemy forces in caves or ravines.

One effective method of engagement was to fire the laser-guided Smel'chak, or Daredevil, round against guerrilla positions which might otherwise require a direct assault by infantry. The Smel'chak was fired by the massive 240mm (9.45in) 2S4 self-propelled mortar, nicknamed the Tyulpan, or Tulip, and known to NATO as the M1975. One battery of 2S4s engaged a Mujahideen stronghold in a deep gorge at a distance of nearly 2400m (2625 yards). After firing conventional high-explosive rounds for ranging, a single Smel'chak was loosed at the target. The resulting direct hit destroyed the guerrilla position.

The BM-21 and BM-27 multiple rocket launchers are direct descendants of the famed BM-13 Katyusha rocket system which gained notoriety during World War II. The BM-21 is mounted atop the Ural 375D 6X6 truck and carries 40 122mm (4.8in) rockets, which may be fired at a rate of two rounds per second. The BM-21 entered service in 1964 and is relatively accurate for an unguided rocket system. It remains a front-line fire-support weapon with the armed forces of more than 50 nations.

The BM-27 multiple rocket launcher appeared in the late 1970s, and its 16 tubes fire a variety of 220mm (8.7in) rockets, including high-explosive fragmentation and chemical warheads, from atop the chassis of the ZIL-135 8X8 launch vehicle. Its crew of four is capable of preparing the system to fire or displacing it within three minutes. The BM-27 was often used in Afghanistan to distribute anti-personnel mines in order to contain the movements of guerrillas during offensive sweeps by infantry units.

▶ 82mm Vasilek Mortar

Soviet Army / 5th Guards Motorized Rifle Division, 1981

The 82mm (3.2in) Vasilek mortar, or Cornflower, was conceived as a weapon which could provide both the plunging fire of a mortar and the flatter trajectory of field artillery. Developed in the early 1970s, it was utilized by mechanized infantry units of the Soviet Red Army in Afghanistan. The Vasilek could be loaded either from the breech or muzzle and was most often towed, although it has been seen fixed to a light vehicle. It remains in use with some airborne units but has largely been replaced by the 120mm (4.7in) mortar.

Specifications

Crew: 4	Range: 4720m (5162 yards)
Calibre: 82mm (3.2in)	Muzzle velocity: 270m/sec (890ft/sec)
Elevation: - 1 degree to + 85 degrees	
Weight: 632kg (1393lb)	

Specifications

Configuration: two-stage; kerosene, solid fuel

Deployment: mobile

Length: 9m (29ft 6in)

Diameter: 800mm (31.5in)

Launch weight: 2500kg (5511lb)

Range: 55km (34 miles)

Launch preparation time: 10 minutes

▲ 2K11 Krug (SA-4 Ganef)

Soviet Army / 8th Guards Surface-to-Air Missile Brigade, 1988

A large ramjet missile powered by kerosene and solid fuel, the SA-4 Ganef long-range air defence missile was deployed with the Red Army in the early 1960s. Mounted atop the GM-123 transporter-erector-launcher, the SA-4 was in service briefly with Soviet forces in Afghanistan. The missile is guided initially by acquisition radar and radio signals, before the SA-4 onboard radar locks onto the target, and the proximity fuse is detonated when range has closed sufficiently. Several nations, including the Czech Republic, Hungary and Bulgaria, operate the system today.

▲ BM-27 Uragan multiple rocket launcher

Soviet Army / 201st Motorized Rifle Division, 1983

Entering service with the Red Army during the early 1970s, the BM-27 Uragan multiple launch rocket system includes the wheeled ZIL-135 8X8 mobile launcher along with 16 tubes which fire 220mm (8.7in) rockets. The weapon is highly mobile and can be prepared for relocation in three minutes. Reloading of the full complement of missiles requires 20 minutes.

Specifications

Crew: 4

Calibre: 220mm (8.7in)

Rocket length: 4.83m (15ft 10in)

Rocket weight: 260kg (573lb)

System combat weight: 18,144kg (40,000lb)

Range: 25,000m (15.5 miles)

Rate of fire: 1 round per second

Falklands War: British forces
1982

When British forces moved to retake the distant Falkland Islands from Argentina, light infantry supported by artillery played a pivotal role in the success of the operation.

IN THE SPRING OF 1982, British forces engaged those of Argentina to reassert their nation's sovereignty over the Falkland Islands, a remote cluster of rocky land thousands of kilometres from Britain itself. Logistics presented an immediate challenge, not to mention the air, naval and ground strength of the Argentinian forces to be confronted. British transport vessels sailed almost halfway around the world to facilitate the establishment of a beachhead at San Carlos Water.

Due to the nature of the conflict, including distance, terrain and available support units, it became apparent that light infantry supported by mobile field and air defence artillery along with a relative few light armoured vehicles could exert the proper force to execute the mission. Success on the ground, however, was dependent on control of the air and the supporting presence of the Royal Navy, which could contribute air assets and provide resupply. Partially due to the fact that the navy could

remain on station for a somewhat short duration, speed was of the essence.

The long march
When British forces landed at San Carlos, they included troops of 3 Commando Brigade, Royal Marines, and the army's 5 Infantry Brigade. The artillery and surface-to-air assets deployed included 29 Commando Regiment, Royal Artillery, which included three six-gun batteries (7, 8, 70) of the 105mm (4.1in) L118 Light Gun, and 148 Commando Forward Observation Battery, Royal Artillery. The Commando Air Defence Troop carried 12 Shorts Blowpipe surface-to-air missiles, while T Battery, 12 Air Defence Regiment, was armed with the Rapier surface-to-air missile. Also there were 105mm (4.1in) L118 Light Guns of 4 Field Regiment, Royal Artillery, as were the surface-to-air missiles of Blowpipe Troop, 43 Air Defence Battery.

▲ **Preparing to fire**
British Army personnel prepare to fire an L118 Light Gun. Although lacking a heavy punch, the L118 proved to be a useful and adaptable gun in adverse conditions, especially the kind of soft terrain British forces encountered in the Falkland Islands.

The Light Gun proved to be a mobile and versatile weapon during the Falklands War, although the wet, marshy conditions often resulted in challenges for displacing and relocating the weapons. During prolonged fire-support missions, it was not unusual for recoil to cause the howitzer to move more than 2.5m (eight feet) from its original location. Innovative measures were taken to further secure the weapon in its correct position. A total of five batteries, including 30 L118s, were deployed by British forces in the Falklands. Their accurate fire was essential to victory in several sharp clashes during the march to the capital at Stanley.

One British soldier fighting at the Battle of Two Sisters remembered, 'There were three [Argentinian] machine guns, and we brought down constant and effective salvoes of our own artillery fire onto them directly, 15 rounds at a time. There would be a pause, and they'd come back at us again. So we had to do it a second time, all over their positions.'

In preparation for the assault of 2 PARA at Wireless Ridge, Light Guns fired 6000 rounds of

Specifications

Crew: 6

Calibre: 105mm (4.1in)

Elevation: - 5.5 degrees to + 70 degrees

Weight: 1860kg (4100lb)

Range: 15,070m (16,480 yards)

Muzzle velocity: 617m/sec (2024ft/sec)

▲ **L118 Light Gun**

British Army / 29 Commando Regiment Royal Artillery, 1982

The L118 Light Gun was introduced to the British Army in 1976 as a replacement for the Italian OTO Melara Mod 56 105mm (4.1in) pack howitzer and became the standard light artillery weapon of the British Army. The Light Gun is served by a crew of six and has a rate of fire of six to eight rounds per minute. Although heavier than the Mod 56, it is airmobile or movable overland by a one-ton Land Rover vehicle.

97 Battery Royal Artillery, Falklands Islands, 1982

During the Falklands War of 1982, 97 Battery Royal Artillery was equipped with six 105mm L118 Light Guns. The battery was one of five which supported British ground operations from San Carlos Water to the final victory at Stanley. The weapons were airlifted by helicopter and often towed by the Land Rover 101 vehicle, which had been designed as the prime mover for both the L118 and the Rapier air defence missile. The L118 proved decisive during several engagements with accurate, sustained fire against Argentinian forces entrenched in positions on high ground.

Battery (6 x 105mm/4.1in L118 Light Guns)

105mm (4.1in) ammunition. As the battles around Stanley progressed, the guns were known to have fired up to 400 rounds per day in support of ground forces.

The Light Gun had been developed in the early 1970s and had entered service with the British Army by 1976 as a replacement for the Italian-made OTO Melara Mod 56, a pack howitzer which could be quickly disassembled and transported with light infantry and airborne units. Based somewhat on the design of the older 25-pounder gun, the L118 was heavier than the Mod 56; however, it provided increased range which had been a prerequisite for the new design and was still airmobile due to improvements in lift aircraft. The L118 has further been deployed to the Balkans and the Middle East.

The performance of the Blowpipe and Rapier air defence missiles in the Falklands has been criticized. The Blowpipe had been developed in the early 1970s

and entered service in 1975. Often, a two-man team would operate the Blowpipe, although one soldier could manage and would have an interval of roughly 20 seconds to sight a target and fire. Nearly 100 of the missiles were fired during the campaign, and the official report of the action stated that only nine of these struck their targets. However, further scrutiny disputed even this claim, and it has been reported that only two aircraft were hit, one of these a British Harrier jump jet.

The Rapier missile entered service in 1971, and with improvements it has since replaced most other air defence systems, missiles or guns, in the British Army. After-action reports from the Falklands indicated disappointing initial results. Only 14 hits had supposedly been confirmed with six probables. However, later studies firmly attributed only one shoot-down – an Argentinian A-4 Skyhawk fighter-bomber – to the Rapier.

▲ **Rapier surface-to-air missile**

British Army / 12 Air Defence Regiment, 1982

The Rapier surface-to-air missile entered service with the British Army in 1971, initially to replace the older English Electric Thunderbird. However, as the air defence requirements of NATO forces evolved, the Rapier took on a larger role and has become the primary air defence weapon of British forces. During favourable weather conditions, the missile is guided by infrared tracking, while the Blindfire tracking and guidance radar allows for use in inclement weather.

Specifications

Configuration: two-stage, solid fuel	Launch weight: 42kg (94lb)
Deployment: fixed or mobile	Range: 7.25km (4.5 miles)
Length: 2.24m (88.2in)	Launch preparation time: 6 seconds
Diameter: 133mm (5.25in)	

Specifications

Configuration: two-stage; solid-fuel booster &	Diameter: 409mm (16.1in)
liquid-fuel sustainer	Launch weight: 2384kg (5256lb)
Deployment: shipboard	Range: 58km (36 miles)
Length: 6.1m (20ft)	

▲ **Seaslug surface-to-air missile**

Royal Navy / HMS Antrim (Destroyer), 1982

The Seaslug missile was introduced to the Royal Navy for shipboard air defence in 1961 and continued in service for 30 years. The missile was deployed during the Falklands War, and at least one incident of its firing was documented. The Seaslug was known as an accurate missile with a probable hit rate of better than 90 per cent. It was guided by radar and carried a 135kg (297lb) warhead.

▲ Blowpipe MANPADS

British Army / Air Defence Troop, 3 Commando Brigade, 1982

The man-portable Blowpipe air defence missile entered service with the British Army in 1975 and was retired a decade later. It includes the launch tube containing the missile and an attached sighting unit. The entire apparatus is then aimed and fired from the shoulder. While aiming is assisted through infrared optics, the operator steers the missile to its target by means of a thumb-operated lever. Its 2.2kg (4.85lb) warhead is detonated by proximity fuse.

Specifications

Configuration: two-stage, solid fuel

Deployment: man-portable

Length: 1.4m (55.1in)

Diameter: 76.2mm (3in)

Launch weight: 11kg (24.5lb)

Range: 3500m (3825 yards)

Launch preparation time: 20 seconds

Falklands War: Argentinian forces
1982

Firing from advantageous positions on high ground, Argentinian artillery performed well during the defence of the Falkland Islands.

AS THE ELITE TROOPS of Britain's 3 PARA assaulted Mount Longdon on the night of 11 June 1982, the soldiers came under intense and accurate fire from Argentinian artillery. For two days, the paras hung on grimly to their hard-won gains, having lost 19 men to artillery and small-arms fire and then another four as the relentless bombardment continued. The artillery fire from the defenders of Mount Harriet and Two Sisters was equally intense that night. The following night on Mount Tumbledown two more British soldiers were killed by Argentinian artillery, and the guns maintained an incessant bombardment of the attacking British at Wireless Ridge throughout the hours of darkness.

Artillery played a major role for both the Argentinians and the British during the brief but bitter war for control of the Falkland Islands. By the

time British forces had overcome major logistical challenges to reach the remote islands in force, the Argentinians had moved substantial military assets to the small, rocky archipelago they referred to as the Malvinas.

The heaviest concentration of Argentinian firepower was with the 3rd Artillery Group and the 4th Airborne Artillery Group, which each fielded at least 18 105mm (4.1in) OTO Melara Mod 56 pack howitzers, which were of Italian manufacture and originally intended to equip mountain troops of the Italian Army. In addition, the 3rd Artillery Group contained four 155mm (6.1in) Model 1977 howitzers. Much of this artillery was situated in or near the capital of Stanley for defensive purposes and due to the fact that the heavier artillery was difficult to transport across the marshy terrain. The 601st Anti-Aircraft

ARGENTINA: ARTILLERY UNITS STATIONED IN THE FALKLANDS, 1982			
Unit	Commander	Equipment	Strength
3rd Artillery Group (GA3), 3rd Infantry Brigade	Lt-Col Martín A. Balza	105mm OTO Melara Mod 56 howitzer 155mm Model 1977 howitzer	18 4
4th Airborne Artillery Group (GA4), 4th Airborne Brigade	Lt-Col Carlos A. Quevedo	105mm OTO Melara Mod 56 howitzer	18

Artillery Group was armed with Roland and Tigercat surface-to-air missiles, the Oerlikon GDF-001 35mm (1.38in) twin cannon, the 30mm (1.2in) Hispano Suiza Hs-831 machine gun, and other light weapons.

Flash and thunder

Argentinian artillery was often located in strong positions along ridges and on high ground which guarded the British route of march. Light mortars and recoilless rifles were placed in order to funnel advancing British troops into the lines of fire of entrenched Argentinian soldiers with their rifles and machine guns. During the bitter clash at Goose Green, troops of the Argentinian 25th Independent

Motorized Infantry Regiment held up British attempts to capture Darwin Ridge for several hours as an officer directed the fire of three 105mm (4.1in) guns and 120mm (4.7in) mortars against the attackers. Argentinian forward observers had been able to track the progress of the British advance and call in accurate coordinates for the gunners. The resulting fire inflicted several casualties on the airborne soldiers of 2 PARA, while British artillery was in action, firing more than 1000 rounds in support of the difficult advance and finally compelling the Argentinians to abandon their positions and surrender at Goose Green.

Although the OTO Melara Mod 56 was a weapon with a long history, it had not been intended for a

▶ OTO Melara 105mm Mod 56

Argentinian Army / 3rd Artillery Group, 1982

The 105mm (4.1in) OTO Melara Mod 56 pack howitzer remains in service half a century after its initial delivery to the Italian armed forces as a light, easily transportable weapon for mountain infantry. The Mod 56 may be dismantled into 12 component pack loads to facilitate movement through rugged country. A versatile weapon, the Mod 56 may be used with a high trajectory to provide plunging fire support for infantry movements or on a flat trajectory in defensive positions against advancing armoured vehicles.

Specifications

Crew: 6	Weight: 1273kg (2806lb)
Calibre: 105mm (4.1in)	Range: 11,100m (12,140 yards)
Elevation: - 7 degrees to + 65 degrees	Muzzle velocity: 416m/sec (1345ft/sec)

4th Airborne Artillery Group (GA4), 4th Airborne Brigade, Falkland Islands, 1982

Participating primarily in the defence of Stanley, the Falklands capital, the 4th Airborne Artillery Group fielded 18 105mm (4.1in) OTO Melara Mod 56 pack howitzers. The Mod 56 was the most numerous field artillery weapon in Argentinian service during the Falklands War and proved a capable and versatile weapon in the hands of Argentinian artillerymen, providing direct fire against advancing British forces during their push from San Carlos in the spring of 1982. These 105mm (4.1in) weapons were heavily engaged at Goose Green, Mount Longdon, Wireless Ridge and other locations.

Airborne Artillery Group (18 x OTO Melara 105mm/4.1in Mod 56 pack howitzer)

prolonged engagement. Given the rocky terrain across the Falklands, this 105mm (4.1in) weapon was well suited to holding high ground and bringing fire on enemy troops engaged in a direct assault against the well-prepared Argentinian positions. As mentioned above, the Mod 56 had been developed 30 years earlier as a pack howitzer for mountain troops. The weapon was appreciated by light infantry and airborne units because of its welcome firepower since it was often the heaviest weapon available to such troops and could be wrestled into position by the soldiers with relative ease due to its light weight.

The Mod 56 could be disassembled into 12 components and carried by the soldiers themselves or by pack animals. Cross-country transport was often accomplished by light vehicles towing the weapon or by carrying the gun inside the modified troop compartment of an armoured personnel carrier. It was also light enough to be lifted by helicopter and transported by air as a single piece. Licence copies of the Mod 56 have been produced in China and Great Britain, where it is known as the L5.

The heaviest-calibre field piece engaged during the Falklands War, the Model 1977 howitzer, was based on an original French design, the 155mm (6.1in) SP Gun F3, a self-propelled weapon. The Argentinians removed the gun from its original tracked mounting and placed it on a carriage with a split trail. During the mid-1970s, the Argentinian Army had sought to replace its aging M114 155mm (6.1in) howitzers, which dated from World War II. Backed by the military junta which had previously taken control of

the Argentinian government, the modification of the Model 1977 to the army's specifications was done in concert with the purchase of substantial quantities of weapons and ammunition from numerous countries.

The Model 1977 was primarily engaged in the defence of the mountains and ridges around Stanley and proved to be the only real land-based artillery counter to the accurate gunfire from warships of the Royal Navy. Fewer than ten of the Model 1977s were in action in the Falklands, and these were transported by aircraft to the islands as the British steadily advanced across East Falkland.

Missile threat

The Tigercat surface-to-air missile was, ironically, a British weapon which was a land-based version of the Royal Navy's Sea Cat air defence missile. The Sea Cat was outdated by the early 1980s and had been replaced by the Sea Dart and Sea Wolf systems on some warships; however, it was still widely used. The Tigercat was a mobile variant which was mounted on a triple launcher. Only one kill was claimed by the Sea Cat during the Falklands War, and more than 80 of the missiles were reported to have been launched. No Tigercat kills were confirmed.

The Argentinians had positioned their Roland missiles at fixed launch points in defence of the airport at Stanley. At least four launchers had been purchased during the late 1970s, and these were captured by the British with the surrender of the Argentinian garrison. Eight of ten Roland missiles deployed were fired, and one British Hawker Sea

Specifications

Crew: 6

Calibre: 155mm (6.1in)

Elevation: - 10 degrees to + 67 degrees

Weight: 8000kg (7.87 tons)

Range: 22,000m (24,060 yards)

Muzzle velocity: 765m/sec (2510ft/sec)

▲ **155mm Model 1977 howitzer**

Argentinian Army / 3rd Artillery Group, 1982

An Argentinian adaptation of the French self-propelled 155mm (6.1in) F3 gun, the Model 1977 included the barrel of the French weapon mounted on a split-trail carriage. In preparation for firing, the wheels were raised and a firing pedestal lowered in order to provide a stable platform. During the Falklands War, the weapon proved too heavy for easy transport across marshy terrain and was engaged primarily in the defence of Stanley.

Harrier fighter-bomber was shot down by a Roland on 1 June 1982. A joint venture between France and Germany, the Roland had become operational by 1977 and was considered a modern, effective weapon during the Falklands War.

In addition to the Roland and Tigercat missiles, the Argentinians had purchased a number of the French Exocet anti-ship missiles, which could be fired from mobile launchers on land, from on board ship and from aircraft. It was the Exocet which inflicted significant losses on the Royal Navy during the Falklands War. An Exocet hit the destroyer HMS *Sheffield*, inflicting damage which later caused the warship to sink, and also damaged the destroyer HMS *Glamorgan*. A pair of Exocets struck the 15,240-tonne (15,000-ton) Cunard roll-on/roll-off container vessel *Atlantic Conveyor*, causing it to sink five days later. The Exocet became the most recognized weapon of the Falklands War and remains in wide use today. It entered service with the French Navy in 1979, and its basic version carries a 165kg (360lb) warhead. The missile skims the surface of the water at 315m (1030ft) per second and locks onto its target with radar.

▲ Oerlikon GDF-001 35mm twin cannon

Argentinian Army / 601st Anti-Aircraft Artillery Group, 1982

The Swiss-manufactured medium-range Oerlikon GDF-001 35mm (1.38in) air defence gun is a twin-mounted weapon deployed atop a wheeled carriage which splits into a four-legged platform for firing. It is fed by an automatic loading system of seven-round clips. The Oerlikon has been in service for many years and forms the Skyguard air defence system when operated in tandem with the Sparrow air defence missile.

Specifications

Crew: 4

Calibre: 35mm (1.38in)

Elevation: - 5 degrees to + 92 degrees

Weight: 6400kg (6.3 tons)

Range: 4000m (13,125 yards)

Muzzle velocity: 1175m/sec (3855ft/sec)

▲ Rheinmetall MK 20 Rh 202 autocannon

Argentinian Army / 601st Anti-Aircaft Artillery Group, 1982

Transported atop a two-wheeled trailer, the 20mm (0.79in) twin guns of the Rh 202 are positioned on a power mounting which can be removed from the trailer and stabilized on a base of three outstretched legs. With a rate of fire of up to 1000 rounds per minute, its close-support capabilities were critical to the Argentinian defences around the airport at Stanley during the Falklands War.

Specifications

Crew: 4

Calibre: 20mm (0.79in)

Elevation: - 5.5 degrees to + 83.5 degrees

Weight: 1650kg (3637lb)

Range: 2000m (6560 yards)

Muzzle velocity: 1050m/sec (3445ft/sec)

Chapter 2

The Korean War, 1950–53

The Cold War erupted into a bloody conflict,
which is still unresolved to this day, when North Korean
troops crossed the 38th parallel on 25 June 1950, in an
attempt to unify the Korean peninsula under communist rule.
Although rumours of war had circulated far and wide, the
defending South Korean Army was ill-prepared to stem the
tide of tanks and troops unleashed by the North. Following a
United Nations resolution which authorized intervention, a
US-led coalition embarked on the arduous task of preserving
the pre-war status quo. Initially, neither side could call upon
artillery support as needed; however, as the war dragged on,
heavy guns gained a prominent role.

◀ Fire in the hole
Men of the 31st Heavy Mortar Company fire their M2 107mm (4.2in) mortar at an enemy position west of
Chorwon, Korea, in early 1953.

Introduction

The Korean War eventually lapsed into a stalemate reminiscent of the trench warfare on the Western Front during World War I, and the firepower of artillery contributed to the deadlock. The frequent use of big guns caused the conflict to become known as 'the artillery war'.

LESS THAN FIVE YEARS after the end of World War II, the prospect of another catastrophic conflict was all too real. North and South Korea were at war, and the forces of numerous countries had joined the fighting either through United Nations mandate or to protect their own national interests. Unlike any previous conflict in world history, however, the Korean War was prosecuted under the ominous prospect of a nuclear cloud, an apocalyptic exchange of weapons so powerful that humankind might destroy itself.

The world had entered the Nuclear Age, and the research and development of atomic weapons was proceeding. Both the United States and the Soviet Union possessed the atomic bomb, and along with strategic considerations there was experimentation into the feasibility of artillery capable of firing tactical nuclear weapons. By the mid-1950s, nuclear-capable artillery was a reality, and US shells as small as 155mm (6.1in) were tipped with nuclear warheads.

In Korea, however, conventional artillery of World War II vintage remained the order of the day. Supplied by the Soviets, the North Korean Army possessed relatively few artillery pieces or self-propelled guns. When the Chinese People's Liberation Army joined the conflict in the autumn of 1950, the same was true. Although field artillery and heavy guns were scarce among the Chinese formations, there was no shortage of manpower. In the South, the Republic of Korea Army was both undermanned and underequipped. Rushed from bases in Japan, the first US forces to reach Korea under the UN flag were woefully understrength as well.

Dash to Seoul

When the North Koreans attacked, their armoured spearheads, including up to 150 of the formidable Soviet-built T-34 medium tanks, which had gained lasting fame on the Eastern Front in World War II, advanced along a traditional invasion route towards the South Korean capital of Seoul. The North Koreans had assembled seven infantry divisions, up to 90,000 combat troops, for the assault. Their progress was rapid.

Opposing the North Koreans, the South Koreans were armed primarily with American weapons. Infantry units were equipped with small arms and some 60mm (2.36in) and 81mm (3.19in) mortars, while the artillery was organized into 22 battalions structured in seven field artillery groups of two battalions each along with an additional eight independent battalions. None of these units possessed any guns heavier than 105mm (4.1in).

The first American artillery unit on the ground in Korea was designated Detachment X and included 33 officers and soldiers of the 507th Antiaircraft Artillery Battalion, which arrived four days after the shooting had begun. A mobile unit equipped with 40mm (1.57in) guns, the 507th accounted for a couple of enemy aircraft, and on 30 June the US government authorized the deployment of two full combat divisions to Korea.

Artillery war

For both the UN and the communist forces, the Korean War presented significant challenges to artillery and mechanized operations. Difficult terrain, which included rugged mountains, undulating hills and swift rivers, was complicated by extremes of climate, with the tremendous heat of summer and sub-zero temperatures in winter. Nevertheless, as the war intensified and the numbers of troops committed continued to grow, artillery units on both sides began to play a more prominent role in the fighting.

In spite of the impediments to mobility, heavy guns were often massed together to break up enemy attacks. Close-quarters, hand-to-hand fighting sometimes prompted soldiers to call artillery fire down upon their own positions.

Although the employment of artillery might prove decisive on a tactical level, it was not capable of dictating the overall outcome of the conflict. In the event, the artillery fire control and precision of the

▲ **Night mission**
A night-time view showing a salvo being fired by the 1st Rocket Battery, 11th Marine Regiment, somewhere in the Marines' front-line sector, April 1953.

United Nations forces were often countered by the sheer weight of numbers of Chinese and North Korean troops engaged.

As the cost of war climbed and neither side sought a widening of the conflict beyond conventional weapons, it became apparent that a negotiated ceasefire would be required to stop the bloodshed. The peace talks at Panmunjom eventually resulted in a tenuous armistice, and the presence of artillery on the battlefield had been instrumental in the result.

United Nations forces
1950–53

Led by the armies of the United States and the British Commonwealth, the armed forces of the United Nations deployed artillery in significant numbers to stem the communist tide in Korea.

FIGHTING AT THE HOOK in the summer of 1953, one US Marine Corps gunner with Battery A, 1st Battalion, 11th Marine Regiment, remembered firing all night long in support of the embattled US 25th Infantry Division. On that particular night, the battery fired in barrage rather than volley, with only an occasional check of target coordinates. Incoming enemy artillery rounds kept most of the crews under cover, and the position was hot. Only two Marines at a time operated the guns. An occasional 155mm (6.1in) round from US Army artillery to the rear fell short, adding to the hazard and the din of combat.

From May to June 1953, the 11th Regiment, which consisted of a total of 72 guns, both 105mm (4.1in) and 155mm (6.1in), fired more than 120,000 rounds. While peace talks were ongoing, so was the business of war. The 105mm (4.1in) howitzer M2A1 was the backbone of the US artillery which served during the Korean War. More than 8500 had been produced during World War II, and the weapon's powerful round coupled with a range of more than 11km (12,200 yards) made it a valuable asset to front-line soldiers in Korea. Along with the 105mm (4.1in) weapon, the 75mm (2.9in) M1A1 pack

howitzer was well suited for the difficult terrain of Korea, while the 155mm (6.1in) M1 (also designated M114) and M3 howitzers, the 155mm (6.1in) M2 Long Tom cannon and the 240mm (9.45in) M1 and 203mm (8in) M115 howitzers were also among the variety of US artillery pieces deployed to Korea.

During three years of combat, more than 60 artillery battalions of the US Army and Marine Corps saw service in Korea. The standard US Army division was equipped with three battalions of the light 105mm (4.1in) howitzer for close fire support and a single battalion of 155mm (6.1in) guns at the divisional level. These were capable of reaching targets at distances of up to nearly 15km (16,000 yards). At the height of the Korean War, four additional US infantry divisions were each given access to another battalion of 155mm (6.1in) weapons, while a pair of combined-arms regimental combat teams each included a battalion of 105s.

Corps artillery in Korea served as something of a large unit fire brigade, dispatched to wherever support was needed, either offensively or defensively. These corps units most often included a battalion of the M7 self-propelled 105mm (4.1in) gun,

▶ **Ordnance ML 3in Mortar**

1st Commonwealth Division / 29th Infantry Brigade, 1951

The remarkable longevity of the 3in mortar (actually 3.2in/81.2mm in calibre) is testament to its durability on the battlefield. This standard British infantry support weapon was developed in the late 1920s, improved with a sturdier barrel which lengthened its effective range and served for four decades until replaced by the modern L16 81mm (3.19in) mortar in the mid-1960s.

Specifications

Crew: 2	Weight: 50.8kg (112lb)
Calibre: 81.2mm (3.2in)	Range: 2560m (2800 yards)
Elevation: + 45 degrees to + 80 degrees	Muzzle velocity: 198m/sec (650ft/sec)

nicknamed Priest during World War II because of its high gun ring; four battalions of 155mm (6.1in) guns, some of which were also self-propelled; a battalion of 203mm (8in) howitzers; and an observation battalion. The mammoth 240mm (9.45in) howitzer appeared late in the war and was assigned to the artillery complements of IX and X Corps. The number of guns in a battery varied

with the size of the weapon. Six guns completed a battery of 105s or 155s, while a 203mm (8in) battery consisted of four guns, and two guns were included in a 240mm (9.45in) battery.

Early arrival

The first US field artillery unit in Korea was a portion of the 52nd Battalion, consisting of Battery A with six

▲ **40mm Bofors L/60 anti-aircraft autocannon**

US Army / 507th Antiaircraft Artillery Battalion, 1950

Of Swedish lineage, the 40mm (1.57in) Bofors L/60 entered service in 1929, and sales to foreign nations began slowly. However, the gun, which became one of the most famous in the history of modern warfare, later sold briskly. By 1941, numerous European countries and the United States had adopted it. The weapon was reliable and versatile, either towed, self-propelled or aboard ship.

Specifications

Crew: 3–4	Weight: 1981kg (4568lb)
Calibre: 40mm (1.57in)	Range: 1525m (5000ft)
Elevation: -5 degrees to + 90 degrees	Muzzle velocity: 823m/sec (2700 ft/sec)

▲ **M114 155mm howitzer**

Eighth United States Army / 11th Field Artillery Battalion, 1952

Originally deployed during World War II and designated the M1 howitzer, the M114 155mm (6.1in) weapon remains in service today. More than 4000 were produced during World War II and more than 10,000 before production ceased in 1953. The weapon was also mounted on the chassis of the M24 Chaffee light tank and designated the M41 self-propelled howitzer.

Specifications

Crew: 11

Calibre: 155mm (6.1in)

Elevation: - 2 degrees to + 63 degrees

Weight: 5600kg (12,000lb)

Range: 14,600m (16,000 yards)

Muzzle velocity: 563m/sec (1847ft/sec)

105mm (4.1in) howitzers and half of the battalion's headquarters and service batteries. This unit was ordered to support a small force under the command of Lieutenant-Colonel Charles B. Smith, which included slightly less than three companies of infantry whose heaviest weapons were the 75mm (2.9in) recoilless rifle and the 107mm (4.2in) chemical mortar.

As the North Korean juggernaut rolled towards them on the morning of 5 July 1950, the 105s opened up on a column of enemy T-34s. Accounts vary as to precisely how much armour-piercing ammunition was available to the US artillerymen; however, all would agree that the number was less than ten rounds. Accurately firing their guns at the oncoming communist armour, the gunners of the 52nd Battalion were dismayed to see their high-explosive rounds glancing harmlessly off the steel hulls of the tanks. When the gunners did use their armor-piercing rounds, they managed to destroy the lead T-34 with a direct hit. A second tank was disabled by a hit to the chassis which resulted in a thrown tread. The North Koreans did not halt,

▲ **75mm M1A1 pack howitzer**

Eighth United States Army / 5th Ranger Infantry Company Airborne, 1952

Developed in the 1920s, the 75mm (2.9in) M1A1 pack howitzer could be disassembled rapidly and transported by mules across mountainous terrain. It could be dropped by parachute and provided airborne and light infantry units with much-needed firepower. Nearly 5000 were manufactured during World War II, and the weapon was in service until the 1960s.

Specifications

Crew: 6	Weight: 607.4kg (1339lb)
Calibre: 75mm (2.9in)	Range: 8787m (9610 yards)
Elevation: - 5 degrees to + 45 degrees	Muzzle velocity: 381m/sec (1250ft/sec)

Specifications

Crew: 7	Speed: 42km/h (26mph)
Weight: 26.01 tonnes (25.6 tons)	Road range: 201km (125 miles)
Length: 6.02m (19ft 9in)	Armament: 1 x 105mm (4.1in) M1A2 howitzer,
Width: 2.88m (9ft 5in)	plus 1 x 12.7mm (0.5in) HMG on 'pulpit'
Height: 2.54m (8ft 4in)	AA mount
Engine: 298kW (400hp) Continental R975 C1	

▲ **105mm Howitzer Motor Carriage (HMC) M7**

Eighth United States Army / 300th Armoured Field Artillery Battalion, 1952

Nicknamed the Priest by British troops due to the prominent machine-gun ring atop the chassis, which resembled a pulpit, the M7 105mm (4.1in) howitzer provided mobile artillery support for infantry.

however, and overran the American positions. The following day, Lieutenant-Colonel Smith could muster only about 250 officers and soldiers. At least 150 men, including 15 soldiers of the 52nd Field Artillery, had been killed, wounded or captured.

Although the mission of Task Force Smith had been realistically only to slow the North Koreans down rather than stop the offensive in its tracks, a resulting lesson of its defeat became readily apparent. More artillery of all calibres would be needed, along with an ample supply of both high-explosive and armor-piercing shells.

Often enough, UN artillerymen were required to fight as infantry during the Korean War. This

Specifications

Crew: 8

Weight: 40.64 tonnes (40 tons)

Length: 9.04m (29ft 9in)

Width: 3.15m (10ft 4in)

Height: 2.69m (8ft 10in)

Engine: 295kW (395hp) Continental 9-cylinder radial petrol

Speed: 39km/h (24mph)

Road range: 161km (100 miles)

Armament: 1 x 155mm (6.1in) M1A1 gun

▲ 155mm Gun Motor Carriage (GMC) M40

Eighth United States Army / 937th Field Artillery Battalion, 25th Infantry Division, 1951

Introduced late in World War II, the US M40 Gun Motor Carriage was built atop the modified chassis of the M4A3 Sherman tank. Its 155mm (6.1in) cannon provided mobile heavy artillery support for infantry.

Specifications

Crew: 7

Calibre: 280mm (11in)

Elevation: + 55 degrees

Weight: 77,383kg (170,600lb)

Range: 32km (20 miles)

Muzzle velocity: 762m/sec (2500ft/sec)

▼ M65 Atomic Cannon

Eighth United States Army, 1953

Nicknamed Atomic Annie, the M65 atomic cannon was test-fired in 1953 and delivered with US forces to both Europe and the Far East during the Cold War. During the first and only test of a nuclear shell fired from a cannon, the result was the detonation of a Type W-9 15-kiloton warhead at a distance of 11.3km (seven miles).

situation occurred for two main reasons. First, due to their lack of organic artillery, communist forces, particularly the Chinese, targeted UN artillery positions and observation posts for early seizure during offensive action. Second, sheer weight of numbers often required the artillerymen to directly defend themselves. Communist infantry was ordered to close with the enemy quickly, causing the artillerymen to cease their devastating fire for fear of hitting their own men.

Commonwealth forces

As part of the 1st Commonwealth Division, the artillery of the British Army and other nations also fought bravely during the Korean War. Several of the 25-pounder (87.6mm/3.45in) guns of 162 Battery, 16th Field Regiment, Royal New Zealand Artillery, fired 300 shells each in a single night during the Battle of Kapyong. At the Battle of the Imjin River in the spring of 1951, the 25-pounders of the 45th Field Regiment, Royal Artillery, and the 107mm (4.2in) mortars of the 170th Heavy Mortar Battery supported the 29th Infantry Brigade and the tanks of the 8th Hussars in a desperate bid to slow down a Chinese offensive. Other British artillery pieces of the Korean War included the 17-pounder (76.2mm/3in) gun, which had developed as the best Allied anti-tank gun of World War II, and the 140mm (5.5in) howitzer.

Numerous other countries fielded artillery batteries during the Korean War in response to the call to arms by the United Nations. One American gunner witnessed the destruction of a battery of Turkish 105mm (4.1in) guns. In the middle of an artillery duel, the Turkish gunners had not safely disposed of their used powder charges, piling them up in close proximity to the weapon while in action. When a direct hit from a North Korean shell destroyed all six of the Turkish guns and killed their crews, the discarded powder charges ignited as well, vaporizing the attached motor transport and ammunition stores.

As in previous wars, it was often the artillery which inflicted the greatest number of casualties. During the Korean War, the superiority of UN artillery often spelled the difference between victory and defeat. The US and British weapons performed admirably amid harsh conditions, while forward observers risked their lives, often in exposed positions, to direct accurate fire on large concentrations of enemy troops. The US and Commonwealth artillery units were, quite possibly, the most proficient in the world at their craft. The Americans, in particular, had recognized their deficiencies in artillery between the world wars, working to perfect their tactics and improve their weapons with telling effect.

NKPA/PLA

1950–53

Both the North Korean People's Army and the Chinese People's Liberation Army relied on the Soviet Union for heavy weapons. Abandoned Japanese guns from World War II were also utilized by the communists during the Korean War.

ON 29/30 OCTOBER 1950, the 27th British Commonwealth Brigade and the 3rd Battalion, Royal Australian Regiment, fought a savage battle with strong North Korean forces at Chongju. Leading the advance of UN troops into North Korea and toward the mouth of the Yalu River, the British, Australians and supporting M4 Sherman tanks of the US 89th Tank Battalion were slowed by the infantry, tanks and self-propelled guns of the North Koreans.

In the gathering darkness, the North Koreans counterattacked with T-34 medium tanks mounting 76.2mm (3in) cannon and SU-76 self-propelled assault guns, which were similarly armed. Several times, the UN force was in danger of being overrun as North Korean soldiers penetrated their line and had to be systematically hunted down and killed. The communist tanks and self-propelled guns, however, were more problematic. Although the British and

Australian soldiers were able to knock out several of the armoured vehicles with shoulder-fired 88mm (3.5in) bazooka rockets, several North Korean units reached within ten metres (33ft) of the UN perimeter before mortar and 105mm (4.1in) artillery fire forced them to retire. Six rounds from a North Korean gun actually landed near the headquarters of the 3rd Battalion, Royal Australian Regiment, killing the commanding officer.

Soviet surplus

Although their effort failed, the North Koreans had skilfully employed their Soviet-built armoured vehicles, both types of which had been proven effective on the battlefields of the Eastern Front during World War II. The T-34 had become a legend, while the SU-76 had earned a reputation as a durable platform for the ZiS-3 76.2mm (3in) field gun. The SU-76 was second only to the T-34 in number of vehicles produced during World War II. As the Korean War progressed, both would become available to the North Koreans in greater numbers.

With the opening of hostilities, the North Korean People's Army had approximately 90,000 troops massed near the border with the South. Throughout the course of the Korean War, at least ten infantry divisions, an armoured brigade and a brigade of mechanized infantry took part in the fighting. The standard North Korean infantry division was triangular in configuration and similar to the arrangement of a US division. Its three infantry regiments comprised three battalions which were supported by one battalion of 122mm (4.8in) howitzers and two battalions of 76.2mm (3in) field guns, each of Soviet manufacture. Anti-tank units and self-propelled artillery were also assigned at varying times. A relative few heavy 152mm (6in) howitzers were also in service.

The North Koreans suffered from a lack of artillery throughout the war, and at times their efficiency was poor. Even as their infantry and tanks rolled swiftly across the 38th parallel, the artillery of the North Korean 2nd Infantry Division was roughly handled by counterbattery action from South Korean artillery, which enjoyed a distinct advantage in fire control and accuracy. The 2nd Division artillery was unable to accompany the infantry during the initial offensive, and its losses were not made good until the following spring when it was withdrawn for training and to prepare newly arrived 76.2mm (3in) guns for use in the field.

Although the 4th Infantry Division had been responsible for the decimation of US Task Force Smith in the opening days of the war and continued its march on Seoul, outflanking and isolating South Korean units and elements of the US 24th Infantry Division, its combat efficiency eroded quickly as casualties mounted. Its divisional artillery component

▲ **SU-76M SP assault gun**

North Korean People's Army / 105th Armoured Brigade

Second only to the T-34 in production during World War II, the SU-76M was the main production variant of the widely used self-propelled 76.2mm (3in) assault gun. The assault gun was based on the obsolete T-70 chassis. Large numbers of these were used by communist forces in Korea.

Specifications

Crew: 4	Engine: 2 x 52kW (70hp) GAZ 6-cylinder petrol
Weight: 10.8 tonnes (10.6 tons)	Speed (road): 45km/h (28mph)
Length: 4.88m (16ft)	Road range: 450km (280 miles)
Width: 2.73m (8ft 11.5in)	Armament: 1 x 76.2mm (3in) gun, plus
Height: 2.17m (7ft 1.4in)	1 x 7.62mm (0.3in) MG

was reduced to a paltry 12 guns during the first six weeks of fighting.

Chinese mobilisation

Threatened by the advance of United Nations forces towards the Yalu River in the autumn and winter of 1950, the People's Republic of China responded with a veritable torrent of infantry, attacking sometimes in human waves which sent the enemy forces reeling southwards. The People's Liberation Army, like its North Korean counterpart, lacked strong organic artillery for much of the Korean War. When communist Chinese forces entered the conflict, their government had only months earlier declared victory over the Nationalists, whom they had fought for years with only a brief respite during which their primary adversary had been the invading Japanese during World War II.

Those Chinese formations designated 'armies' were roughly equivalent in manpower to a US corps and included troop strength of up to 8500 men organized in three divisions. Their equipment, however, was either generally inferior or non-existent. It has been reported that the typical Chinese army could field fewer than 40 artillery pieces of 76mm (3in) or larger in 1950. In some instances, the heaviest weapon available was the Soviet-made 120mm (4.7in) M1938 mortar.

▲ **76.2mm Field Gun M1942 (ZiS-3)**

North Korean People's Army / 2nd Artillery Regiment, 1950

The M1942 was one of the most famous field guns to emerge from World War II, and more than 100,000 examples of this 76.2mm (3in) weapon were produced in the Soviet Union from 1941 to 1945. Design work was undertaken in 1940, and it was manufactured in greater numbers than any other field artillery weapon of the Red Army. Stalin himself referred to the 76.2mm (3in) M1942 as a masterpiece.

Specifications

Crew: 7	Weight: 1116kg (2460lb)
Calibre: 76.2mm (3in)	Range: 13,300m (14,545 yards)
Elevation: - 5 degrees to + 37 degrees	Muzzle velocity: 680m/sec (2230ft/sec)

▲ **152mm Howitzer M1943 (D-1)**

North Korean People's Army / 5th Artillery Regiment, 1951

By combining the carriage of the 122mm (4.8in) M1938 howitzer and the barrel of the 152mm (6.1in) M1938 howitzer, Soviet weapons designers were successful in an attempt to speed up artillery production during World War II. The result was the 152mm Howitzer M1943 (D-1), which features a distinctive muzzle brake on the barrel to assist the carriage in dealing with the recoil. The weapon was exported widely to Soviet client states.

Specifications

Crew: 8	Weight: 3600kg (7937lb)
Calibre: 152.4mm (6in)	Range: 12,400m (13,560 yards)
Elevation: - 3 degrees to + 63.5 degrees	Muzzle velocity: 508m/sec (1666ft/sec)

Chinese industrial capacity was exceptionally low during the Korean War, and it is estimated that enough heavy equipment – including field and self-propelled artillery – to equip 20 divisions was purchased from the Soviet Union. Meanwhile, the communists attempted to compensate for their lack of artillery via adapted tactics. Attacking in overwhelming numbers or at night minimized the effectiveness of United Nations artillery. Infiltrators slipped through enemy lines and emerged at predetermined times to attack artillery emplacements and command-and-control centres. Tunnels and bunkers were sometimes dug into hillsides to escape UN bombardment, and when the barrage lifted, the soldiers emerged to confront the attackers. If the high ground was taken, the communists disengaged, returning to their bunkers. Then, if the effort was coordinated properly, North Korean or Chinese artillery would shell the United Nations soldiers in their exposed positions, forcing their withdrawal.

Today, the Korean peninsula remains a flashpoint of hostility between North and South. The United States maintains a contingent of approximately 29,000 troops in South Korea, including up to six air defence and field artillery battalions with the latest in sophisticated weaponry such as the MLRS multiple launch rocket system. By comparison, the North Korean People's Army is estimated to possess at least 2500 towed artillery pieces, 3500 self-propelled guns, and 4400 multiple launch rocket systems.

◀ ZPU-2 Type 58 anti-aircraft artillery

People's Liberation Army / 112th Mechanized Infantry Division, 1953

The People's Liberation Army of China fielded the ZPU-2 Type 58 heavy machine gun in the 1950s as an air defence weapon. A copy of the Soviet 14.5mm (0.57in) machine gun, it was deployed during the Korean War and with North Vietnamese and Viet Cong forces during the Vietnam War. A twin-barrelled weapon, the ZPU-2 was towed on a two-wheeled carriage. Its wheels were removed to place it in its firing position on a stabilized three-pronged platform.

Specifications

Crew: 5	Weight: 621kg (1369lb)
Calibre: 14.5mm (0.57in)	Range: 1400m (1531 yards)
Elevation: - 15 degrees to + 90 degrees	Muzzle velocity: 995m/sec (3264ft/sec)

▶ 120mm M1938 mortar

North Korean People's Army / 4th Infantry Division, 1950

Often towed by a light vehicle, the 120mm (4.7in) M1938 mortar could also be carried by infantry to provide close support. The weapon was fired either by a lanyard or by dropping the round down the muzzle and was deployed in combat during the Korean War and later in Vietnam. For many North Korean and Chinese infantry units, it was their heaviest weapon.

Specifications

Crew: 4	Weight: 280kg (617lb)
Calibre: 120mm (4.7in)	Range: 6000m (6560 yards)
Elevation: + 45 degrees to + 80 degrees	Muzzle velocity: 272m/sec (892ft/sec)

Chapter 3

Vietnam, 1959–75

One of the longest wars in human history, the Vietnam conflict actually traced its origins to a curious blend of Marxist theory and fervent nationalism, which was championed by a charismatic leader, Ho Chi Minh. During the course of the war, the North Vietnamese Army became a highly skilled fighting force, proficient in the use of Soviet-made artillery, while Viet Cong guerrillas in the South conducted raids and kept the French and then the Americans off balance. For their part, the armies of these traditional powers were confronted with a new kind of war. Strategy and tactics were modified, and the role of artillery was adapted to the changing circumstances of unconventional battle against a determined enemy.

◀ 'The thing'

Designed as multibarrel rapid fire tank killer, the M50 Ontos (Ancient Greek for 'the thing') proved to be an excellent close fire support weapon for the US Marine Corps in Vietnam. It mounted six M40 106mm (4.17in) recoilless rifles, which could be fired in rapid succession.

Introduction

As early as 1959, the government of the United States had determined that the spread of communism in Southeast Asia must be contained. France had vacated Indochina, its former colonial possession, and an increasing American military presence was undertaken.

BY THE TIME AMERICAN advisers were on the ground with South Vietnamese forces, the ranks of the North Vietnamese Army and the Viet Cong guerrillas included combat veterans who had resolved to unite their country whatever the cost. Experts in hit-and-run tactics, fighting when and where they chose, communist insurgents would strike in ambush and then melt into the dense jungle before heavy firepower could be brought to bear against them. North Vietnamese troops were instructed to close swiftly with their enemy, hold tightly to his belt, and prevent US artillery from inflicting heavy casualties due to the risk of friendly fire.

Mobility and firepower

The terrain of Vietnam, with its flat coastal areas, Mekong Delta, dense jungle of the Central Highlands, and extensively irrigated rice paddies and farmland, presented obstacles to the free movement of artillery by both communist forces and the US and South Vietnamese armies. Towed and self-propelled artillery were utilized by each, but often these weapons were restricted in their areas of operation. Towed artillery, for example, was often unable to

follow infantry on the ground. Therefore, airmobile artillery, light enough to be transported by helicopter, was deemed a viable alternative by US military planners. The light 75mm (2.9in) pack howitzer and M1A2 (also designated the M101) and M102 105mm (4.1in) howitzers were moved by air in support of infantry operations.

Although US artillery had performed superbly during World War II and again during the Korean War, traditional tactics were also deemed ineffective in prosecuting a war against guerrilla forces and an organized army which had learned its lesson on the value of artillery during years of fighting against the French. In Vietnam, there was no defined front line. Therefore, offensive operations were frequently conducted by relatively small units which were dispersed across a wide area.

Traditional US doctrine rarely dictated direct artillery support by a unit smaller than a battalion, which generally consisted of three batteries. In Vietnam, each battery was placed within range of the other in order to provide mutual support for one another in case any of them were threatened. These batteries would then coordinate with the infantry

▲ **20mm Tarasque (53 T2) towed anti-aircraft gun**
French Far East Expeditionary Corps / 1st Colonial Far East Anti-Aircraft Artillery, 1953
Mounting the F1 20mm (0.79in) cannon, the Tarasque is a towed, single-barrelled anti-aircraft weapon developed for the French Army as a light gun which could be easily transported and deployed. From towing to deployment the elapsed time for an experienced crew is as little as 20 seconds. The weapon has also proven effective against ground targets.

Specifications

Crew: 3	Range: 2000m (6560ft)
Calibre: 20mm (0.79in)	Muzzle velocity: 1050m/sec (3445ft/sec)
Elevation: - 8 degrees to + 83 degrees	
Weight: 650kg (1433lb)	

▲ Heavy howitzer
The mobile M107 howitzer could provide long-range fire support at distances of up to 30 kilometres (18 miles).

battalions which were on the move. Fire control was pushed down from the battalion level to the battery commander in tactical situations. At times, a single battery was required to split into sections, and in such cases fire control followed suit to the lowest operational level.

Often, the heavy guns of the US divisional artillery, such as the 155mm (6.1in) and 203mm (8in) weapons, were employed in support situations where they were most needed. However, the great distances covered and the need to provide support to several dispersed units at one time potentially lessened the effectiveness of the artillery at the divisional level.

Inexperienced forces

As US forces prepared to leave Vietnam in the early 1970s, an aggressive programme of 'Vietnamization' was enacted in order to train and equip units of the South Vietnamese Army to defend themselves against the communists. The experience of Vietnamization as it relates to artillery may be considered a microcosm of the comprehensive effort. At the end of 1970, a total of 1116 guns had been delivered to the South Vietnamese Army.

Extensive training had already taken place. However, the crucial element of time was working against both the South Vietnamese and their American instructors. It became the rule rather than the exception for South Vietnamese gunners to observe Americans servicing artillery rather than stepping into a hands-on role. On several occasions, the inexperienced South Vietnamese were unable to utilize their artillery effectively, and during the communist Easter Offensive of 1972, dozens of artillery pieces were abandoned to the enemy.

The North Vietnamese artillery during the Vietnam War included field weapons such as the proven Soviet 76.2mm (3in) gun of World War II design and the heavier 105mm (4.1in), 130mm (5.1in), and 152mm (6in) weapons, which were known for their considerable range and durability. Soviet-made 60mm (2.36in), 82mm (3.2in) and 120mm (4.7in) mortars were complemented by 57mm (2.2in) and 82mm (3.2in) recoilless rifles. Later in the war, 122mm (4.8in) rockets were commonly used.

US/ARVN forces
1959–75

Firepower and mobility were key elements of the US and South Vietnamese artillery deployment during the Vietnam War. Mutual support of infantry and field artillery units proved critical.

SOON AFTER US TROOPS began to arrive in Vietnam in significant numbers, it became readily apparent that they would be fighting a different kind of war – one without defined lines of battle or enemy positions which might be easily identified and attacked. Infantry tactics were refined with the concept of air mobility and other innovations, and supporting artillery followed suit.

Mobility was acknowledged as a critical element for success against an insurgency, particularly due to the fact that the enemy was resourceful, familiar with the countryside and usually chose the time and place of a confrontation. Counterinsurgency efforts required much larger numbers, with a preferred ratio of as many as ten US and South Vietnamese troops for every Viet Cong guerrilla, in order to reconnoitre areas for evidence of insurgent activity, to find and fix targets and to provide sufficient security. Mobile artillery was essential in bringing firepower to bear against an elusive enemy; however, mobile units were also potentially exposed to ambush or counterattack.

Typically, each brigade of US combat infantry sent to Vietnam was to be supported by two battalions of field artillery, one ordered in direct fire support of the infantry while the other provided an umbrella of area coverage or joined in as needed to leverage offensive operations or break up enemy attacks. During the course of the war, an extensive training programme was established to instruct South Vietnamese soldiers in the proper coordination and utilization of artillery assets. The results of this component of the Vietnamization programme were mixed at best. Although the South Vietnamese did perform well at times, their lack of training contributed to poor performance in the field. Therefore, the lion's share of the artillery in combat during the Vietnam War was fired and maintained by experienced US troops.

Mutual support

US and ARVN (Army of the Republic of Vietnam; the South Vietnamese Army) infantry rarely ventured outside the range of covering artillery, while it was evident that artillerymen were ill-equipped for or ill-disposed to defending themselves in the event of a direct attack by communist troops on their positions. In hostile country, both forward-positioned artillery and infantry

▲ **Talos surface-to-air missile**

US Navy / USS Long Beach *(Cruiser), 1966*

Talos was one of the first surface-to-air missile systems to be mounted aboard warships of the US Navy. Its development was undertaken in the late 1940s, and the system was in use until 1979. The Talos missile rode a radar beam towards its target and then engaged a radar homing system to reach the target. A variant was deployed in Vietnam to attack enemy SAM missile sites.

Specifications

Configuration: two-stage, kerosene fuel	Launch weight: 3450kg (7105lb)
Deployment: US Navy cruisers	Range: 120km (75 miles)
Length: 6.78m (22ft, 3in)	Launch preparation time: unknown
Diameter: 762mm (30in)	

could be vulnerable to an enemy which could mass substantial force and attack from virtually any direction.

Whether airlifted or transported on the ground, artillery and infantry required mutual support. Therefore, strong positions which accommodated both infantry and artillery were established in combat zones throughout Vietnam. Such positions came to be known as fire bases. Several considerations went into the selection of a fire base location, including the ability of the artillery to support manoeuvring infantry and the proximity of other field artillery, located at nearby fire bases within range of the subject location or at the divisional level to assist with fire support if necessary. Some of the most ferocious combat of the Vietnam War erupted with the defence of these forward positions.

AIR DEFENCE ARTILLERY UNITS IN VIETNAM, 1967			
Duster	Attached	Based	Area of operation
1st Battalion, 44th Artillery	Battery G, 65th Artillery (M55) Battery G, 29th Artillery (Searchlight)	Dong Ha Da Nang	Phu Bai in the south to Con Thien in the north and Khe Sanh in the west
5th Battalion, 2nd Artillery	Battery D, 71st Artillery (M55) Battery I, 29th Artillery (Searchlight)	Long Binh	North of Saigon
4th Battalion, 60th Artillery	Battery E, 41st Artillery (M55) Battery B, 29th Artillery (Searchlight)	Qui Nhon An Khe Tuy Hoa	

▲ M2A1 105mm Howitzer

US Army / 1st Battalion, 21st Field Artillery Regiment, 1966

Appearing in greater numbers than any other US artillery weapon of the Vietnam War, the 105mm (4.1in) M2A1 howitzer had already been battle-tested during World War II and in Korea. Its high rate of fire and ease of operation endeared the weapon to the artillerymen who served it. The M2A1 remains active today with the armed forces of numerous countries.

Specifications

Crew: 6

Calibre: 105mm (4.1in)

Elevation: - five degrees to + 66 degrees

Weight: 2030kg (4475lb)

Range: 11,200m (12,248 yards)

Muzzle velocity: 472m/sec (1548ft/sec)

Field Artillery Battery, United States Army, 1969

The US Army field artillery battery of the Vietnam era typically included four to six 105mm (4.1in) M2A1 howitzers. The howitzer is noted for its short barrel and steep firing angle, and in Vietnam these weapons served as critical direct fire support for infantry. The M2A1 was airmobile, facilitating the penetration of infantry units into hostile territory and the establishment of forward fire bases. During the course of the Vietnam War, the M2A1 was gradually replaced by the lighter 105mm (4.1in) M102.

5 x 105mm/4.1in Howitzer M2A1

The surrounding terrain and weapons available dictated the organization of the fire base. Infantry drew a close perimeter around the artillery firing positions to defend against large assaults and infiltrators. Usually 105mm (4.1in) and 155mm (6.1in) guns, in batteries of six, would be placed in a star formation, with five of the guns at each point of the star and the sixth in the centre. Other formations, depending on the number and calibre of the guns involved, included the box or diamond. Typically these were used with four-gun batteries of 203mm (8in) or 175mm (6.9in) weapons.

Base camp protection

Other positions, housing headquarters elements larger than the size of a battalion, were known as base camps. These were also protected by artillery, which often fired at distant targets to prevent enemy troops from closing with the command centre. Common missions also included firing on call when requested by manoeuvring infantry, disrupting enemy lines of supply and reinforcement, and direct fire against attacking enemy formations.

A variety of artillery was deployed by the United States in Vietnam, and though it had been in service for three decades, the 105mm (4.1in) M1A2 howitzer, which was later also designated the M101, continued to serve as the backbone of the American field artillery. First developed during the 1930s at the recommendation of a review board which identified weaknesses in the performance of US artillery during World War I and the dependence on weapons produced in France and Great Britain, the M101 was virtually unchanged from its appearance in World War II. It provided a high rate of fire in direct support of infantry movement and was also supplied to the South Vietnamese forces in large numbers. Light enough to accompany infantry in the field, the M1A2/M101 could also be airlifted to forward positions.

In March 1966, the US began to deliver the improved M102 howitzer to front-line units in Vietnam, and elements of the 21st Field Artillery were the initial recipients of the weapon meant to replace the aging M101. Although it was initially received with scepticism by the veteran gunners who had come to love the M101, the M102 was cheaper to produce. Weighing approximately 1.52 tonnes (1.5 tons), it was considerably lighter and easier to transport, particularly by air, than its predecessor. The maximum rate of fire for the M102 was an impressive ten rounds per minute, while its sustained rate of fire was up to three rounds per minute at a range of 11,500m (12,576 yards).

The 155mm (6.1in) howitzer was fielded in the towed configuration as the M114A1 or deployed as

▲ M107 175mm SP gun

US Army / 8th Battalion, 4th Field Artillery Regiment, 1967

The M107 175mm (6.9in) self-propelled gun was often the heaviest weapon engaged in artillery support during the Vietnam War. Its heavy calibre and long range were utilized in area fire support missions and against command-and-control centres. The weapon was sometimes criticized due to perceived inconsistent accuracy at long range.

Specifications

Crew: 13	Engine: 302kW (405hp) General Motors 8V71T
Weight: 28,304kg (62,400lb)	diesel
Length: 6.46m (21ft 2in)	Speed: 80km/h (50 mph)
Width: 3.15m (10ft 4in)	Road range: 725km (450 miles)
Height: 3.47m (11ft 4in)	Armament: 1 x 175mm (6.9in) gun

Specifications

Crew: 6

Weight: 23,723kg (52,192lb)

Length: 6.612m (21ft 8.25in)

Width: 3.295m (10ft 9.75in)

Height: 3.289m (10ft 9.5in)

Engine: 302kW (405hp) Detroit Diesel
Model 8V-71T diesel

Speed: 56km/h (35mph)

Road range: 390km (240 miles)

Armament: 1 x 155mm (6.1in) howitzer, plus
1 x 12.7mm (0.5in) AA HMG

▲ M109 155mm SP howitzer

1st Infantry Division / 1st Squadron, 4th Cavalry Regiment, 1967

The M109 self-propelled howitzer, mounting a 155mm (6.1in) main weapon, was first delivered to the US Army in 1962 and served in numerous armoured formations throughout the Vietnam War, adding heavy artillery capability to combined-arms operations.

3rd Battalion, 13th Field Artillery Regiment, Fire Support Base 'Stuart', June 1969

Deployed in forward positions such as fire-support bases, field artillery battalions sometimes combined a complement of 18 self-propelled M109 155mm (6.1in) howitzers organized in three batteries and a single battery of towed 105mm (4.1in) M2A1 howitzers. The mobile M109 was sometimes able to provide heavy, direct fire support for infantry. Meanwhile, the towed 105s offered a protective umbrella of artillery coverage to units within range. In turn, infantrymen guarded the fire-base perimeter against ground attack.

Battery A (M109 SP howitzers)

Battery B (M109 SP howitzers)

Battery C (M109 SP howitzers)

Battery D (105mm/4.1in howitzers)

the self-propelled M109. Although the towed version was considered past its prime, it did deliver effective supporting fire and was called upon at times to participate in direct fire against enemy formations. Surprisingly, it was light enough for air transport. However, it was far less manoeuvrable than the self-propelled M109, which could provide powerful direct fire support on the spot. With a crew of six, the operational range of the M109 was 390km (240 miles). The most widely used self-propelled howitzer in the world in the 1960s, the M109's 155mm (6.1in) weapon could fire a heavy projectile 14,600m (15,967 yards). It was powered by a Model 8V-71T 302kW (405hp) Detroit diesel engine.

Larger self-propelled artillery, such as the M107 175mm (6.9in) gun and the M110 8in (203mm) howitzer were the most powerful weapons of their kind deployed by the US to Vietnam. The maximum range of the M107's heavy weapon was 33,000m (36,089 yards), and it shared a common chassis with the M110, which fired up to an effective range of 17,000m (18,591 yards). The M107 and M110 were both powered by a 302kW (405hp) eight-cylinder General Motors diesel engine. The M108 105mm (4.1in) self-propelled gun was developed in the early 1950s and believed too light to effectively support infantry in Vietnam. However, some of these

weapons were supplied to a few units and fired in general area support missions.

US air defence artillery consisted of several weapons systems. The M42A1 Duster mounted twin 40mm (1.57in) Bofors cannon and a 7.62mm (0.3in) machine gun atop the chassis of the M41 Walker Bulldog light tank. The main weapons could fire at a cyclical rate of 120 rounds per minute to a ceiling of 5000m (16,404ft). The M55 Quad 50 was known to both friend and foe as the Whispering Death and consisted of a quadruple mount of four Browning M2 .50-caliber (12.7mm/0.5in) machine guns with a rate of fire up to 1500 rounds per minute. These weapons were sometimes called upon to deliver direct fire against enemy ground forces. The effect was predictably devastating.

The M168 Gatling gun was mounted atop the chassis of the M113 armoured personnel carrier, designated the M163 Vulcan Air Defense System and deployed to Vietnam; however, the system proved less than satisfactory in jungle conditions and its high silhouette was particularly vulnerable to communist rocket-propelled grenades (RPGs).

The HAWK (Homing All the Way Killer) anti-aircraft missile system, developed during the early 1950s, was deployed to Vietnam with several battalions of four batteries each. Its mobile configuration was

Specifications

Crew: 5	Engine: 302kW (405hp) Detroit Diesel V8
Weight: 28,350kg (62,512lb)	Speed: 56km/h (35mph)
Length: 5.72m (18ft 9in)	Road range: 520km (325 miles)
Width: 3.14m (10ft 4in)	Armament: 1 x 203mm (8in) howitzer
Height: 2.93m (9ft 8in)	Radio: n/a

▲ **M110A2 SP howitzer**

15th Field Artillery Regiment / Battery A, 7th Battalion, 1969

The M110 self-propelled howitzer was the largest weapon of its kind in the US arsenal during the Vietnam era. The 203mm (8in) main weapon of the M110A2 was distinguished from the M110A1 model by its double-baffle muzzle brake.

mounted on a trailer with a hard point holding three missiles in position. In addition to field, heavy and air defence artillery, infantry units were armed with mortars and recoilless rifles, while aerial rocket artillery also came into its own in Vietnam. The 69.85mm (2.75in) rockets were often mounted in pods of 48 aboard helicopters and provided tremendous ground support.

US and South Vietnamese artillery units were severely tested on a number of occasions. During the siege of Khe Sanh, artillery reinforcements were flown in regularly. At the height of the battle, nearly 50 artillery pieces, mostly the ubiquitous M101 105mm (4.1in), and up to 100 six-barrel Ontos mounted or single 106mm (4.17in) recoilless rifles were engaged. East of Khe Sanh, 175mm (6.9in) artillery at Camp Carroll also joined in the effort to hold the base against repeated communist attacks which occurred over an 11-week period while the base itself was under relentless fire from North Vietnamese artillery. During the bitter struggle at Khe Sanh, US Marine artillerymen fired nearly 159,000 rounds in defence of the base, which was later abandoned.

▲ M56 Scorpion SP gun

US Army / 101st Airborne Division, 1968

Designed as a light, airmobile anti-tank gun which packed the offensive firepower of a tank, the M56 was manufactured by Cadillac from 1953 to 1959. Introduced to Vietnam with the 82nd and 101st Airborne Divisions, the M56 proved a disappointment in action as the chassis was insufficient for the recoil of the main 90mm (3.5in) gun.

Specifications

Crew: 4	Engine: 150kW (200hp) Continental 6-cylinder
Weight: 7000kg (15,400lb)	petrol
Length: 5.84m (19ft 2in)	Speed: 45km/h (28mph)
Width: 2.577m (8ft 5in)	Road range: 225km (140 miles)
Height: 2.067m (6ft 9in)	Armament: 1 x 90mm (3.5in) gun

Specifications

Crew: 3	Engine: 108kW (145hp) General Motors
Weight: 8640kg (19,051lb)	302 petrol
Length: 3.82m (12ft 6in)	Speed: 48km/h (30mph)
Width: 2.6m (8ft 6in)	Road range: 240km (150 miles)
Height: 2.13m (6ft 11in)	Armament: 6 x 106mm (4.17in) recoilless rifles;
	4 x 12.7mm (0.5in) M8C spotting rifles

▲ Rifle, Multiple 106mm, Self-propelled, M50 Ontos

1st Marine Division / 1st Anti-Tank Battalion, 1969

An airmobile tank destroyer, the M50 Ontos was lightly armoured but offered heavy firepower with six 106mm (4.17in) recoilless rifles and was utilized primarily as an infantry-support weapon in Vietnam. The M50 was withdrawn from service by the mid-1970s.

▲ M167 Vulcan Air Defense System (VADS) towed short-range anti-aircraft gun

US Army / 82nd Airborne Division, 1970

Designed for easy transport by air, road or rail, the M167 Vulcan Air Defense System (a towed version of the M163) was deployed with US forces for nearly 30 years. Its six-barrel, 20mm (0.79in) M168 Gatling gun was well suited to defence against low-flying enemy aircraft. The system was guided by radar, and targeting was accomplished via fire-control computer.

Specifications

Crew: 4	Weight: 1569kg (3458lb)
Calibre: 20mm (0.79in)	Range: 1200m (3935ft)
Elevation: - 5 degrees to + 80 degrees	Muzzle velocity: 1030m/sec (3380ft/sec)

▲ M163 Vulcan Air Defense System (VADS)

US Army / 5th Battalion, 2nd Artillery, 1969

The self-propelled version of the Vulcan Air Defense System, the M163 combined the 20mm (0.79in) Gatling gun with the chassis of the M113 armoured personnel carrier. These units were designed for either anti-aircraft or ground-defence duties, and their rate of fire could be adjusted depending on the type of target.

Specifications

Crew: 4	Engine: 161kW (215hp) Detroit 6V-53 6-cylinder diesel
Weight: 12,310kg (27,082lb)	
Length: 4.86m (15ft 11in)	Speed: 67km/h (42mph)
Width: 2.85m (9ft 4in)	Road range: 482.8km (300 miles)
Height: 2.736m (9ft 11in)	Armament: 1 x 20mm (0.79in) M168 Gatling gun

Specifications

Crew: 6	Engine: 373kW (500hp) Continental AOS-895-3 6-cylinder air-cooled petrol
Weight: 22,452kg (49,394lb)	
Length: 6.35m (20ft 10in)	Speed: 72.4km/h (45mph)
Width: 3.225m (10ft 7in)	Road range: 161km (100 miles)
Height: 2.847m (9ft 4in)	Armament: 2 x 40mm (1.57in) anti-aircraft guns, plus 1 x 7.62mm (0.3in) MG

▲ M42 SP anti-aircraft gun

3rd Marine Division / 1st Battalion, 44th Artillery Regiment

The self-propelled M42 Duster anti-aircraft gun was developed during the 1950s and deployed to Vietnam in response to disappointing results from early anti-aircraft missile systems. The 40mm (1.57in) guns of the M42 also proved outstanding in an infantry-support role.

North Vietnamese Army (NVA)
1964–75

Supplied by both the Soviet Union and the People's Republic of China, North Vietnamese military leaders understood the capabilities of efficient artillery and utilized it to its fullest wherever possible.

AS THE UNITED STATES escalated its military involvement in Vietnam, the communist forces under General Vo Nguyen Giap had been at war for years. Giap's veterans remembered the stunning victory of the Viet Minh against the French airhead at Dien Bien Phu in 1954. Their memories were of a systematic reduction of the French capacity to resist and that this had been achieved in large part by the concentrated, sustained fire of artillery.

Taking control of the high ground surrounding the French positions, the communists had manhandled heavy artillery into the surrounding hills and pounded the French without ceasing. When he realized that his own guns were in no position to reply effectively, the French artillery commander committed suicide.

Soviet style
Through combat experience, the North Vietnamese were well aware of the power of artillery and respected the devastating potential of American guns. Therefore, when possible, they positioned their own guns just outside the range of the American weapons. While the US 105mm (4.1in) and 155mm (6.1in) weapons reached out to 11,200m (12,248 yards) and 14,600m (16,000 yards) respectively, the Soviet-made 130mm (5.1in) and 152mm (6in) guns had longer ranges at 14,995m (16,399 yards) and 31,000m (33,902 yards). Thus the North Vietnamese guns were often able to take US and South Vietnamese positions under fire with little concern for counterbattery activity.

Until the mid-1960s, the North Vietnamese Army depended heavily on infantry weapons such as mortars and recoilless rifles. Although these remained significant and were actually included in North Vietnamese and Viet Cong artillery units on a limited basis, access to heavier weapons increased. Older model guns, some dating to the French colonial period and the Japanese occupation during World

War II, were replaced or augmented by the 76.2mm (3in) field piece, and guns of 85mm (3.3in), 100mm (3.9in), 122mm (4.8in) and larger calibre. North Vietnamese artillery regiments were generally equipped with 36 guns, including at least 24 guns or howitzers of up to 105mm (4.1in) and as many as 12 130mm (5.1in) or 152mm (6in) weapons.

Captured hardware
The North Vietnamese and Viet Cong training programmes also included lessons on the operation of captured US artillery pieces. The use of rockets increased steadily as the war progressed. These included Soviet 122mm (4.8in) and 140mm (5.5in) and Chinese 107mm (4.2in) weapons. Each of these was ideally suited for attacking large targets, although it became imperative for the shooters to scoot away quickly since US observers might pinpoint the exhaust trails of the rockets and call for retaliatory fire.

A North Vietnamese training manual explained that the 'main purpose of firing rockets is to attack objectives of large area, usually 400 meters by 400 meters, such as enemy strongholds, airfields, storage areas, or towns and to support the infantry and to attack distant objectives that may affect the combat mission of the infantry.'

One North Vietnamese officer who was taken prisoner commented during interrogation that the rockets were to be used in 'hit-and-run tactics adhering to the principles of guerrilla warfare. No more than five rounds were to be fired from a single tripod launcher … and evacuation from the scene could usually be accomplished within five minutes.'

Ke Sahn
Such was the case on numerous occasions as Viet Cong infiltrators launched rockets against such major US installations as Da Nang air base and the forward combat base at Khe Sanh near the Laotian border.

During the 77-day siege of Khe Sanh from January until April 1968, North Vietnamese guns pounded the US positions on an almost daily basis. Often this artillery fire was from communist guns situated across the Laotian frontier. At Khe Sanh, the North Vietnamese undoubtedly believed that a victory on the scale of Dien Bien Phu was within reach. Artillery had proven decisive 14 years earlier, and the pounding of Khe Sanh and US Marine positions in the surrounding hills was relentless. Estimates of the number of North Vietnamese shells of all calibres fired at Khe Sanh top 11,000. During one eight-hour period, more than 1300 shells, mostly 130mm (5.1in) and 152mm (6in), were fired.

▲ **Type 54-1 SP 122mm gun**

North Vietnamese Army / 304th Division, 1972

Based on a modified chassis of the YW-31 armoured personnel carrier and mounting a variant of the Soviet 122mm (4.8in) howitzer developed during the 1930s, the Type 54-1 SP 122mm (4.8in) gun was supplied to the North Vietnamese Army in limited numbers. The weapon was used in support of infantry attacks, providing mobile direct fire.

Specifications

Crew: 7

Weight: 15.4 tonnes (34,000lb)

Length: 5.65m (18ft 6in)

Width: 3.06m (10ft)

Height: 2.68m (8ft 9in)

Engine: 192kW (257hp) Deutz 6150L 6-cylinder diesel

Speed: 56km/h (35mph)

Road range: 500km (310 miles)

Armament: 1 x 122mm (4.8in) howitzer

Specifications

Crew: 5

Calibre: 132mm (5.2in)

Rocket length: 1.42m (53.9in)

Rocket weight: 42.5kg (93.7lb)

System combat weight: varied

Range: 8500m (9300 yards)

Rate of fire: multiple in 7–10 seconds

▲ **BM-13 Katyusha rocket launcher**

North Vietnamese Army / 4th Regiment Rocket Battalion, 1968

Of World War II vintage, the Soviet-built BM-13 rocket launcher was a platform for the famous Katyusha rocket which was prominent on the Eastern Front. The majority of the BM-13 systems were mounted atop ZiS-6 6X4 trucks. Several later variants of the famous system were produced in the coming decades.

Anti-Aircraft Battery, North Vietnamese Army, 1970

The standard North Vietnamese Army self-propelled anti-aircraft battery included four ZSU-57-2 guns mounting twin 57mm (2.2in) cannon. The first Soviet weapon of its type to see combat on a large scale since World War II, the ZSU-57-2 fired at a sustained rate of 70 rounds per minute. Later replaced by the ZSU-23-4, the system was widely exported to Warsaw Pact countries and Soviet client states in the Middle East and Africa.

Battery (4 x ZSU-57-2 SP anti-aircraft guns)

Air defence curtain

Although the SAM 1 and SAM 2 surface-to-air missiles received a lot of attention in the Western media, light anti-aircraft weapons were responsible for shooting down far more US aircraft than the high-profile missiles. At Khe Sanh, the light-weapons fire was so intense that resupply aircraft were forced to drop materiel by parachute and maintain altitude rather than risk a landing.

Among the most lethal anti-aircraft weapons in the North Vietnamese order of battle were the ZSU-57-2 and ZSU-23-4 self-propelled guns. The former mounted a pair of 57mm (2.2in) cannon atop the chassis of the T-54 tank, while the ZSU-23-4 Shilka was a quadruple mount of 23mm (0.9in) cannon. Meant to replace the older ZSU-57-2, the Shilka incorporated the modified chassis of the PT-76 amphibious tank.

During the war, the North Vietnamese and Viet Cong also deployed large numbers of 37mm (1.45in) anti-aircraft guns, of both Soviet and Chinese manufacture, along with the 14.5mm (0.57in) ZPU-4 heavy machine gun, which was effective against low-flying helicopters.

The Vietcong were also supplied with the Chinese-built Type 63 anti-aircraft gun. Mounting twin 37mm (1.45in) guns on the hull of a T-34 tank, the Type 63 proved ineffective as the gun had to be manually elevated and loaded: a severe drawback against fast, low-flying aircraft.

▲ Type 63 SP anti-aircraft gun
North Vietnamese Army / 24th Viet Cong Anti-Aircraft Battalion, 1966
Combining the chassis of the Soviet T-34 medium tank and an open turret with a pair of 37mm (1.5in) anti-aircraft cannon, this Chinese-produced self-propelled anti-aircraft weapon was mediocre at best. During the 1960s, the Type 63 was supplied to both North Vietnamese Army and Viet Cong guerrilla forces.

Specifications

Crew: 6	Engine: 372kW (493hp) V-2 V12 diesel
Weight: n/k	Speed: 50km/h (31mph)
Length: 5.9m (19ft 7in)	Road range: 300km (186 miles)
Width: 3m (9ft 10in)	Armament: 2 x 37mm (1.45in) Type 63 AA guns,
Height: 2.6m (8ft 6in)	plus 1 x 7.62mm (0.3in) DT MG

Chapter 4

Cold War in Asia

The phenomenon of the Cold War shaped
the formation and government of nations across the globe
for half a century. The power vacuum created at the end of
World War II gave rise to movements of self-determination,
and the Third World was born. Developing nations in Asia
and elsewhere shook off the yoke of colonial rule, often
through bloody, prolonged military conflict. They settled old
scores and vied for possession of rich natural resources.
National armies and guerrilla forces were supplied by the
superpowers and utilized weapons abandoned by Allied
and Japanese forces following World War II. Prominent
among these were field guns, heavy artillery
and air defence weapons.

◀ **Barrage gun**
The 155mm (6.1in) L/45 Type 89 towed artillery gun was built in China to serve the needs of both the
People's Liberation Army and the export market. It was based on Western technology, being similar to the
Austrian GHN-45 and firing a Western-standard calibre shell.

Introduction

Artillery, more than any other weapon system, offered the armies of Asian nations the ability to alter the course of a battle and even an entire war.

A N IRRESISTIBLE TIDE of armed conflict swept the continent of Asia during the latter half of the twentieth century. Nationalism, ideology, religious fervour and the global ambitions of the Soviet Union and the United States contributed to instability in the region. With the ascent of its communist regime in 1949, the People's Republic of China gained a prominent role in the geopolitical future of the continent as well.

Spheres of influence, control of natural resources, the security of national borders, ethnic tensions and the abstract ideals of freedom versus totalitarianism made Asia a tinderbox and a proving ground for modern weapons systems developed by the superpowers and other arms-exporting nations. The proliferation of nuclear and chemical weapons in the region increased the likelihood of open war, which erupted with regularity, and in some cases remains unresolved to this day.

Proxies and projectiles

Among the detritus of World War II lay hundreds of thousands of abandoned artillery pieces and millions of rounds of ammunition. Often, Japanese forces which were vacating the Asian continent turned their weapons over to Allied authorities or local governments or simply walked away from them. Allied weapons had also been abandoned far and wide. These provided the seeds of the artillery corps of new national armies, guerrilla forces and militias.

Soon enough, these weapons, particularly examples of the venerable Japanese Type 35 75mm (2.9in) gun, were in action on the Korean peninsula in the 1950s and during the Vietnam conflict which persisted for 30 years after the eviction of the Japanese from Indochina. Simultaneously, advancing technology enhanced the mobility and accuracy of heavy guns, while radar-controlled air defence artillery proved deadly, and tactical missiles of various types were introduced.

Driven by the perceived exigencies of the Cold War, the United States and the Soviet Union embarked upon a calculated programme of arms sales and support for their proxy nations and fighting forces in Asia. The US was intent on curbing the spread of communism, while the Soviets took advantage of a volatile blend of previously repressed nationalism and Marxist philosophy to expand the limits of their influence. The ubiquitous Soviet-made 76.2mm (3in) field gun, produced in greater numbers than any other artillery piece in World War II, remains active to this day and was supplied to Soviet clients in great numbers, while the 152mm (6.1in) gun-howitzer was also in common use. The US 105mm (4.1in) M2A1 howitzer was a workhorse in Asia for decades, as vast quantities were exported to the armies of friendly countries.

By the 1980s, a report published by the US Central Intelligence Agency disclosed the magnitude

▲ **Type 75**

The Type 75 multiple rocket launcher mounts 32 130mm (5.1in) rockets on top of the hull of a Type 73 armoured personnel carrier. Introduced in the mid 1970s, in the early twenty-first century the Japanese armed forces were still operating more than 60 of these vehicles.

▲ Indian WMD

Prithvi truck-mounted missiles are paraded on India's Republic Day. The Prithvi was India's first indigenously developed ballistic missile. First test-fired in 1988, it is not a particularly sophisticated missile, incorporating propulsion technology from the Soviet SA-2 surface-to-air missile.

of the Cold War involvement of the superpowers, including their arms sales on the Asian continent. In 1980 alone, the report stated, the Soviet Union had supplied $7 billion in military aid, particularly arms, to Third World countries, while more than 50,000 Soviet military advisers had been deployed around the world to instruct the recipients in the efficient use of these weapons.

Although the report had been generated by the CIA, the United States was also active in the global arms trade along with most of the developed countries of Eastern and Western Europe. A black market in arms thrived in Asia, particularly with the rise of insurgencies, civil war and revolution.

Elsewhere in Asia, the People's Republic of China slowly weaned itself away from dependence on Soviet artillery and embarked on a programme of developing and producing its own such weapons, some of which were nearly identical to original Soviet designs. Territorial disputes between Muslim Pakistan and predominantly Hindu India boiled over into major conflicts twice during the Cold War, pitting large quantities of US and Soviet weaponry against each other; and some of the largest land battles since World War II took place between the Pakistani and Indian armies.

Meanwhile, the Shah of Iran was deposed, and the Islamic fundamentalist power structure which succeeded him came into bloody conflict with the Baathist regime of Saddam Hussein of Iraq. Large quantities of artillery, both towed and self-propelled, were engaged, and widespread reports of the use of chemical weapons were confirmed. Many of these lethal weapons were delivered by modified artillery shells.

China

1950–PRESENT

The People's Republic of China fields the largest army in the world and contains numerous artillery divisions assigned to group armies, as well as unattached artillery regiments of various types.

ONE OF THE PRE-EMINENT NUCLEAR POWERS on the world stage, the People's Republic of China was actively involved in military operations in Southeast Asia during the Cold War, intervening on behalf of North Korea during the bitter Korean War; fighting periodically with neighbouring Vietnam during border disputes and for control of the Spratly and Paracel islands in the South China Sea; and clashing with the Soviet Union on its northern border during the late 1960s.

During the Cold War, the People's Liberation Army evolved significantly, from a low-technology force which had conducted human-wave assaults during the Korean War to a high-tech mechanized army competing for global arms sales and fielding weapons systems, including artillery, on a par with those of other nations. Following the victory of Mao's communist forces over the Nationalists of Chiang Kai-shek in 1948, the Chinese depended largely on Soviet weapons and equipment, particularly systems which had been produced in great quantities during World War II.

Gradually, however, Chinese engineers began to develop their own designs and to modify and adapt their own weapons as needed. For example, the Type 63 self-propelled anti-aircraft gun married the chassis of the famed Soviet T-34 medium tank with an open turret and a pair of 37mm (1.45in) cannon.

By the 1980s, the Chinese Harbin First Machinery Building Group Ltd, previously known as state-run 674 Factory, was producing such weapons as the Type 83 self-propelled 152mm (6in) gun-howitzer, a combination of the towed Type 66 artillery piece and the Type 321 artillery chassis.

The Type 89 155mm (6.1in) field gun-howitzer, also known as the PLL01, was based on an original design known as the CG-45 by Gerald Bull's Space Research Corporation. The Type 89 was introduced in 1987 and was the first Chinese field gun to utilize the Western standard 155mm (6.1in) shell rather than the Soviet standard 122mm (4.8in) projectile. Its existence was originally noted by Western observers during the Chinese National Day military parade in 1999, and while only a relative handful of them are confirmed to have been built, it is known that towed and truck-mounted versions are operational.

Early artillery

Among the earlier light artillery systems manufactured by the Chinese was the Type 63 107mm (4.2in) rocket launcher, which was introduced in 1963. The towed weapon comprised a dozen rocket tubes and provided intense direct fire support to infantry regiments in the field in companies of six units, which were attached to field artillery battalions.

▶ **Type 63 107mm multiple rocket launcher**

People's Liberation Army / 121st Infantry Division, 1965

In service with the People's Liberation Army for over 30 years, the Type 63 107mm (4.2in) multiple rocket launcher was manufactured in large numbers and proved to be a durable and versatile weapon. Requiring three minutes to reload, its rate of fire is 12 rounds in seven to nine seconds.

Specifications

Crew: 5
Diameter: 107mm (4.2in)
Tubes: 12
Weight: 613kg (1351lb)
Range: 8.5km (5.28 miles)

▲ CSS-1 ballistic missile

PLA / 51 Base / 806 Brigade, 1965

China's first home-developed ballistic missile, the Dongfeng-2, known to NATO as the CSS-1, was undertaken by the Chinese Academy of Launch Vehicle Technology in the late 1950s. A variant, the Dongfeng-2A, was successfully launched in June 1964. The weapon was withdrawn from service by the 1980s.

Specifications

Configuration: single-stage, liquid fuel	Body diameter: 1.65m (5ft 5in)
Deployment: believed road-mobile on towed	Launch weight: 31,900kg (31.4 tons)
trailer	Range: believed 1250km (776.71 miles)
Length: 20.61m (67ft 7in)	Launch preparation time: 120–180 minutes

▲ CSS-2 ballistic missile

PLA / 51 Base / 810 Brigade, 1975

A single-stage intermediate-range ballistic missile, the CSS-2 is known to the Chinese as the Dongfeng-3. Designed specifically to bring US military bases in Southeast and East Asia within range of the Chinese nuclear arsenal, the Dongfeng-3 entered service in 1971 and was improved in the early 1980s. Some of these missiles have been conventionally armed, and the missile's nuclear payload is up to 3000 kilotons.

Specifications

Configuration: single-stage, liquid fuel	Launch weight: 64,000kg (63 tons)
Deployment: launch pad and road mobile	Range: 2500km (1553.43 miles)
Length: 21.2m (69ft 6in)	Launch preparation time: 120–180 minutes
Diameter: 2.25m (7ft 5in)	

▲ CSS-3 ballistic missile

PLA / 55 Base / 814 Brigade, 1984

The CSS-3, or Dongfeng-4, intermediate-range ballistic missile entered service with the Second Artillery Corps of the People's Liberation Army in the early 1980s. The missile carries a warhead of up to 3000 kilotons, and it is estimated that up to 20 of them are currently deployed in China. The Dongfeng-4 rocket was used to send China's first satellite into orbit in 1970.

Specifications

Configuration: two-stage, believed liquid fuel	Launch weight: 82,000kg (80.7 tons)
Deployment: silo and semi-mobile (towed trailer)	Range: 4750km (2951.51 miles)
Length: 28m (91ft 10in)	Launch preparation time: 3–5 hours (mobile);
Diameter: 2.25m (7ft 4in)	2–3 hours (silo)

▲ CSS-4 ballistic missile

PLA / 54 Base / 801 Brigade, 1980

A two-stage intercontinental ballistic missile, the CSS-4 is known in China as the Dongfeng-5. Requirements for an ICBM capable of reaching targets in North America were issued by the Chinese government in 1965, and the first test flight was conducted in September 1971. The weapon carries a single 3000-kiloton warhead. Three bases are known to house the Dongfeng-5, each with up to ten missiles.

Specifications

Configuration: two-stage, liquid fuel	Launch weight: 183,000kg (180.1 tons)
Deployment: silo or launch pad	Range: 12,000km (7456 miles)
Length: 33m (108ft 3in)	Launch preparation time: 3–5 hours (launch
Diameter: 3.4m (11ft 2in)	pad); 1–2 hours (silo)

Spurred by the need to produce its own weaponry and to take advantage of arms sales to other countries, the Chinese government has supported investment in private ventures, such as China North Industries Corporation, known as NORINCO in the West, to develop and produce modern weapons systems. Established in 1980 and rigidly controlled by the country's Commission on Science, Technology and Industry for National Defence, NORINCO manufactures anti-aircraft, anti-missile and other artillery systems.

Specifications

Crew: 5	Engine: 391.4kW (525hp) diesel
Weight: 32,000kg (70,560lb)	Speed: 56km/h (35mph)
Length: 6.1m (20ft)	Road range: 450km (280 miles)
Width: 3.2m (10ft 6in)	Armament: 1 x 155mm (6.1in) WAC-21 howitzer,
Height: 2.59m (8ft 6in)	plus 1 x 12.7mm (0.5in) anti-aircraft MG
	Radio: n/k

▲ **155/45 NORINCO SP howitzer**

People's Liberation Army / 1st Armoured Division, 1997

The NORINCO-designed PLZ 155/45 self-propelled howitzer was conceived in the early 1990s for the Chinese armed forces and the export market. Its 155mm (6.1in) howitzer was modified by Chinese designers from an Austrian weapon. The vehicle also mounts a 12.7mm (0.5in) anti-aircraft machine gun and grenade launchers.

PLA Self-Propelled Artillery Battalion, 1997

The People's Liberation Army self-propelled artillery battalion consists of 18 gun-howitzers divided into three companies of six weapons each. The primary function is infantry support, although a combined-arms strategy is emerging. The firepower of the 155mm (6.1in) guns is also available in numerous unattached armoured regiments; however, organic motorized infantry support is considered to be lacking and may cause undue vulnerability to armoured vehicles and artillery on the battlefield.

1 Company (6 x 155mm/45 SP howitzers)

2 Company (6 x 155mm/45 SP howitzers)

3 Company (6 x 155mm/45 SP howitzers)

The People's Liberation Army grew in numbers and strength through the 1980s, and by 1989 it was estimated to include up to 35 army groups with 118 infantry, 13 armoured, 17 artillery and 16 anti-aircraft artillery divisions. These were augmented by a large number of support regiments and battalions, many of which included field and anti-aircraft artillery. The armoured divisions often included self-propelled assault and artillery weapons as well.

In the late 1990s, the army was restructured, with a number of People's Liberation Army units being transferred to the People's Armed Police, which had been created in 1983, or relegated to the equivalent of Category B or 'national guard' status. At the same time, a doctrine of combined arms was instituted, revising an old system in which an army division included approximately 12,000 soldiers and contained an organic artillery regiment and anti-aircraft artillery battalion along with an armoured regiment and three infantry regiments. The new arrangement included 'group armies' of four divisions totalling nearly 180,000 troops and containing artillery support at appropriate levels. With the new alignment, the combined number of artillery divisions in the People's Liberation Army was reduced from 33 to eight.

Specifications

Crew: 4

Calibre: 130mm (5.1 inch)

Weight: 14,000kg (13.77 tons)

Rocket length: 1.063m (41.85in)

Rocket weight: 32.80kg (72.3lb)

Warhead: high-explosive fragmentation;
   14.73kg (32.47lb)

Range: 10,115m (11,060 yards)

▲ **Type 70 multiple launch rocket system**

People's Liberation Army / 112th Mechanized Infantry Division, 1980

The 19-barrel, 130mm (5.1in) Type 70 multiple launch rocket system mounted on the Type YW 531 armoured personnel carrier provides intense close support for People's Liberation Army infantry over a reasonably large coverage area. The mount above the crew compartment is rotated and elevated to fix the target area. The Type 70 was replaced by the Type 89 as recently as 1990.

Specifications

Crew: 5

Calibre: 155mm (6.1in)

Weight: 12,000kg (11.8 tons)

Range: 39km (24.23 miles)

Rate of fire: 2–4 rounds per minute

▲ **Type 89 155mm towed howitzer**

People's Liberation Army / 118th Artillery Division, 1996

Developed during the 1980s as a variant of an original design by Gerald Bull's Space Research Corporation, the Type 89 155mm (6.1in) towed howitzer incorporated the standard NATO shell rather than the 122mm (4.8in) Warsaw Pact ordnance and was evidence of a temporary warming in Chinese relations with the West. An auxiliary power unit provides limited self-propulsion.

Recognizing the necessity of obtaining nuclear defensive capability, the People's Republic of China began the development of strategic missiles in 1956,

 The emblem of the People's Liberation Army is used across all branches of the Chinese armed forces, including the army, navy, air force, artillery and reserve units.

and late in the following year a core group of 600 military personnel began training and development in the deployment of nuclear weapons. As early as 1960, the Chinese nuclear programme had undergone several organizational revisions. Nevertheless, the first successful test-firing of a nuclear-capable missile occurred in October 1963, followed in June 1964 by the launch of the short-

Specifications

Crew: 3

Weight: 22,861kg (22.5 tons)

Length: 6.71m (22ft)

Armament: 4 x 25mm (0.98in) cannon;
  MANPAD missiles

Range: guns – 2.5km (2734 yards);
  missiles – 6km (6562 yards)

Rate of fire: gun – 3200 rounds per minute

▲ **Type 95 SPAAG**

People's Liberation Army / 116th Mechanized Infantry Division, 2004

The Type 95 self-propelled anti-aircraft gun provides the backbone of division-level mobile anti-aircraft defence for the People's Liberation Army. Its four 25mm (0.98in) cannon or MANPAD missiles are controlled by a relatively basic radar tracking system. The Type 95 was initially an attempt to produce a weapon equivalent to the performance of the Soviet ZSU-23-4 Shilka and entered service in the late 1990s. Its tracked chassis is common to numerous other vehicles.

Specifications

Crew: 5

Calibre: 122mm (4.8in)

Number of tubes: 40

Rocket length: 2870mm (9ft 5in)

Rocket weight: 67kg (147.71lb)

System combat weight: 30,000kg
  (29.5 tons) estimated

Range: 30km (28.64 miles)

Rate of fire: 40 rounds in 20 seconds

▲ **Type 89 multiple launch rocket system**

People's Liberation Army/ 124th Motorized Infantry Division, 1998

Entering service with the People's Liberation Army in 1990, the 40-tube, 122mm (4.8in) Type 89 multiple launch rocket system was developed by the China North Industries Group. Its rocket tubes are mounted atop the Type 321 utility chassis. The Type 89, which also served as a replacement for the Type 70, included improvements such as nuclear, biological and chemical defences and automatic loading operations. The weapon may be reloaded in three minutes.

Specifications

Crew: 6–7

Calibre: 122mm (4.8in)

Number of tubes: 40

Rocket length: 2870mm (9ft 5in)

Rocket weight: 66.8kg (147.27lb)

System combat weight: 15,532kg (15.3 tons)

Range: 20km (12.43 miles)

Rate of fire: 40 rounds in 20 seconds

▲ **Type 81 122mm rocket launcher**

People's Liberation Army / 123rd Infantry Division, 1997

Developed from the Soviet BM-21 Grad system, the Type 81 multiple rocket launcher entered service with the People's Liberation Army in 1982. The weapon can be reloaded in eight minutes, and its 40 rocket tubes fire projectiles carrying warheads of 18.3kg (40lb). Outstanding performance led to the Type 81 being deployed from corps level to division and then to artillery battalions attached to motorized infantry units. It replaced the older Type 70.

PLA Artillery Battalion, 1997

The Chinese version of the highly successful Soviet BM-21 Grad close-support multiple launch rocket system, the Type 81 was deployed to motorized infantry divisions of the People's Liberation Army during the 1980s. The Grad has been acknowledged as the most widely used system of its kind in the world, and the Type 81 provides concentrated firepower against fixed targets and infantry concentrations, delivering 122mm (4.8in) rockets from 40 tubes. The Type 81 was originally derived from examples of the Grad captured from North Vietnamese forces in 1979.

Battalion (18 x Type 81 rocket launchers)

range Dongfeng-1 missile, a licensed copy of the Soviet SS-2 Sibling.

On 1 July 1966 China's strategic nuclear force was placed under the control of the somewhat euphemistically named Second Artillery Corps. Successive generations of ballistic missiles have improved range and payload. The Dongfeng-5, known in NATO nomenclature as the CSS-4, is a two-stage intercontinental ballistic missile which can deliver a 3200kg (7055lb) three-megaton thermonuclear warhead at a maximum range of 10,000 to 12,000km (6214 to 7456 miles), placing the Western United

States and most of Western Europe within range. As recently as 2008, it was estimated that up to 30 Dongfeng-5 missiles were deployed in three brigades, each with six to ten missiles.

Although the number of nuclear warheads currently in the Chinese arsenal is unknown, the tally is well into the hundreds. The Second Artillery Corps is controlled by the Chinese Central Military Commission and headquartered at Qinghe near the capital city of Beijing, while the warheads are dispersed among six missile divisions supported by security, technical and communications regiments. These divisions are based in the main military regions throughout the vast country, including Shenyang, Qimen, Kunming, Luoyang, Huaihua, Xining and Baoji. The total number of personnel assigned to the Second Artillery Corps is believed to exceed 215,000.

PLA II ARTILLERY CORPS (2009)				
Unit	Cover Designator	Province	City/Region	Equipment
51 Base	96101 Unit	Liaoning	Shenyang	
806 Brigade	96111 Unit	Shaanxi	Weinan (Hancheng)	DF-31A (CSS-9)
810 Brigade	96113 Unit	Liaoning	Dalian (Jinzhou)	DF-3A (CSS-2)
816 Brigade	96115 Unit	Jilin	Tonghua	DF-15 (CSS-6)
822 Brigade	96117 Unit	Shandong	Laiwu	DF-21C (CSS-5)
?	96623 Unit	Shandong	Laiwu	Support
52 Base	96151 Unit	Anhui	Qimen (Huangshan)	
807 Brigade	96161 Unit	Anhui	Chizhou	DF-21 (CSS-5)
811 Brigade	96163 Unit	Anhui	Huangshan (Qimen)	DF-21 (CSS-5)
815 Brigade	96165 Unit	Jiangxi	Jingdezhen (Leping)	DF-15B (CSS-6)
817 Brigade	96167 Unit	Fujian	Yongan	DF-15 (CSS-6)
818 Brigade	96169 Unit	Guangdong	Meizhou	DF-15 (CSS-6)
819 Brigade	96162 Unit	Jiangxi	Ganzhou	DF-15 (CSS-6)
820 Brigade	96164 Unit	Zhejiang	Jinhua	DF-15 (CSS-6)
?	96172 Unit	Anhui	Huangshan (Qimen)	Support
Signal Regiment	96173 Unit	Jiangxi	Jingdezhen	Signal
Factory	96174 Unit	Anhui	Huangshan (Xiuning)	Maintenance
53 Base	96201 Unit	Yunnan	Kunming	
802 Brigade	96211 Unit	Yunnan	Jianshui	DF-21 (CSS-5)
808 Brigade	96213 Unit	Yunnan	Chuxiong	DF-21 (CSS-5)
821 Brigade	96215 Unit	Guangxi	Liuzhou	DH-10
?	96217 Unit	Guizhou	Qingzhen	?
?	96219 Unit	Yunnan	Kunming	?
54 Base	96251 Unit	Henan	Luoyang	
801 Brigade	96261 Unit	Henan	Lingbao	DF-5A (CSS-4)
804 Brigade	96263 Unit	Henan	Luanchuan	DF-5A (CSS-4)
813 Brigade	96265 Unit	Henan	Nanyang	DF-31A (CSS-9)
55 Base	96301 Unit	Hunan	Huaihua	
803 Brigade	96311 Unit	Hunan	Huaihua (Jingzhou)	DF-5A (CSS-4)
805 Brigade	96313 Unit	Hunan	Huaihua (Tongdao)	DF-4 (CSS-3)
814 Brigade	96315 Unit	Hunan	Huaihua (Huitong)	DF-4 (CSS-3)
824 Brigade	96317 Unit	Hunan	Shaoyang (Dongkou)	?
?	96321 Unit	Hunan	Shaoyang (Dongkou)	Support
56 Base	96351 Unit	Qinghai	Xining	
809 Brigade	96361 Unit	Qinghai	Datong	DF-21 (CSS-5)
812 Brigade	96363 Unit	Gansu	Tianshui	DF-31A (CSS-9)
823 Brigade	96365 Unit	Xinjiang	Korla	DF-21 (CSS-5)
Training Unit	96367 Unit	Qinghai	Delingha	-
Training Unit	96367 Unit	Xinjiang	Ruowu	-
22 Base	96401 Unit	Shaanxi	Baoji	Logistics support

▲ AR1A multiple launch rocket system

People's Liberation Army / 113th Infantry Division, 2010

Initially demonstrated in 2009, the AR1A multiple launch rocket system was developed from the earlier A-100, which was never adopted by the People's Liberation Army. Its 300mm (11.8in) rockets are contained in ten launching tubes. A full salvo is discharged in 60 seconds. Designed to saturate ground targets, the AR1A is similar to the Russian 9A52-2T Smerch. Carried atop an 8X8 truck chassis, the system is reloaded with an exchange of preconfigured pods.

Specifications

Crew: 4

Weight: 38,555kg (37.9 tons)

Rocket weight: 840kg (1852lb)

Range: 130km (80.78 miles)

Reloading time: 20 minutes

India and Pakistan in conflict

1965–PRESENT

At odds for decades, these South Asian rivals have fought for control of the Kashmir region and accused one another of inciting rebellion and supporting terrorist organizations.

DURING THE WARS BETWEEN INDIA AND PAKISTAN in 1965 and 1971, artillery played a key role on the battlefield. Supported by US advisers, Pakistani artillery was massed in support of Operation Grand Slam in 1965, enabling Pakistani infantry to break through Indian lines behind a heavy barrage, although neither side possessed adequate firepower for a decisive victory. Pakistani artillery was distributed across two infantry divisions and also comprised one independent brigade of two heavy regiments and three medium regiments plus one each of light anti-aircraft artillery and field artillery. The 7th Division Artillery consisted of two field regiments, the 27th and the 2nd, along with a locating battery, while the 12th Division Artillery consisted of three additional regiments.

Indian artillery had been dispersed across a relatively great distance and was unable to reply with concentrated effect. When Indian ground forces counterattacked, the Pakistani artillery was superbly handled and thwarted the Indian advance on more than one occasion. It has been said that the commander of a Pakistani artillery brigade attached to the IV Army Corps achieved a reputation as an outstanding gunnery officer.

By the outbreak of the 1971 war, the Pakistani Army had organized its 1st Armoured Division's mobile artillery into four regiments of self-propelled guns, a light anti-aircraft regiment plus numerous field artillery and anti-aircraft artillery battalions assigned as needed. The 11th Infantry Division was supported by two field and two medium regiments and a heavy artillery regiment. Future Pakistan president Pervez Musharraf served as a lieutenant of artillery with the 16th Self-Propelled Field Regiment of the 1st Armoured Division.

During the Battle of Assal Uttar in September 1965, a Pakistani offensive was blunted by Indian forces; however, this was due in part to superior Indian tactical manoeuvring and the inept handling of Pakistani armour. Pakistani artillery, including at one point up to 140 massed guns, was of greater range and firepower than the 106mm (4.17in) recoilless rifles, 75mm (2.9in) pack howitzers and 120mm (4.7in) mortars available to the Indians.

While tensions have continued to smoulder, India and Pakistan have modernized their artillery capabilities steadily. Today's Indian Army includes two artillery divisions, an artillery brigade attached to each of its 18 infantry divisions and a total of nearly 200 regiments of field artillery. Primary towed weapons include 105mm (4.1in) light field guns; the Soviet-made 122mm (4.8in) D-30, 130mm (5.1in) M-46 and modified 155mm (6.1in) M-46; as well as the 155mm (6.1in) Bofors FH-77B. Air defence capabilities include more than 12 regiments of surface-to-air missiles plus flak regiments fielding such proven guns as the ZSU-23-4 Shilka.

In response to India's purchase of the Russian 9A52-2T Smerch ground-support rocket system, Pakistan was reported to have procured at least a battalion of the Chinese AR1A, totalling 36 launchers, and is considering manufacturing the modern multiple launch rocket system under licence. Both nations also possess nuclear missiles.

Specifications

Crew: 8	Weight: 4000kg (3.93 tons)
Calibre: 75mm (2.9in)	Effective ceiling: 8565m (28,000ft)
Elevation: - 5 degrees to + 85 degrees	Muzzle velocity: 840m/sec (2755ft/sec)

▲ 75mm Bofors Model 29

Indian Army / 312th Air Defence Brigade, 1965

Similar in design to the German 88mm (3.5in) Flak 18, which served in multiple roles in World War II, the Swedish-manufactured Bofors Model 29 anti-aircraft gun preceded the 88mm (3.5in) weapon by several years. However, several German designers were working in Sweden at the time the weapon was developed. It was exported to numerous countries and remains in service in limited numbers today.

▲ Ordnance BL 5.5in Medium Gun Mk 2

Pakistani Army / 12th Medium Artillery Regiment, 1965

Manufactured first in 1942 as an improvement over the 60-pounder cannon then in service, the 5.5in (140mm) gun was distinguishable by the characteristic horns alongside the barrel, which were components of the spring support for the gun's weight. Serving with British forces for more than 40 years, it was retired in the early 1980s; however, the weapon remains active with the Pakistani Army today.

Specifications

Crew: 10

Calibre: 140mm (5.5in)

Elevation: - 5 to + 45 degrees

Weight: 6190kg (6.09 tons)

Range: 14,813m (16,200 yards)

Muzzle velocity: 510m/sec (1673ft/sec)

▲ **FH-77 155mm field howitzer system**

Indian Army / 261st Artillery Brigade, 1971

A truly modern field howitzer of Swedish manufacture, the FH-77 was designed in the early 1980s and utilizes hydraulic power generated by an auxiliary engine system for short-distance movement and to assist in numerous operations, such as loading and ramming, elevating the weapon and lowering the trailing wheels. More than 400 are said to be in service with the modern Indian Army.

Specifications

Crew: 5

Calibre: 155mm (6.1in)

Elevation: - 3 degrees to + 50 degrees

Weight: 11,500kg (11.32 tons)

Range: 22,000m (24,050 yards)

Muzzle velocity: 774m/sec (2450ft/sec)

Japan
1960–PRESENT

Since the end of World War II, the scope of the Japanese armed forces has been limited and largely dependent upon the United States for support in the event of hostilities of long duration.

IMMEDIATELY FOLLOWING WORLD WAR II, the Japanese nation was forbidden to rearm or to raise a standing army of any consequence. However, as war erupted on the Asian continent, it became apparent to the United States that Japan might serve as a valuable ally and continuing base of operations against the spread of communism. Indeed, from bases in Japan, the United States has, over the years, preserved a Cold War balance of power with the Soviet Union, opposed the aggression of North Korea and staged military assets to Vietnam.

Although the Japanese Ground Self-Defence Force maintains limited manpower and levels of equipment, its weapons are modern and, in many cases, of Japanese design and manufacture. Strictly controlled through a series of National Defence Program Outlines, the number and types of weapons to be deployed are modified periodically. As of 1976, a total of 1000 artillery pieces were in the Japanese arsenal. This number has been reduced by ten per cent since then, while the number of self-propelled

artillery pieces and vehicles used in the transport of artillery was decreased by 30 per cent, from 900 to 600, in 2005. Eight anti-aircraft artillery groups with surface-to-air-missile capabilities are also maintained.

The latest organizational changes in the Japanese Ground Self-Defence Force were accompanied by a restructuring from divisional to brigade alignment. Prior to the organizational change, an infantry division was usually supported by an artillery regiment of four battalions, each with two batteries of howitzers, and a reserve battalion of four batteries. Each battery typically fielded four guns. Mechanized divisions included an air defence battalion and a field artillery regiment. The current organization consists of a single artillery brigade with three groups and two air defence brigades with three groups.

Towed artillery includes the 155mm (6.1in) FH-70 howitzer, while self-propelled models include the Japanese Type 75 and Type 95 155mm (6.1in) guns and the US MLRS rocket system. Together with several armoured vehicles, the Japanese have

Specifications

Crew: 3

Weight: 36,000kg (79,400lb)

Length: 7.99m (26ft 2in)

Width: 3.18m (10ft 5in)

Height: 4.4m (14ft 5in)

Engine: 536kW (718hp) 10F22WT 10-cylinder
   diesel

Speed: 60km/h (37mph)

Road range: 500km (310 miles)

Armament: 2 x 35mm (1.38in) autocannon

▲ Type 87 SPAAG

Japan Ground Self-Defence Force / 2nd Combined Brigade, 1995

The Type 87 self-propelled anti-aircraft gun mounts a pair of radar-directed 35mm (1.38in) autocannon. Developed during the 1980s as a replacement for the outmoded American M42 Duster, the Type 87 has a chassis by Mitsubishi, while its weapons, similar to the Swiss Oerlikon, were produced by Japan Steel Works.

Specifications

Crew: 3

Calibre: 130mm (5.1in)

Elevation: 0 to + 50 degrees

Weight: 18,695kg (18.4 tons)

Length: 5.8m (19ft)

Range: 15,000m (16,404 yards)

Engine: 224kW (300hp) Mitsubishi 4ZF diesel

Speed: 53km/h (33mph)

▲ Type 75 multiple launch rocket system

Japan Ground Self-Defence Force / 1st Artillery Brigade, 1984

The Type 75 multiple launch rocket system was developed by the Aerospace Division of Nissan Motor Company during the mid-1970s. Its 130mm (5.1in) rockets are carried in a boxlike frame of 30 barrels, which is mounted on the chassis of the Type 73 armoured personnel carrier. More than 60 remained in service two decades after deployment.

▲ Type 81 Tan-SAM

Japan Ground Self-Defence Force / 2nd Anti-Aircraft Artillery Brigade, 1988

Developed by the Toshiba Corporation, the Type 81 Tan-SAM went into design in 1966. The system was originally deployed in 1981 and has undergone several upgrades. Its 160mm (6.3in) radar-controlled missiles replaced the outmoded 75mm (2.9in) M51 and 37mm (1.5in) M15A1 anti-aircraft systems while complementing the shoulder-fired FIM-92 Stinger and MIM-23 HAWK missiles. The Type 81 battery, or firing unit, includes a fire-control vehicle capable of tracking two targets simultaneously and two launching vehicles.

Specifications

Crew: 15

Missile weight: 100kg (220.46lb)

Missile length: 2.7m (8ft 10in)

Range: 10km (6.21 miles)

Warhead: 9.2kg (20.3lb)

developed notable weapons systems such as the Type 87 self-propelled anti-aircraft gun and the Type 75 multiple launch rocket system. The radar-directed 35mm (1.38in) autocannon of the Type 87 replaced the 1960s-vintage US-made M42 Duster, while the Type 75 was designed to provide close support for infantry. The Type 81 Tan-SAM complements shoulder-fired and heavier platform-launched anti-aircraft missiles and was designed by the Toshiba Corporation.

Singapore
1965–PRESENT

The tiny Republic of Singapore has developed into a manufacturer of modern artillery, and its weapons are in demand around the world.

WHEN THE REPUBLIC OF SINGAPORE gained independence in 1965, its armed forces consisted of only two infantry regiments; however, the newly formed government solicited assistance from Israel and patterned its modern armed forces in similar fashion to the Israeli Defence Forces. Today, the Singapore Armed Forces (SAF) comprises more than 72,000 active personnel and over 300,000 reservists. The SAF includes two artillery battalions and an air defence artillery battalion assigned at the divisional level.

Among the primary artillery weapons of the SAF are the French 105mm (4.1in) GIAT LG-1 towed light howitzer and the FH-88 and FH-2000 155mm (6.1in) howitzers, both of which were designed by engineers in Singapore. The FH-88 was designed in the early 1980s and has been delivered to the Indonesian armed forces as well, while the FH-2000 variant is a product of Singapore Technologies Corporation which entered service in 1993 and was field-tested in New Zealand.

Self-propelled weapons fielded include the 155mm (6.1in) SSPH Primus and the 155mm (6.1in) SLWH Pegasus, both developed in Singapore. The Pegasus entered service in the autumn of 2005 and is intended eventually to replace the LG-1, while the Primus was introduced in 2004 and was developed following an extensive survey of US, British, Japanese and Russian types. In 2007, Singapore ordered at least 18 units of the US HIMARS (High Mobility Artillery Rocket System), and deliveries began in 2009. One notable aspect of the sale was the absence of unguided rockets in the deal, as Singapore apparently is intent on deploying the first fully GPS-guided HIMARS unit known to exist.

Specifications

Crew: 8

Calibre: 155mm (6.1in)

Elevation: - 3 degrees to + 70 degrees

Weight: 12,800kg (12.59 tons)

Range: 19,000m (20,780 yards)

Muzzle velocity: 765m/sec (2510ft/sec)

▲ **155mm ODE FH-88**

Singapore Armed Forces / 21st Artillery Division, 1992

Ordnance Development and Engineering of Singapore developed five prototypes of the FH-88 beginning in 1983, and production of the service model was undertaken four years later. The first howitzer designed in Singapore for the republic's own army, the FH-88 has been a successful replacement for the Soltam M-71. The FH-2000 was a later upgrade of the original production model.

Chapter 5

The Middle East and Africa

The Middle East and the continent of Africa
have been torn by strife for centuries. The rise and fall of
mechanized armies have brought regime change, the births
of nations, guerrilla warfare and civil turmoil. Throughout
these periods of unrest, the firepower and range of artillery
have been deciding factors in the course of events. The
outcome on the battlefield dictates the tenor of negotiations
and overtures for peace. Artillery provides a decided edge in
the continuation of diplomacy by other means, as armed
conflict has been described by some. Its mere presence,
let alone its utilization, may tip the military
and political balance.

◀ **SP bombardment**

An Israeli M107 self-propelled howitzer fires on Syrian positions somewhere near the Golan Heights,
October 1973.

Introduction

As European colonialism waned, independent Arab states and the Jewish nation of Israel armed for the series of conflicts which would define the modern era in the Middle East.

THE NATION OF ISRAEL came into being with a declaration of independence on 14 May 1948, and almost immediately it was attacked by neighbouring Arab states. The conflict had deep roots, stretching back more than 2000 years, and the United Nations endorsement of the partition of Palestine sparked a renewal of old antagonisms. While the Arab nations of Egypt, Syria, Iraq, Lebanon and Trans-Jordan had raised standing armies with some degree of mechanization, the fledgling Israeli Defence Forces (IDF) began its storied history as the Haganah, a makeshift, underequipped militia organization facing an enemy which was attacking from several directions.

Elementary artillery

Many of the heavy weapons utilized by both the Arab and Israeli armed forces during the war of 1948 had been abandoned or relinquished to local military control by Allied or Axis forces following World War II. Common among the Arab forces were the British Bren Gun Carrier; the French Lorraine 38L chassis which often mounted a small artillery piece, anti-tank gun or machine gun; and the light British 2-pounder and 6-pounder anti-tank weapons. Armoured vehicles included the Marmon-Herrington armoured car, often mounting the 2-pounder gun with a secondary Browning .30-cal (7.62mm) or .50-cal (12.7mm) machine gun.

The Trans-Jordanian Arab Legion entered the war with at least 7000 soldiers grouped in infantry and mechanized infantry brigades and two fully mechanized brigades with armoured cars and artillery. Its heaviest weapon was the venerable British 25-pounder gun, with a complement of at least four organized into a single battery. The legion's armoured car troop fielded 12 Marmon-Herrington vehicles.

The two brigades of the Egyptian Expeditionary Force included a hotchpotch of pre-World War II French tanks of Hotchkiss and Renault manufacture, the British Matilda and Crusader types and even a few German Mark IV panzers. Its mechanized infantry complement included nearly 300 Bren Gun

Carriers capable of towing light artillery pieces; a variety of armoured cars such as the Humber Mk III and Mk IV; and the Loyd Carrier, which often towed a 6-pounder anti-tank gun.

The Syrian Army of 1948 was noted for its complement of 65mm (2.6in) mountain guns carried on the Lorraine 38L chassis – which in effect produced a makeshift self-propelled artillery piece – and for the anti-aircraft or anti-tank 25mm (0.98in) gun mounted atop the Bren Gun Carrier. Its few artillery pieces were also remnants of the French colonial presence in the Levant and included 75mm

▲ **Soviet mortar**
Amir El Hassan (foreground), prime minister of Yemen, examines a Soviet-supplied 82mm Model 1941 mortar captured from the Egyptian Army during the North Yemen Civil War, 1962–70.

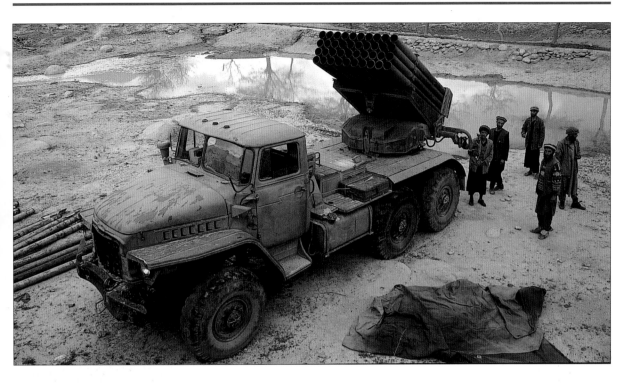

▲ **Mobile launcher**
Afghan irregulars man a Soviet-built BM-21 rocket launcher, probably captured after the withdrawal of Soviet troops in 1989. The BM-21 is highly mobile: a trained crew can emplace the system and have it ready to fire in three minutes, and packed up and ready to move in two minutes if encountering counter-battery fire.

(2.9in) and 105mm (4.1in) models. Most of these were well-worn Vichy weapons, which had served pro-Axis forces during the Allied offensive operations of 1941.

The Bren Gun Carrier, or Universal Carrier, was produced in Great Britain from 1934 to 1960, and during that time more than 113,000 were manufactured. The tracked vehicle had originally been intended to transport infantry and support weapons such as heavy machine guns and mortars which were too large to be man-portable. Early models mounted the .303-cal (7.7mm) Bren light machine gun or the Boys 0.55in (13.97mm) anti-tank rifle, and even the British 3in (actually 3.2in/81.2mm) mortar. The carrier was protected by seven to ten millimetres (0.28–0.39in) of armour and powered by a 64kW (85hp) Ford V-8 petrol engine. Its crew of two was often complemented by a contingent of onboard infantrymen. In time, the Bren Gun Carrier was employed by artillery units as the prime mover for the 6-pounder gun, and this was the case with Syrian forces in Palestine.

The Haganah had its origins in the 1920s during the British mandate in Palestine, and by the time of the 1948 war its brigades included British Cromwell and Valentine tanks and the French Hotchkiss H39. Among its most versatile weapons were the numerous variants of the US-built M3 half-track. The M3 was deployed in mechanized infantry units in a troop carrier role, with heavy machine guns or mortars in a modified troop compartment to provide direct infantry fire support, or with a 75mm (2.9in) or 90mm (3.54in) gun used in an artillery or anti-tank function. The British-manufactured Daimler armoured car and a number of improvised mobile weapons, such as the machine-gun-equipped jeep called the Negev Beast, equipped Haganah units.

Along with light weapons of European and US manufacture, the Israelis also utilized the 81mm (3in) Davidka, or Little David, mortar. Only six of these were known to have seen service; however, their presence was considered a tribute to the resourcefulness of the Haganah and its determination to stand up to the vastly superior Arab forces arrayed against it.

Suez Crisis to Six Day War
1956–67

From the Suez Crisis to the Six Day War, the armed forces of the Middle Eastern nations grew in power and performance. The emergence of the Cold War further precipitated the export of modern artillery and other technology to a global hotspot.

INTERNATIONAL TENSIONS grew exponentially with the rise of nationalism and communism around the world, and with the intricacies of politics armed confrontation became an almost inevitable consequence. High-stakes bargaining for the financing of the Aswan Dam resulted in a breakdown of negotiations between Egypt and the Western democracies. When the Egyptian government recognized the People's Republic of China and nationalized the Suez Canal in 1956, Britain, France and Israel responded militarily. This was followed in 1967 by Israel's lightning pre-emptive strike at the start of the Six Day War, during which IDF armour and artillery were skilfully handled and Israel gained control of the Golan Heights on the Syrian frontier and wrested the entire Sinai Peninsula from Egypt.

Egyptian forces had been substantially augmented by the addition of Soviet-manufactured artillery and the licensed production of rocket systems. Among the most common of the mobile artillery organic to Egyptian Army units were the SU-100 and Archer

17-pounder self-propelled guns. The SU-100 had been developed by the Soviets late in World War II and deployed extensively during the last year of the war. Its 100mm (3.9in) D10S gun was initially installed in an enclosed turret on the chassis of the T-34/85 medium tank and later the chassis of the T-54/55 tank. Characteristic of Soviet armoured vehicles of the late World War II and post-war eras, the SU-100 was distinguished by its low silhouette which presented a minimal target to the enemy but restricted its effectiveness in the hull-down position.

The lighter Archer 17-pounder was of British manufacture and combined the chassis of the Valentine tank and the QF 17-pounder (76mm/3in) gun. Introduced in the autumn of 1944, the Archer was an open-topped gun due to the narrow Valentine chassis, which resulted in the recoil of the weapon into the driver's compartment. Its low silhouette and rear-mounted gun allowed the Archer to lie in ambush, fire at an approaching enemy and make its escape with a minimum of manoeuvre.

▲ SU-100 SP gun

Egyptian Army / 4th Armoured Division, Port Said, Suez Canal,
November 1956

The SU-100 self-propelled gun was developed by the Soviet Union during World War II and remained in service with Arab armies in the Middle East until the 1970s. Modifications for service in the desert resulted in the SU-100M variant.

Specifications

Crew: 4	Engine: 370kW (500hp) V-2-34 12-cylinder
Weight: 31.6 tonnes (69,665lb)	4-stroke diesel
Length: 9.45m (31ft)	Speed: 48km/h (30mph)
Width: 3m (10ft)	Road range: 320km (200 miles)
Height: 2.25m (7ft 5in)	Armament: 1 x 100mm (3.9in) D-10S gun
	Radio: R-113 Granat

Among the towed artillery prevalent at the time of the Suez Crisis and the Six Day War a decade later were the French-designed 155mm (6.1in) Howitzer Model 1950 and the Soviet-built 152mm (6in) Howitzer M1943, better known as the D-1. The Model 1950 was utilized by both Arab and Israeli forces during the period and was one of the first newly manufactured weapons of its kind to emerge on the international arms market following World War II. Its four-wheeled carriage was towed behind a half-track or large truck, and the howitzer was also modified by the Israelis to fit the chassis of the M4 Sherman medium tank, resulting in the M50 self-propelled assault gun.

The D-1 was the result of a need to expedite Soviet artillery production at the height of World War II and comprised the larger 152mm (6in) howitzer mounted on the light carriage of the 122mm (4.8in) M1938 weapon. As a result, Soviet designers had to fit a large muzzle brake on the gun to decrease the recoil. One of the most enduring artillery pieces of the Cold War era, the D-1 served into the 1980s with the armed forces of several Arab nations and was exported around the world.

▲ **Walid APC rocket launcher**

Egyptian Army / 2nd Infantry Division / 10th Brigade, Abu Ageila, Sinai, 1967

A variant of the Soviet-produced BTR-152 armoured personnel carrier, the Walid was manufactured in Egypt and exported to other Arab countries. The Walid carried a crew of two and a complement of up to ten combat infantrymen. Some were fitted with 80mm (3.15in) rocket launchers.

Specifications

Crew: 2	Speed: 86km/h (54mph)
Weight: not available	Road range: 800km (500 miles)
Length: 6.12m (20ft)	Armament: 12 x 80mm (3.15in)
Width: 2.57m (8ft 5in)	rocket-launcher tubes
Height: 2.3m (7ft 6in)	Radio: n/k
Engine: 125kW (168hp) diesel	

◀ **155mm Howitzer Mle 1950**

Egyptian Army / 53rd Artillery Battery, 1967

A post-war French design, the Mle 1950 155mm (6.1in) howitzer remained in service with the armed forces of numerous countries into the 1990s. The weapon features a recoil system of individual cylinders arranged around the barrel in order to provide rapid cooling during sustained action. The stable firing platform consists of a pedestal which is lowered in the carriage centre along with the two legs of a split trail.

Specifications

Crew: 5	Weight: 8100kg (7.97 tons)
Calibre: 155mm (6.1in)	Range: 18,000m (19,685 yards)
Elevation: - 4 degrees to + 69 degrees	Muzzle velocity: 650m/sec (2133ft/sec)

Specifications

Crew: 4

Weight: 18.79 tonnes (18.5 tons)

Length: 6.68m (21ft 11in)

Width: 2.64m (8ft 8in)

Height: 2.24m (7ft 4in)

Engine: 123kW (165hp) GMC M10 diesel

Speed: 24km/h (15mph)

Road range: 145km (90 miles)

Armament: 1 x 76mm (3in) 17pdr OQF,

plus 1 x 7.7mm (0.303in) Bren MG

▲ **Archer 17pdr SP gun**

Egyptian Army / 4th Armoured Division, Port Said, Suez Canal, November 1956

The open-turret self-propelled-gun variant of the British Valentine tank, the Archer tank destroyer was deployed by the Egyptian Army during the Suez Crisis. Its 17-pounder (76mm/3in) gun was effective against Israeli armoured vehicles in the Sinai.

94th Anti-Tank Battery, Egyptian Army, 1956

Typical of an Egyptian Army anti-tank battery at the time of the 1956 Suez Crisis, the 94th fielded a complement of nine Archer 17-pounder self-propelled anti-tank guns. The Archer was manufactured by the British firm of Vickers, and fewer than 700 were actually constructed. Although it was somewhat lighter than other self-propelled artillery in service at the time, the Archer proved adept at fire and manoeuvre. Its 17-pounder (76mm/3in) main gun was powerful enough to engage Israeli M4 Sherman tanks from camouflaged positions and then displace rapidly.

Battery (9 x Archer SP guns)

▲ **152mm Howitzer M1943 (D-1)**

Syrian Army / 42nd Mechanized Brigade, 1967

One of the longest-serving field artillery weapons in modern history, the 152mm (6in) M1943 howitzer combined the two-wheeled carriage of the 122mm (4.8in) M1938 howitzer with the barrel of the heavier 152mm (6in) howitzer. Its large muzzle brake minimized destabilizing recoil during long periods of operation. The product of Soviet manufacturing expediency during World War II, the M1943 served with the armed forces of numerous Warsaw Pact and Soviet client states into the 1990s.

Specifications

Crew: 8

Calibre: 152mm (6in)

Elevation: - 3 degrees to + 63.5 degrees

Weight: 3600kg (7937lb)

Range: 12,400m (13,560 yards)

Muzzle velocity: 508m/sec (1666ft/sec)

Yom Kippur War
1973

Coordinated weapons technology initially gave the Egyptian and Syrian armed forces the upper hand. However, Israeli forces rallied to stem the Arab bid to regain control of territory lost in 1967.

WHEN EGYPTIAN FORCES breached the Bar-Lev Line and took Israeli commanders by surprise in October 1973, their well-coordinated capabilities of air and ground defences provided a decided edge during the opening days of the conflict. A centrepiece of the Egyptian tactics was the employment of air defence artillery, ground artillery and man-portable anti-tank missiles. Although the Israeli Defence Forces rallied in the later weeks of the war, the Egyptians had taught the world a lesson in the employment of complementary capabilities of multiple weapons systems.

Integral to the Egyptian offensive was the ingenuity of using high-pressure water hoses which blasted exits for infantry and armoured units through the high sand berms on the eastern bank of the Suez Canal. Once across in force, the Egyptian infantry pierced the Bar-Lev Line and took on the counterattacking Israeli tanks with the potent 9K11 Malyutka anti-tank missile, known to NATO forces as the AT-3 Sagger.

The effectiveness of the Sagger came as a rude shock to the Israelis and accounted for heavy losses in Israeli armour during the three-week war. Specially trained in the use of anti-tank weapons, including the AT-3 and the RPG-7 rocket-propelled grenade, tank-killer teams were among the first Egyptian troops across the Suez Canal, assisting in the capture of isolated posts along the Bar-Lev Line.

Sagger power

The Sagger was an MCLOS (Manual Command Line Of Sight) man-portable missile which was developed in the Soviet Union in the early 1960s and entered service with the Red Army by the autumn of 1963. Weighing 10.9kg (24.3lb), the light missile system was wire-guided and controlled by the operator, who corrected the path to the target with a joystick. The shaped warhead was capable of penetrating the armour of Israeli M48 tanks and other fighting vehicles at distances of up to 3000m (3280 yards).

While the Sagger was an initial shock to the Israelis, it was determined that the operator was able

▲ **AT-3 Sagger**

Egyptian Army / 3rd Mechanized Infantry Division, 1973

The MCLOS 9K11 Malyutka anti-tank missile was known to NATO as the AT-3 Sagger. This man-portable wire-guided missile is one of the most widely produced and exported systems of its kind in the world and destroyed a number of Israeli armoured vehicles during the Yom Kippur War of 1973.

Specifications

Configuration: single-stage, shaped charge	Launch weight: 10.9kg (24.3lb)
Deployment: man-portable	Range: 3000m (3280 yards)
Length: 860mm (33.86in)	
Diameter: 125mm (4.92in)	

64th Artillery Brigade, Syrian Army, 1973

During the Yom Kippur War of 1973, the Syrian Army's 64th Artillery Brigade fielded both the towed and self-propelled variants of the 122mm (4.8in) D-30 howitzer which had been developed by the Soviet Union in the early 1960s. The Syrian conversion of the D-30 to a self-propelled weapon set the howitzer atop the chassis of the T-34 medium tank. Firing from prepared positions, the towed D-30 proved to be an outstanding anti-tank weapon. Large numbers of these guns remain in service today.

Brigade (54 x 122mm/4.8in D-30 howitzers; 18 x 122mm/4.8in D-30 SP Howitzers)

to maintain control of the missile within only 4.6m (15ft) of the firing point. Therefore, as the Yom Kippur War progressed, Israeli tanks and infantry concentrated their fire on the position of the Sagger operator, forcing him to displace rapidly and alter the course of the missile. In the intervening time, however, estimates of the number of Israeli vehicles destroyed by the Sagger range from 800 to more than 1000, with the higher figure possibly including vehicles which were disabled and returned to service.

When the Egyptian infantry was forced on the defensive, the troops typically deployed adjacent to dug-in positions with the Sagger at the ready. Advancing Israeli tank crews were well aware of the

▲ ZSU-23-4 SPAAG

Egyptian Army / 2nd Infantry Division / 51st Artillery Brigade, 1973

With radar-directed quad-mounted 23mm (0.9in) autocannon, the ZSU-23-4 self-propelled anti-aircraft vehicle, commonly called the Shilka, was attached to numerous Egyptian armoured brigades during the Yom Kippur War. Along with surface-to-air missiles, they accounted for a number of low-flying Israeli aircraft.

Specifications

Crew: 4	Engine: 210kW (280hp) V-6R diesel
Weight: 19,000kg (41,800lb)	Speed: 44km/h (27mph)
Length: 6.54m (21ft 5in)	Road range: 260km (162 miles)
Width: 2.95m (9ft 8in)	Armament: 4 x 23mm (0.9in) AZP-23
Height (without radar): 2.25m (7ft 4in)	anti-aircraft cannon
	Radio: n/k

Specifications

Crew: 7	Engine: 372kW (493hp) V-2 V12 diesel
Weight: n/k	Speed (road): 55km/h (33mph)
Length (hull): 6m (19ft 7in)	Road range: 360km (223 miles)
Width: 3m (9ft 10in)	Armament: 1 x 122mm (4.8in) D-30 howitzer
Height: n/k	

▲ T-34 with 122mm D-30 SP howitzer

Syrian Army / 64th Artillery Brigade, 1973

With its turret removed, the chassis of the World War II-vintage T-34 medium tank provided a stable platform for the 122mm (4.8in) D-30 self-propelled howitzer of the Syrian Army during the Yom Kippur War. In order to keep pace with advancing mechanized infantry units and provide much-needed supporting fire, the Syrians adapted the two Soviet weapons into a capable system.

prowess of the Sagger after the first few days of the Yom Kippur War, and its mere presence altered their method of attack. Israeli armoured doctrine emphasized rapid movement; however, the Sagger required a more cautious approach. Infantry was deployed to take out the Sagger positions, exacting a toll in both time and lives.

At the Battle of the Chinese Farm, elements of General Ariel Sharon's 143rd Armoured Division encountered stiff resistance and lost approximately 70 of its 250 tanks in one night of savage fighting on 15 October. During the fighting around the Suez Canal as Egyptian forces attempted to disengage, a single tank-killing team of the Egyptian 19th Infantry Division was reported to have destroyed at least nine Israeli tanks with Sagger missiles.

In the air, the dominance of the Israeli Air Force, which had decimated Egyptian armour and infantry

▲ Soltam Systems L33 155mm SP howitzer
Israeli Defence Forces / 188th Armoured Brigade, 1973

Distinguished by its large, boxlike turret structure and based on the chassis of the M4A3E8 Sherman tank, the Soltam Systems L33 mounted a 155mm (6.1in) cannon. After trials in 1968, the L33 entered production in 1970. The vehicle was deployed shortly before the Yom Kippur War.

Specifications

Crew: 8	Engine: 331kW (450hp) Ford GAA V8 petrol
Weight: 41.5 tonnes (40.8 tons)	Speed: 38km/h (24mph)
Length (hull): 5.92m (19ft 5in)	Road range: 260km (162 miles)
Width: 2.68m (8ft 9in)	Armament: 1 x 155mm (6.1in) L33 howitzer, plus
Height: n/k	1 x 7.62mm (0.3in) MG

▲ Soltam Systems M-68 155mm howitzer
Israeli Defence Forces / 75th Armoured Infantry Battalion, 1973

Based on an earlier Finnish design, the Soltam M-68 155mm (6.1in) howitzer was mounted on a four-wheeled carriage. The wheels at the forward end of each trail leg moved in order for the weapon to be positioned for firing. To stabilize the platform, spades were pounded into the ground and then locked in place.

Specifications

Crew: 8	Weight: 8000kg (7.87 tons)
Calibre: 155mm (6.1in)	Range: 22,000m (24,060 yards)
Elevation: - 10 degrees to + 67 degrees	Muzzle velocity: 765m/sec (2510ft/sec)

concentrations during the Six Day War of 1967, was challenged by the combination of Soviet-made surface-to-air missiles and rapid-firing self-propelled air defence guns allied with modern radar detection systems. The Soviet 2K12 Kub air defence missile, known to NATO as the SA-6 Gainful, was a state-of-the-art surface-to-air missile system at the time of the Yom Kippur War. Development of the SA-6 was undertaken in the summer of 1958, and the system was deployed to units of the Red Army by 1970.

Mounted on a tracked chassis which carried a triple launcher and sophisticated radar codenamed Straight Flush by NATO, the SA-6 took a heavy toll on Israeli aircraft, particularly the American-built A-4 Skyhawk and F-4 Phantom. In response to the deadly success of the SA-6 batteries, Israeli aircraft adopted a tactic of flying low, beneath the trajectory of the radar. In doing so, however, the Israeli aircraft were engaged by the self-propelled ZSU-57-2 and highly effective ZSU-23-4 Shilka anti-aircraft guns of the Egyptian Army.

The Shilka

The ZSU-23-4 Shilka, named for a river in southeastern Russia, consists of a quadruple battery of 23mm (0.9in) radar-directed autocannon mounted on a modified chassis similar to that of the PT-76 amphibious tank and the SA-6 air defence missile. The ZSU-23-4's combined rate of fire is up to 4000 rounds per minute, creating a veritable curtain of fire against low-flying aircraft. Developed in the late 1950s, the Shilka was produced in large numbers from the early 1960s to the 1980s, and many of these weapons were placed in service with the armed forces of Soviet client states. At least five Israeli Phantoms were shot down by the ZSU-23-4 during one fighter sweep against mobile SA-6 sites on 7 October 1973.

The Shilka had been designed as a replacement for the older ZSU-57-2, which mounted a pair of 57mm (2.2in) autocannon. Although the 57mm (2.2in) guns were of heavier calibre, the ZSU-57-2's combined rate of fire was approximately 240 rounds per minute, substantially lower than that of the Shilka. The ZSU-57-2 was the first self-propelled air defence gun produced in substantial numbers by the Soviet Union. Nicknamed Sparka, or Pair, it proved considerably less effective than its successor during the Yom Kippur War.

The Israeli Defence Forces countered Egyptian self-propelled artillery with the Soltam L33 155mm (6.1in) howitzer, which mounted the potent L33 barrel atop the chassis of the American-designed M4A3E8 'Easy Eight' Sherman tank. This self-propelled howitzer was easily distinguished by its high silhouette and boxlike turret which held eight crewmen. The Soltam M-68 155mm (6.1in) towed howitzer, meanwhile, was designed and built in Israel, entering service with the IDF in 1970. With a range of 22,000m (24,060 yards), it provided much-needed firepower which slowed advancing Egyptian and Syrian troops during the critical opening days of the Yom Kippur War. Based on a pair of Finnish designs from the early 1960s, the M-68 underwent firing trials in 1968 and was later upgraded to the M-71, which featured a longer barrel.

Specifications

Configuration: two-stage, solid fuel	Diameter: 370mm (14.5in)
Deployment: fixed and mobile	Launch weight: 626kg (1380lb)
Length: 5.12m (16ft 9in)	Range: 40km (25 miles)

▲ **MIM-23 HAWK surface-to-air missile**
Israeli Air Force / Southern Air Defence Regiment, 1973

At the outbreak of the Yom Kippur War, the Israeli Air Force had acquired up to 12 batteries of the US-made MIM-23 HAWK surface-to-air missile. Deployed in 1960, the HAWK is still in use as a medium-range air defence missile system. HAWK (Homing All the Way Killer) missiles have also been mounted on mobile tracked vehicles by the Israelis.

Specifications

Crew: 3

Calibre: 20mm (0.79in)

Elevation: - 10 degrees to + 90 degrees

Weight: 1350kg (2976lb)

Range: 2000m (6560ft)

Muzzle velocity: 844m/sec (2770ft/sec)

▲ **TCM-20 AA gun (Hispano-Suiza HS.404)**

Israeli Defence Forces / 14th Infantry Brigade, 1973

Basically, the Israeli TCM-20 served during the Yom Kippur War as an updated version of the US towed twin-mount .50-calibre (12.7mm) Browning air defence machine gun. The TCM-20's updated armament consists of two 20mm (0.79in) Hispano-Suiza cannon mounted on a two-wheeled carriage which is easily towed by a light vehicle.

Lebanon
1982–2006

Various factions vied for control of Lebanon for several years, and civil war devastated the country. The artillery of the Israeli and Syrian armies and the indiscriminate rocket attacks by insurgents became symbolic of the nation's suffering.

AS CIVIL WAR WRACKED LEBANON beginning in the mid-1970s, neighbouring countries were inexorably drawn into the conflict. While control of the country was at stake, old antagonisms came to the fore, with the Palestine Liberation Organization (PLO) openly inciting unrest between Christian and Muslim militia groups and in turn provoking Israel and Syria to military action. During the same period, the Hezbollah terror organization was founded by Islamic extremists and Palestinian nationalists supported by the government of Iran.

During periods of unrest, the Israeli Defence Forces have invaded or occupied portions of Lebanon, most notably during the 1982 offensive which evicted the Palestine Liberation Organization from the country. Israeli involvement stemmed largely from continuing terror and guerrilla rocket and infiltration attacks against settlements in northern Israel from havens in southern Lebanon. These operations were often backed by the PLO and later by Hezbollah. At the height of its strength in

Lebanon, the PLO fielded up to 200 artillery pieces and rocket launchers in the country, organized into seven artillery battalions.

Antagonism old and new

At various times, the Syrian Army deployed at least 200 tanks and artillery pieces, including as many as 19 batteries of air defence missiles such as the SA-6 Gainful, in the region of the Bekaa Valley, while the Israeli Defence Forces committed more than 1200 tanks and armoured personnel carriers along with supporting field artillery and defence units. Numerous paramilitary forces, both Christian and Muslim, numbered in the thousands, and throughout the course of the war these groups were allied with one another, betrayed those alliances, and fought in a confusing tangle of allegiances during which thousands of civilians were killed, wounded or made homeless. While artillery fire is often a deciding factor in the outcome of a battle, during the Lebanese Civil War, it was sometimes employed

THE MIDDLE EAST AND AFRICA

indiscriminately by several factions against civilian targets which were suspected of harbouring guerrilla fighters or as an instrument of terror in its own right.

Among the most prominent artillery weapons employed by the Syrian Army, the PLO and other forces in Lebanon were the Soviet-made 130mm (5.1in) M1954 and 152mm (6in) field artillery pieces and the BM-21 truck-mounted rocket launcher. Also known as the M-46, the 130mm (5.1in) M1954 was an aging weapon at the time of the Lebanese Civil War but was no less effective. Its crew of eight was capable of firing six rounds per minute under standard combat conditions, eight rounds in burst mode and five rounds in a sustained engagement. Its effective range of 27.5km (17 miles) with unassisted ammunition provided a weapon which could be used against Israeli forces and other targets at a considerable distance. The People's Republic of China has manufactured a copy of the M-46 under licence for a number of years and designated it the Type 59-1.

The 152mm (6in) M1955 D-20 towed gun-howitzer was introduced to the Red Army in 1955 as a nuclear-capable long-range field artillery weapon.

Its crew of eight could fire up to six rounds per minute in burst situations and one round per minute during sustained combat operations. Its range with conventional ammunition was approximately 17.4km (11 miles). Manufactured by the People's Republic of China as the Type 66, the D-20 was the first Soviet field artillery piece to employ a semi-automatic vertical sliding wedge breech block.

A descendant of the original BM-13 Katyusha rocket launchers of the World War II era, the BM-21 Grad 122mm (4.8in) rocket launcher entered service in 1964 and is still in widespread use today. It consists of 40 tubes and is mounted atop the 6X6 Ural 375D truck chassis. With a rate of fire of two rounds per second and a maximum range of 40km (25 miles), the BM-21 battery is capable of saturating a large area of territory and disrupting troop concentrations and armoured formations. Its crew of five can deploy the system into firing position in as little as three minutes, while the reload time is approximately ten minutes. In a barrage situation, all 40 rockets may be airborne in as little as 20 seconds.

While the launchers themselves have been utilized by the PLO and the Syrian Army, guerrilla

Specifications

Crew: 7	Engine: 372kW (493hp) V-2 V12 diesel
Weight: n/k	Speed (road): 55km/h (33mph)
Length (hull): 6m (19ft 7in)	Road range: 360km (223 miles)
Width: 3m (9ft 10in)	Armament: 1 x 122mm (4.8in) D-30 howitzer
Height: n/k	

▲ **T-34 with 122mm D-30 SP howitzer**

Syrian Army / 1st Armoured Division / 58th Mechanized Brigade, Lebanon, 1982

This artwork shows the Syrian 122mm (4.8in) D-30 SP howitzer in winter camouflage and in firing position. The crew's firing platform unfolded from the side of the tank chassis. When the vehicle was in motion, the platform folded back.

organizations such as Hamas or Hezbollah have been known to fire the same 122mm (4.8in) rocket used with the BM-21 from improvised tubes during attacks on Israeli settlements.

Battleship bombardment

The United States became involved in the Lebanese Civil War during the early 1980s as United Nations peacekeepers and multinational forces were introduced to the war-torn country. Frequently these troops were the targets of suicide bombers and insurgent activity. In October 1983, a pair of truck bombings hit a US Marine Corps barracks and a French military installation in the Lebanese capital of Beirut, killing nearly 300 servicemen. Syrian and Druze artillery shelled Christian positions routinely, while the Christians responded in kind and often enough instigated the duels as well. US aircraft attacked Syrian artillery emplacements on several occasions in retaliation for Syrian air defence missiles having been fired against US and French planes.

The 406mm (16in) guns of the battleship USS *New Jersey* fired for the first time on hostile positions near the Lebanese capital on 14 December 1983. On 8 February 1984, the *New Jersey* conducted the heaviest naval bombardment of shore targets since the Korean War, firing 300 406mm (16in) shells at positions occupied by the Syrian Army and its allied Druze militia. After-action reports indicated that at least 30 of these massive shells destroyed a Syrian

command post, killing at least one general, reported to have been the commander of all Syrian forces in Lebanon, and several senior staff officers.

During their numerous incursions into Lebanon, the Israeli Defence Forces have adapted their use of armour and mechanized infantry to the rigours of urban combat while also utilizing artillery fire to suppress the small arms and rockets of guerrilla forces and to duel with Syrian guns. Along with the M-50 self-propelled assault gun, the Israelis deployed their Soltam M-68 155mm (6.1in) artillery and the M-71, an improved version of the M-68 which incorporated not only a longer barrel but also a compressed-air-driven rammer which facilitated rapid loading and firing under combat conditions. The Israelis also modified the chassis of the M4 Sherman tank to carry a number of artillery pieces, including the 155mm (6.1in) L39, a longer version of the L33 gun.

Israeli-made self-propelled artillery

Along with using US-made artillery such as the M109 self-propelled howitzer and the M107 175mm (6.9in) self-propelled gun, the Israelis developed their own self-propelled artillery. In the mid-1980s, the Soltam company experimented with a 155mm (6.1in) self-propelled howitzer known as the Sholef, or Gunslinger, which mounted the heavy weapon atop the modified chassis of the Merkava main battle tank; however, the 45.7-tonne (45-ton) vehicle never entered production. During the 1982 Lebanon

▲ **Rascal light SP howitzer**

Israeli Defence Forces / Southern Regional Command / 366th Division / 55th Artillery Battalion 'Draken' ('Dragon'), 1990

The light self-propelled Rascal 155mm (6.1in) howitzer was designed and built by Soltam Ltd. Weighing only 20.3 tonnes (20 tons), the Rascal was the lightest of the Soltam 155mm (6.1in) self-propelled weapons. It was capable of transport by air, truck or rail.

Specifications

Crew: 4	Engine: 261kW (350hp) diesel
Weight: 19,500kg (43,000lb)	Speed: 50km/h (31mph)
Length (with gun): 7.5m (24ft 7in)	Road range: 350km (220 miles)
Width: 2.46m (8ft 1in)	Armament: 1 x 155mm (6.1in) howitzer
Height: 2.3m (7ft 7in)	

invasion, the MAR-290 was deployed, with four 290mm (11.4in) rocket tubes capable of firing high-explosive fragmentation or cluster ammunition.

The Soltam Rascal light self-propelled 155mm (6.1in) howitzer is contemporary with the Sholef but much lighter at 20.3 tonnes (20 tons) and easily transported by air. The barrel is mounted on a hydraulic turntable at the rear of the chassis, which adds to the Rascal's stability. In preparation for firing,

the Rascal deploys two hydraulically operated spades. Its 36 rounds of ammunition are stored externally.

An innovative infantry weapon of the period is the Soltam 120mm (4.7in) mortar. Adopted by the US Army in the early 1990s, the Soltam 120mm is capable of firing a maximum of 16 rounds per minute or four rounds in a sustained environment. Operated by a crew of four or five, the weapon is either towed or mounted on a light vehicle.

▲ **Soltam 120mm Mortar**

Israeli Defence Forces / Golani Infantry Brigade, 1982

A heavy infantry mortar which is often towed on a two-wheeled carriage, the Soltam 120mm (4.7in) mortar has been accepted by several armies, including that of the United States, as a replacement for lighter weapons. Its fin-stabilized ammunition provides accurate plunging fire against enemy positions. Deployment is rapid and involves first tipping the trailer so that the baseplate drops to the ground, and then lifting the tube.

Specifications

Crew: 5	Weight: 231kg (510lb)
Calibre: 120mm (4.7in)	Range: 6500m (7100 yards)
Elevation: + 43 degrees to + 85 degrees	Muzzle velocity: 310m/sec (1017ft/sec)

▲ **MAR-290**

Israeli Defence Forces / 211th Armoured Brigade, 1982

An improved version of an Israeli-built copy of the Soviet BM-24 multiple launch rocket system, the MAR-290 consists of four 290mm (11.4in) backward-facing rocket tubes mounted on the modified chassis of the M4 Sherman tank. Its combat debut occurred during the 1982 Israeli invasion of Lebanon, and the weapon is capable of firing high-explosive fragmentation or cluster ammunition.

Specifications

Crew: 4	System combat weight: 29,465kg (29 tons)
Calibre: 290mm (11.4in)	Range: 22km (24,059 yards)
Rocket length: 5.45m (17ft 10in)	Rate of fire: 4 rockets in 10 seconds
Rocket weight: 600kg (1322lb)	

▲ Fire support

An Israeli M109A6 self-propelled howitzer bombards positions in Lebanon from northern Israel during the 2006 Lebanon War.

▲ M109 SP howitzer

Israeli Defence Forces / 212th Artillery Regiment / 405th Artillery Battalion / 2nd Platoon, 2006

The US 155mm (6.1in) M109 self-propelled howitzer was developed in the early 1950s and has been upgraded on numerous occasions to include automatic fire control, an improved gun mount, a longer barrel and improved explosive reactive armour protection. More than 4000 have been manufactured, and the weapon today is fielded by the armed forces of more than 30 nations.

Specifications

Crew: 6	Engine: 302kW (405hp) Detroit Diesel
Weight: 27.9 tonnes (27.5 tons)	Model 8V-71T diesel
Length: 6.61m (21ft 8.25in)	Speed: 56km/h (35mph)
Width: 3.26m (10ft 9.75in)	Range: 390km (240 miles)
Height: 3.29m (10ft 9.5in)	Armament: 1 x 155mm (6.1in) howitzer

Iran–Iraq War
1980–88

A horrific war of attrition developed between neighbouring countries following the invasion of Iran by Saddam Hussein's Iraq. Both sides fired ballistic missiles, and the horror of chemical weapons was revealed to the world.

WHEN PRE-EMPTIVE AIR STRIKES hit bases of the Iranian Air Force and troops of the Iraqi Army surged across the frontier with the Islamic Republic, Saddam Hussein had hoped for a quick victory. However, the two nations became locked in a bloody war of attrition with each gaining the upper hand temporarily. Neither, in the end, was able to overcome the other decisively.

Although the Iraqi military had been professionally trained, somewhat modernized and augmented with equipment purchased from a number of nations, and prepared for war, the Iranian force which confronted it possessed equipment, including field artillery and a small number of self-propelled guns, of US manufacture which had been sold to Iran under the regime of the Shah. As the war dragged on, it became apparent that the Iraqis did possess towed and self-propelled artillery in greater numbers than the Iranians, whose armoured vehicles

and infantry were often at a decided disadvantage on the battlefield. However, the sheer weight of Iranian infantry numbers countered the Iraqi advantage in heavy equipment.

At the outset of hostilities, the Iranian Army deployed four independent artillery groups and an air defence command of four HAWK missile battalions. Iranian towed artillery included the US-manufactured M2A1 105mm (4.1in) and M114 155mm (6.1in) howitzers. Self-propelled artillery included the M107 175mm (6.9in) self-propelled gun and the M108 203mm (8in) self-propelled howitzer. At the height of its capability, Iranian artillery numbered approximately 5000 guns of various types.

In 1980, the Iraqi Army could muster more than 7300 towed and self-propelled artillery pieces, some of which had been in service for more than 30 years. Among the towed pieces were the Italian OTO Melara 105mm (4.1in) Mod 56 pack howitzer, the Soviet

▲ **Canon de 155mm Mle F3 Automoteur**

Iraqi Army / 5th Mechanized Division, 1980

During the Iran–Iraq War, the Iraqi military received 85 examples of this French self-propelled artillery weapon. The gun, also known as the GCT 155mm (6.1in), went into production in 1977, and more than 400 were constructed by the mid-1990s. With a maximum rate of fire of eight rounds per minute and upgraded nuclear, biological and chemical defences, it was one of the most modern self-propelled guns of the Iran–Iraq War.

Specifications

Crew: 4	Engine: 540kW (720hp) Hispano-Suiza 110
Weight: 41,949kg (92,288lb)	12-cylinder multifuel
Length: 10.25m (33ft 7.5in)	Speed: 60km/h (37mph)
Width: 3.15m (10ft 4in)	Range: 450km (280 miles)
Height: 3.25m (10ft 8in)	Armament: 1 x 155mm (6.1in) cannon

152mm (6in) D-20 Model 1955 and 122mm (4.8in) D-30 developed in the 1960s, the US M114, and the Type 59-1, a Chinese copy of the Soviet 130mm (5.1in) M1954 gun. Among the self-propelled artillery in the Iraqi arsenal were the Soviet 122mm (4.8in) 2S1 and 152mm (6in) 2S3 howitzers along with a relative few examples of the American M109.

The Iraqi Army was also equipped with Soviet tactical surface-to-surface FROG (Free Rocket Over Ground) missiles, AT-3 Sagger and AT-4 Spigot anti-tank missiles, and the French MILAN anti-tank missile. Several rocket-launcher systems, including the ubiquitous Soviet BM-16 and BM-21 truck-mounted systems, were also available. The Iraqi ballistic-missile inventory included the Soviet Scud B and a modified Scud known as the Al Hussein, with increased range. Iran responded to Iraqi Scud attacks against Tehran with its own launches of Scud missiles purchased from Syria and Libya directed towards Baghdad. By the end of the war, Iraq had expended more than 500 standard and Al Hussein Scuds, while the Iranians had fired more than 170.

The bull's eye

While the war with Iran was under way, Canadian engineer Gerald Bull was employed by the government of Iraq to produce a generation of artillery weapons with great range and the capability of firing conventional, chemical and nuclear

IRANIAN ARTILLERY UNITS, 1980	
Unit	Base
11th Independent Artillery Group	Khuzestan, Iran
22th Independent Artillery Group	Khuzestan, Iran
44th Independent Artillery Group	Khuzestan, Iran
55th Independent Artillery Group	Khuzestan, Iran
4 HAWK missile battalions	Khuzestan, Iran

weapons. Among the most prominent of the Bull guns developed for the Iraqis and utilized during the war with Iran were approximately 300 new 155mm (6.1in) weapons similar in design to the GC-45, which Bull had developed in the 1970s for several nations, primarily Austria and South Africa. The GC-45 was considered one of the finest weapons of its kind in the world, with a maximum range of 39,600m (24.6 miles) and maximum and sustained rates of fire of five and two rounds per minute respectively. Reports have surfaced that in 1985 Austria shipped 200 of these guns, designated the GHN-45, through Jordan to Iraq for use in the war. By the time of the 1991 Gulf War, these guns were still worrisome to the Coalition partners.

Bull was also commissioned to design two self-propelled guns, the 210mm (8.27in) Al Fao and the 155mm (6.1in) Majnoon. Although the Al Fao was first seen in public in Baghdad in 1989, neither is

Specifications

Crew: 6

Weight: 28,100kg (61,820lb)

Length: 8.48m (27ft 10in)

Width: 3.27m (10ft 9in)

Height: 2.75m (9ft)

Engine: 388kW (520hp) Model V-54 V12 diesel

Speed: 50km/h (31mph)

Road range: 420km (260 miles)

Armament: 2 x 57mm (2.2in) anti-aircraft guns

▲ **ZSU-57-2 SPAAG**

Iraqi Army / 113th Infantry Brigade, 1980

The ZSU-57-2 originally entered service with the Soviet Red Army in World War II and was later modified to fit the chassis of the T-54 main battle tank. Mounting a pair of 57mm (2.2in) anti-aircraft cannon, the weapon produced a sustained rate of fire of approximately 70 rounds per minute per gun. Its excellent mobility and range contributed to its service longevity into the 1990s.

known to have entered service with the Iraqi Army. The Al Fao is a similar design to the South African G6 howitzer and has been estimated to weigh 48.8 tonnes (48 tons). Its range of 56,000m (35 miles) is astonishing, particularly considering that its rate of fire is four rounds of 109kg (240lb) ammunition per minute. Most troubling is the capability of the Al Fao to fire chemical rounds containing sarin, mustard or phosgene gases.

Chemical consternation

On numerous occasions during the war with Iran, Saddam Hussein demonstrated a ruthless willingness to use chemical weapons. These deadly weapons of mass destruction were delivered by Scud missiles, aerial bombs, or artillery shells. Series G nerve agents and Series H blister agents were both used. The US Central Intelligence Agency estimated in 1991 that Iran had suffered at least 50,000 casualties due to chemical weapons during the war; however, other estimates exceed 100,000.

In battle, the Iraqis integrated chemical weapons into their defensive schemes. Often, chemical shells would be fired at Iranian troop concentrations and artillery emplacements to disrupt the progress of large Iranian infantry attacks and supporting fire. Offensively, the Iraqis fired conventional high-explosive fragmentation shells at distant targets, while hitting Iranian forward positions, command-and-

control centres and marshalling areas near the front line with chemical shells. Iraqi aircraft dropped bombs filled with mustard gas and tabun, a highly toxic nerve agent, and it was also reported that spray devices were affixed to helicopters to disperse chemicals over a wide area of the battlefield.

In March 1986, Javier Pérez de Cuéllar, Secretary General of the United Nations, accused the Iraqis of using chemical weapons in direct violation of the 1925 Geneva Protocol. Although Saddam Hussein continued to deny their use, the evidence began to mount, and independent reports confirmed thousands of casualties. Particularly horrific was the apparent use of nerve gas on the civilian population of the Kurdish town of Halabjah in northeastern Iraq.

Man versus machine

In mid-1982, control of the Iranian military was vested in the country's Islamic clergy. In turn, massive human-wave attacks were ordered against entrenched Iraqi troops and artillery. The results were predictable as Iranian soldiers, many of them as young as nine and as old as 50, were slaughtered. The Iraqis also flooded low-lying areas to impede the progress of Iranian tanks. However, in most instances the combat-effectiveness of tanks on both sides was limited due to the preference of commanders for digging the vehicles in and employing them primarily as artillery.

▲ 152mm Towed Gun-Howitzer M1955 (D-20)

Iraqi Army / 12th Armoured Division, 1980

The Model 1955 152mm (6in) D-20 gun-howitzer was developed in the Soviet Union just after World War II and entered service with the Red Army by the mid-1950s. Intended as a replacement for the 152mm (6in) Model 1937 howitzer, the D-20 featured a split-rail carriage and maximum rate of fire of up to six rounds per minute. The gun was also mounted on a tracked chassis to produce the 2S3 self-propelled assault weapon.

Specifications

Crew: 8

Calibre: 152mm (6in)

Elevation: - 5 degrees to + 63 degrees

Weight: 5700kg (12,566lb)

Range: 17.4km (11 miles)

Muzzle velocity: 650m/sec (2132ft/sec)

▲ **Dragon ATGM**

Islamic Republic of Iran Army / 30th Infantry Brigade, 1981

Developed in the United States as a shoulder-fired wire-guided anti-tank missile, the Dragon was designed in the mid-1960s and entered service with the US Army in 1975. Designed specifically to eliminate Soviet main battle tanks, the weapon could be fired by a single soldier and was used effectively against Iraqi armour during the war of 1980–88.

Specifications	
Configuration: two-stage, hollow charge	Diameter: 292mm (11.5in)
Deployment: man-portable	Launch weight: 14.57kg (32.1lb)
Length: 1154mm (45.4in)	Range: 1000m (1094 yards)

Middle East today

1990–PRESENT

In this volatile region, the military forces of numerous nations have continued to arm and equip with vast amounts of artillery. Although many of these systems have been in service for decades, they remain lethal.

THE PROLIFERATION of artillery throughout the armies of Middle Eastern countries and in the hands of guerrilla and militia organizations has contributed to the instability of the region during the past quarter-century. Following the bloody war with Iran, Saddam Hussein's Iraq embarked on a substantial programme of rearmament, purchasing equipment and technology from numerous countries and posing a threat to neighbouring nations such as tiny Kuwait, which Iraqi forces invaded in August 1990. Countering the Iraqi threat, moderate Arab nations such as Saudi Arabia and Egypt modernized the artillery components of their land forces as well. While each of these remained primarily dependent on foreign technology, some organic modifications to existing systems did occur as each country sought to complement its existing arsenal.

Among the major purchases made by the Iraqis were the American M198 155mm (6.1in) towed and the M109 155mm (6.1in) self-propelled howitzers; the GHN-45 155mm (6.1in) towed howitzer designed by Canadian engineer Gerald Bull and sold to Iraq via Austria; and the modern French GCT 155mm (6.1in) self-propelled gun. The GCT 155mm was developed in the early 1970s, and Saudi Arabia was the first nation to deploy the weapon after accepting deliveries in the 1980s. Iraq quickly followed suit, purchasing 85 of the GCTs during the Iran–Iraq War. Many of these remained in service with the Iraqi Army into the next decade, and more than 400 were manufactured by the French by 1995. Developed as a replacement for the F3 155mm (6.1in) gun, the GCT provided better armour protection for the four-man crew, enhanced night-vision technology, protection against nuclear, chemical and biological weapons, and an automatic loading system.

The artillery capabilities of the Royal Saudi Land Forces have been substantially improved in recent years with the introduction of more than 300 examples of the US M109A6 Paladin 155mm (6.1in) self-propelled howitzer. The Paladin constitutes a substantial upgrade to earlier versions of the M109,

▲ AMX-13 DCA

Royal Saudi Land Forces / 10th Mechanized Brigade, 1990

Developed in response to the French Army's need for a self-propelled air defence gun, the AMX-13 DCA entered service with the French Army in 1969. Its twin 30mm (1.2in) Hispano-Suiza cannon were mounted on the chassis of the AMX-13 light tank, with the three-man crew protected by an enclosed turret of cast steel. The same turret was later mounted on the AMX-30 tank chassis, and these were also purchased by Saudi Arabia.

Specifications

Crew: 3	Engine: 187.5kW (250hp) SOFAM Model 8Gxb
Weight: 17,200kg (37,840lb)	8-cylinder petrol
Length: 5.4m (17ft 11in)	Speed: 60km/h (37mph)
Width: 2.5m (8ft 2in)	Range: 300km (186 miles)
Height: 3m (9ft 10in)	Armament: 2 x 30mm (1.2in) cannon

▲ Shahine SAM

Royal Saudi Air Defence Forces / Dhahran Battery, 1991

The Shahine air defence missile system combines the chassis of the French AMX-30 main battle tank and a variant of the French Crotale air defence missile. Seventeen mobile batteries of the Royal Saudi Air Defence Forces were equipped with the Shahine in the 1990s, and other Crotale missiles were posted in static firing positions.

Specifications

Crew: 3	Engine: 517.5kW (690hp) Hispano-Suiza 110
Weight: 38,799kg (85,554lb)	12-cylinder multifuel
Length: 6.59m (21ft 7.4in)	Speed: 65km/h (40mph)
Width: 3.1m (10ft 2in)	Range: 600km (370 miles)
Height: 5.5m (18ft)	Armament: 6 x Crotale SAMs

which date to the late 1950s. The M109A6 includes upgraded armour protection, fire direction control and quicker displacement.

Several hundred M198 and FH-70 155mm (6.1in) field howitzers were acquired by the Saudis during the early 1980s to equip the army's five artillery battalions. The M198 entered service with the US Army in 1979, and a well-trained crew of nine is capable of a maximum rate of fire of four rounds per minute. Although the armed forces of the United States and Great Britain have been replacing their M198s with the Global Combat Systems M777 howitzer, the M198 remains widely used by Middle Eastern countries. The FH-70 entered service in 1978 and was a joint venture between Germany, Italy and the United Kingdom. Its crew of eight can fire as many as six 155mm (6.1in) rounds per minute to a maximum range of 30km (32,808 yards).

Israeli ignition

The modern Israeli Defence Forces remain true to their fundamental doctrine of armour-heavy striking power. However, the lessons of the 1973 Yom Kippur War have influenced the thinking of Israeli commanders to the extent that artillery, both towed and self-propelled, has evolved into a major component of battlefield operations. Israeli tanks had

been largely unsupported by self-propelled artillery during the 1973 war, and losses against Egyptian tank-killer units armed with man-portable missiles had been exceptionally high. Since then, Israeli artillery has played a key role in the fighting in southern Lebanon against Syrian and guerrilla forces.

Fielding at least 15 armoured and nine mechanized infantry brigades, the Israelis have augmented their artillery capabilities in recent years with the acquisition of updated US M109 155mm (6.1in) self-propelled howitzers while maintaining their older M-71 towed howitzers and other systems as well. More recent additions include the ATMOS 2000 152mm (6in) and Rascal 155mm (6.1in) self-propelled howitzers.

At the same time, the Israeli military has invested in nuclear-capable weaponry, including field artillery and surface-to-surface missile systems such as the Jericho, which originated during the early 1960s as a joint effort between the Israeli government and the French firm of Dassault. The most recent of the Jericho series, the Jericho III, is reportedly a three-stage, solid-propellant ballistic missile with a range of up to 11,500km (7180 miles) and a nuclear payload of a single warhead of 750kg (1653lb) or three smaller MIRV warheads. Potentially, the Jericho brings the entire Middle East within range of Israeli nuclear weapons.

▲ **AMX-13/LAR160 MLRS**

Israeli Defence Forces / 334th Artillery Battalion, 1993

The AMX-13/LAR multiple launch rocket system incorporates the chassis of the French AMX-13 light tank with the LAR 160 rocket launcher. The LAR 160mm (6.3in) rocket is typically carried in pods of 13 and can be adapted to other platforms such as trucks, light armoured vehicles or trailers. The LAR 160 rocket is fin-stabilized and powered by solid propellant. It may be carried by helicopters to provide long-range fire support to airborne and light infantry units.

Specifications

Crew: 6

Calibre: 160mm (6.3in)

Rocket length: 3477mm (11ft 5in)

System combat weight: 16,765kg (16.5 tons)

Range: 45km (49,213 yards)

Rate of fire: unknown

▲ Palmaria SP howitzer

Libyan Army, 1992

Developed solely for the export market, the OTO Melara Palmaria 155mm (6.1in) self-propelled howitzer included an automatic loading system. The heavy weapon was mounted on the chassis of the OF 40 main battle tank. The first prototypes were built in the late 1970s. Production commenced in 1982 and ceased in the early 1990s.

Specifications

Crew: 5	Engine: 559kW (750hp) 8-cylinder diesel
Weight: 46,632kg (102,590lb)	Speed: 60km/h (37mph)
Length: 11.474m (37ft 7.75in)	Road range: 400km (250 miles)
Width: 2.35m (7ft 8.5in)	Armament: 1 x 155mm (6.1in) howitzer, plus
Height: 2.874m (9ft 5.25in)	1 x 7.62mm (0.3in) MG

Specifications

Crew: 6	Engine: 391kW (525hp) diesel
Weight: 47,000kg (103,600lb)	Speed: 90km/h (56mph)
Length (chassis): 10.2m (33ft 4.3in)	Road range: 700km (435 miles)
Width: 3.4m (11ft 2in)	Armament: 1 x 155mm (6.1in) cannon
Height: 3.5m (11ft 6in)	

▲ G6 Rhino 155mm SP howitzer

United Arab Emirates Union Defence Force, 1997

The G6 155mm (6.1in) self-propelled howitzer is an autonomous system with a 700km (435-mile) vehicle fuel range. Developed in South Africa by Denel Land Systems, the G6 is in service with the South African Army (43 systems) and has also been exported to the United Arab Emirates (78 systems) and Oman (24 systems). The crew members are protected against landmines, gunfire and bombardment fragments.

133

▲ **Spike AT missile**

Israeli Defence Forces / Golani Brigade, 1998

A man-portable anti-tank missile incorporating fire-and-forget technology, the Spike entered service with the Israeli Defence Forces in 1997. While the missile is line-of-sight oriented, some variants are also capable of targeting through fire-and-observe guidance. The missile carries a tandem HEAT (high-explosive anti-tank) warhead and is powered by a solid-fuel rocket. It is also mounted on light vehicles.

Wars in Africa
1960–2000

Since 1960, Africa has been wracked by more than 20 civil wars, far more than any other continent on the planet. Ethnic strife, territorial ambitions and political strongmen have fuelled the flames of unrest.

THE WAR-TORN CONTINENT OF AFRICA has been the modern scene of locally driven civil war, battles for control of natural resources and the settling of centuries-old tribal and ethnic accounts. Since 1960, major conflicts have been fought in Rwanda, Congo, Somalia, Sudan, Liberia, Burundi and Angola among others, while millions of civilians and paramilitary and military personnel have been killed or made homeless, suffering the twin spectres of starvation and disease in the wake of war. In 1998, at least 11 major armed conflicts were in progress on the continent simultaneously.

Proxy wars

The rise of the Third World created a power vacuum on the African continent, facilitating a surge of nationalism and unrest. Often enough, foreign nations have exacerbated these conflicts through ideological proxy wars or attempts to extend their own influence through puppet governments. Former colonial powers have funnelled arms and equipment to rebel warlords, to legitimate governments fighting for survival and to oppressive regimes bent on crushing opposition.

Outside suppliers

From 1950 to 1989, the United States alone supplied $1.5 billion to various governments and political or military factions in Africa. In 1991, a total of $4.5 million in military hardware was shipped by the US to the government of what was then the nation of Zaire. Soviet military advisers and Cuban troops participated in the long-lasting civil war in Angola. During each of the wars on the African continent, various old and new artillery systems have been primary dealers of death and destruction.

Angolan Civil War
1975–2002

In a confusing tangle of alliances and ideologically charged confrontations, a 27-year civil war in Angola did not end before at least 500,000 people were killed and the superpowers had been drawn into a developing proxy war.

LONG A COLONIAL POSSESSION of Portugal, Angola became an independent nation in the autumn of 1974, and civil war broke out shortly thereafter. The communist-backed ruling party, the MPLA (Popular Movement for the Liberation of Angola), and its military wing, the FAPLA (People's Armed Forces for the Liberation of Angola), opposed the anti-communist UNITA (National Union for the Total Independence of Angola). These were the principal warring factions, and during the course of the fighting the Soviet Union, the United States, Cuba and the neighbouring African countries of Zaire, Mozambique and South Africa were drawn either directly into the fighting or provided material support to one side or the other. United Nations efforts to bring about peace were continually frustrated, and civilian populations were often caught in the crossfire. Three distinct periods of fighting were punctuated by brief intervals of peace, and from 1994 to 1998 the United Nations invested more than $1.6 billion to maintain a peacekeeping force in the country.

During the Angolan Civil War, numerous heavy artillery bombardments were experienced, and many of these were conducted by regular army and paramilitary groups. Soviet military aid to Marxist forces in the country topped $1 billion in 1986, while

Fidel Castro's Cuba not only supplied arms and equipment but also introduced combat troops to the conflict. As the war dragged on, Cuban troop strength approached 40,000. At the same time, the United States sent millions of dollars in aid to UNITA, along with advanced weapons such as the shoulder-fired FIM-92 Stinger air defence missile.

Angola became nothing short of an arms marketplace during the war as numerous countries sold military aircraft, missiles, small arms and artillery to the warring factions. UNITA was known to have purchased a number of FROG (Free Rocket Over Ground) missile systems from North Korea. The Soviet-designed FROG-7 entered service in the mid-1960s and consists of a transporter-erector-launcher atop the wheeled 8X8 ZIL-135 platform. The missile itself packs a 550kg (1200lb) high-explosive warhead with a range of up to 90km (56 miles).

Cold War calamity

Both East and West considered the Angolan Civil War a contest of political and armed will. Angola would prove to be a prime example of proxy warfare with political and ideological prestige at stake for the major powers. The Battle of Cuito Cuanavale in early 1988 proved to be the largest battle on the African

▲ **9K33 Osa (SA-8 Gecko)**
Cuban Revolutionary Armed Forces / Revolutionary Army Command SAM Brigade, 1988
The 9K33 Osa surface-to-air missile, known as the SA-8 Gecko to NATO personnel, is a single-stage solid-fuel low-altitude surface weapon developed in the Soviet Union and deployed in 1972. It was the first mobile air defence system to deploy missiles and onboard radar on the same platform, which includes the 9A33 amphibious 6X6 transporter-erector-launcher. Nicknamed Land Roll by NATO, the sophisticated radar of the SA-8 system allows tracking of multiple targets and minimizes the effects of jamming by electronic countermeasures.

Specifications
Configuration: single-stage, solid fuel
Deployment: mobile
Length: 3.15m (19ft 4in)
Diameter: 210mm (8.26in)
Launch weight: 130kg (287lb)
Range: 12km (7.5 miles)
Launch preparation time: 4 minutes

continent since the World War II fight at El Alamein in far-off Egypt. Both sides claimed a victory; however, the result was indecisive.

Concerned with its border security, the government of South Africa opted to intervene militarily in Angola on several occasions. Among the weapons deployed by the South African Defence Force was the relatively new G5 155mm (6.1in) howitzer, produced in South Africa and based initially on the design of the Gerald

Bull GC-45. A lengthy development and modification phase was conducted in the late 1970s, and the G5 entered service with the South African armed forces in 1982. Its eight-man crew could fire at a sustained rate of three rounds per minute, and the weapon was also exported to Iran, Iraq, Malaysia and Qatar.

The South West African Territorial Forces, formed in 1980 under the control of the South African Defence Force, mounted the US-manufactured M40

Specifications
Crew: 3
Calibre: 180mm (7.1in)
Rocket length: 4.2m (13ft 9in)
Rocket weight: 152kg (335lb)
System combat weight: 10,000kg (22,046lb)
Range: 16,000m (17,500 yards)
Rate of fire: 450–550rpm/cyclic

▲ **ASTROS II MLRS**

FAPLA / Mechanized Infantry Brigade Artillery Battalion, 1987

The ASTROS II MLRS (multiple launch rocket system) was developed in Brazil by defence contractor Avibrás and entered service with the Brazilian Army in 1983, while also being exported to several countries. Capable of firing rockets of 127mm (5in), 180mm (7.1in) and 300mm (11.8in), the ASTROS utilizes the Tectran Enginharia 10-ton 6X6 wheeled chassis mounting the AV-LMU launcher. Depending on the rocket loaded, the launcher's maximum capacity is from four to 32 missiles. Specifications here are for the 180mm (7.1in) SS-40 rocket.

Specifications
Crew: 4
Calibre: 300mm (11.8in)
Rocket length: 4.85m (15.91ft)
Rocket weight: 645kg (1422lb)
System combat weight: 17,273kg (17 tons)
Range: 68km (42.25 miles)
Rate of fire: unknown

▲ **Avibrás X-40**

FAPLA / Mechanized Infantry Brigade Artillery Battalion, 1976

The predecessor of the ASTROS II MLRS, the Brazilian Avibrás X-40 was a single-stage solid-fuel free flight rocket launcher mounted on the chassis of the Bernardini X1A1 light tank. The X-40 was a cumbersome system. Target acquisition, launching sequence and reloading were time-consuming functions. The X-40 was eventually retired from service in the 1990s.

106mm (4.17in) recoilless rifle atop a variety of 4X4 vehicles including the Toyota Land Cruiser and the Land Rover Defender. The M40 had been developed in the mid-1950s as a replacement for the earlier M27 105mm (4.1in) recoilless rifle. While it is generally referred to as 106mm (4.17in), the M40 is actually also a 105mm (4.1in) weapon. The slight variation in the name was to avoid confusion with other 105mm (4.1in) ammunition which was not compatible with the weapon. Used extensively in Vietnam, it was eventually replaced in the anti-tank role by missiles such as the BGM-71 TOW.

Marxist forces in Angola deployed a variety of Soviet Bloc-supplied towed artillery, and despite its age the 130mm (5.1in) M1954 was among the best. Developed during the mid-1950s as a replacement for older pre-World War II weapons, the M1954 served

with FAPLA forces along with the 122mm (4.8in) D-30 field howitzer of 1960s origin. Officially called the M-46 by the Soviets, the M1954 was light enough for reasonable mobility in the jungles and grasslands of Angola, while its sustained rate of fire of six rounds per minute and maximum rate of eight rounds per minute were formidable. With a maximum range of up to 37.8km (23.5 miles) with performance-assisted ammunition, it is capable of taking opposing forces under fire at a great distance. Although the Soviet Army replaced the M-46 with the 152mm (6in) 2A36 Giatsint B in the late 1970s, the older weapon is still in use around the globe.

In the air

To defend against South African aircraft, the Cuban forces in Angola were equipped with the Soviet-made

▲ **Toyota Land Cruiser with 106mm recoilless rifle**

South West African Territorial Forces / 201st Infantry Battalion 1980

The all-terrain Toyota Land Cruiser was an ideal mobile mount for the US-manufactured 106mm (4.17in) recoilless rifle, an effective anti-tank weapon deployed by the South West African Territorial Forces. The 106mm (4.17in) recoilless rifle was developed during the mid-1950s as a replacement for the older M27 weapon and was later supplanted by anti-tank missiles such as the BTM-71 TOW system.

Specifications

Crew: 3

Calibre: 105mm (4.1in)

Elevation: - 17 degrees to + 65 degrees

Weight: 209.5kg (462lb)

Range: 1350m (1476 yards)

Muzzle velocity: 503m/sec (1650ft/sec)

Specifications

Crew: 8

Calibre: 130mm (5.1in)

Elevation: - 2.5 degrees to + 45 degrees

Weight: 7700kg (16,975lb)

Range: 27.5km (17 miles) unassisted

Muzzle velocity: 930m/sec (3051ft/sec)

▲ **130mm Towed Field Gun M1954 (M-46)**

FAPLA / Mechanized Infantry Brigade Artillery Battalion, 1975

The 130mm (5.1in) towed field gun, known to the Soviets as the M-46 and to NATO as the M1954, is a durable field artillery piece which is still in service with numerous nations after half a century. The M-46 proved a stable firing platform and relatively manoeuvrable towed artillery piece during the Angolan Civil War, and its large numbers were augmented with examples of the newer 122mm (4.8in) D-30 weapon.

9K33 Osa, or Wasp, a potent air defence missile with an effective range of up to 12km (7.5 miles) and delivering a high-explosive warhead of 19kg (42lb). Known to NATO as the SA-8 Gecko, this missile entered service with the Red Army in 1972 and was produced for nearly a decade. Its 9A33 6X6 wheeled transporter-erector-launcher carries sophisticated radar which allows the tracking of two missiles simultaneously fired at the same target. A full Gecko battery includes four 9A33 vehicles along with two 9T217 transporter vehicles carrying additional missiles.

Brazilian rockets

One of the most effective weapons of the MPLA was of Brazilian manufacture, and the country became one of the leading arms exporters in the world during the 1980s. The ASTROS II MLRS (multiple launch rocket system) entered service in 1983 with the Brazilian Army and rapidly became the most profitable weapons system sold by its manufacturer, the Avibrás company. Prior to the deployment of the ASTROS II (ASTROS stands for Artillery Saturation Rocket System), Avibrás had marketed the X-40 300mm (11.8in) mobile rocket system, which comprised a single-stage solid fuel rocket launcher mounted atop the chassis of the Bernardini X1A1 light tank.

The ASTROS II consists of the AV-LMU launcher atop the Tectran Enginharia 10-ton 6X6 truck, while rockets of 127mm (5in), 180mm (7.1in) and 300mm (11.8in) are compatible with the system. A full ASTROS II battery consists of six launcher vehicles, six ammunition resupply vehicles and a fire-control vehicle. At the battalion level, command-and-control centres are capable of directing up to four batteries.

FAPLA Mechanized Infantry Brigade artillery elements, 1986

The artillery component of the FAPLA mechanized infantry brigade included HQ and field artillery observation personnel along with a pair of batteries equipped with the 122mm (4.8in) D-30 field howitzer and 76mm (3in) ZIS-3 field gun, the latter a Soviet anti-tank gun dating from World War II. The Soviet-made BM-21 multiple launch rocket system was capable of saturating an area with high-explosive 122mm (4.8in) rockets, while the 120mm (4.7in) mortar team provided plunging fire against hardened enemy positions and troop concentrations. FAPLA operational units were organized similarly to the Soviet Red Army, although the term brigade may be misleading. FAPLA mechanized infantry brigades were smaller versions of the Red Army mechanized infantry regiments.

HQ (1 x truck)

Field Artillery Observation (1 x truck)

Artillery Battery (2 x 122mm/4.8in D-30 howitzers, 2 x trucks)

Artillery Battery (2 x 76mm/3in ZIS-3 guns, 2 x trucks)

MLR Battery (2 x BM-21 rocket launchers)

Mortar Battery (1 x 120mm/4.7in mortar unit, 1 x truck)

Cuban Motor Rifle Regiment artillery element, 1986

At its height during the late 1980s, Cuban military strength in Angola neared 40,000 troops. The artillery element of a Cuban Revolutionary Armed Forces motor rifle regiment included three artillery batteries, each consisting of a single 122mm (4.8in) D-30 field howitzer along with a pair of BM-21 truck-borne multiple launch rocket systems. The well-equipped Cuban forces brought modern anti-tank missiles such as the AT-3 Sagger and air defence missiles such as the SA-8 Gecko to Angola as well. These were typically organic to infantry battalions, as were the self-propelled FROG-7 surface-to-surface missile and the heavy 120mm (4.7in) mortar.

HQ (1 x truck) **Field Artillery Observation (1 x truck)**

1 Battery (1 x 122mm/4.8in D-30 howitzer, 1 x truck, 2 x BM-21 rocket launchers)

1 Battery (1 x 122mm/4.8in D-30 howitzer, 1 x truck, 2 x BM-21 rocket launchers)

1 Battery (1 x 122mm/4.8in D-30 howitzer, 1 x truck, 2 x BM-21 rocket launchers)

South Africa
1970–PRESENT

The South African Artillery Formation has participated in territorial actions in Angola and Namibia and as a peacekeeping force in Central Africa.

SINCE ITS INVOLVEMENT IN the Angolan Civil War, the South African Defence Force has maintained a modern complement of weaponry, including the 155mm (6.1in) G5 towed and 155mm (6.1in) G6 self-propelled howitzers, the 40-barrel 127mm (5in) Bateleur MLRS (multiple launch rocket system), the M5 120mm (4.7in) mortar and smaller infantry support weapons.

The South African Artillery Formation is organized as a regular component consisting of the artillery school and the composite 4 Artillery Regiment at Potchefstroom, an airborne artillery battery with the 44 Parachute Regiment located at Bloemfontein and an artillery mobilization centre. Designated as reserve, seven artillery regiments are maintained at cadre strength. Reports currently indicate that a full deployment of the South African Artillery Formation would be a difficult task due to a lack of manpower and the fact that some reserve artillery personnel have been pressed into service as infantry peacekeepers in Central Africa. The 10 Air Defence Regiment is maintained as a separate force.

Contemporary firepower

The primary towed weapon of the South African Artillery Formation is the 155mm (6.1in) G5 howitzer, which has been in service for nearly 30 years and has undergone several improvements during that time. The weapon was designed by the South African firm of Denel Land Systems during the late 1970s. Based on Gerald Bull's GC-45 howitzer, the original 45-calibre version has been upgraded to a 52-calibre weapon designated the G5 2000.

SP version

A self-propelled version of the G5, the G6 Rhino, entered production in the late 1980s and is mounted on a heavy, wheeled 6X6 chassis. The Rhino has been praised for its outstanding mobility, which reduces the effectiveness of enemy

▲ **G5 howitzer (Armscor)**

South African Artillery Formation / Natal Field Artillery, 1985

The G5 howitzer was developed during the late 1970s by Denel Land Systems, a former arms-manufacturing facility of the Armscor company. The G5 incorporated much of the design of the GC-45 howitzer, which had been developed by Canadian engineer Gerald Bull. The G5 is adapted to fire conventional ammunition or an extended-range type with stabilizing fins. Its crew of eight soldiers is capable of a sustained rate of fire of three rounds per minute. An updated G5, designated the G5 2000, made its debut in 2002.

Specifications

Crew: 8

Calibre: 155mm (6.1in)

Elevation: - 3 degrees to + 75 degrees

Weight: 13,750kg (13.56 tons)

Range: 30,000m (32,810 yards)

Muzzle velocity: 897m/sec (2942ft/sec)

Artillery Battery, 61st Mechanized Infantry Battalion, South African Defence Force, 1988

At this time a typical South African Defence Force artillery battery consisted of either two G5 155mm (6.1in) howitzers (with two trucks) or two 120mm (4.7in) M5 mortars. Some artillery batteries were equipped with both, and which weapon was used depended on the task the battery was asked to carry out. The 61st Mechanized Infantry Battalion served under the command of the 82nd Mechanized Brigade in 1988.

Artillery Battery (2 x G5 155mm/6.1in howitzers, 2 x M5 120mm/4.7in mortars, 4 x trucks)

counterbattery fire, and the protection which the armoured hull affords the crew of six against anti-tank mines.

Reports indicate that Denel embarked on the development of a light 105mm (4.1in) howitzer, the G7, in 1995 and that the weapon has undergone extensive tests and modifications related to its weight. A self-propelled version of the G7 was tested jointly with the US Army following a partnership between Denel and General Dynamics Land Systems. The General Dynamics LAV III armoured

vehicle chassis and the G7 gun mount produced a light, air-transportable self-propelled weapon which may outfit units of the American Stryker Brigade. The towed version of the G7 is served by a crew of five and is capable of a sustained rate of fire of six rounds per minute. Its effective range is up to 32km (20 miles) – a long reach for a weapon of its calibre. An even more advanced version of the G7 is planned under a contract designated the Advanced Multirole Light Artillery Gun Capability (AMLAGC) programme.

<table>
<tr><td colspan="2">Specifications</td></tr>
<tr><td>Crew: 6</td><td>Engine: 391kW (525hp) diesel</td></tr>
<tr><td>Weight: 47,000kg (103,600lb)</td><td>Speed: 90km/h (56mph)</td></tr>
<tr><td>Length (chassis): 10.2m (33ft 4.3in)</td><td>Road range: 700km (430 miles)</td></tr>
<tr><td>Width: 3.4m (11ft 2in)</td><td>Armament: 1 x 155mm (6.1in) cannon</td></tr>
<tr><td>Height: 3.5m (11ft 6in)</td><td></td></tr>
</table>

▲ **G6 Rhino 155mm SP howitzer**

South African Army / 8th Mechanized Infantry Battalion, 1997

The wheeled G6 Rhino self-propelled howitzer has been noted for its excellent mobility and protection against anti-tank mines. It has a crew of six, and its 155mm (6.1in) L52 cannon is intended for direct mechanized infantry fire support as well as the protection of advancing tank columns.

▲ **Valkiri multiple launch rocket system**

South African Army / 61st Mechanized Infantry Battalion, 1982

Patterned after the highly successful Soviet-designed BM-21 MLRS (multiple launch rocket system), the Valkiri was introduced to the South African Army in 1982 and deployed to Angola. The system consists of a 4X4 light truck mounting 24 127mm (5in) rocket tubes in three rows of eight. The solid-fuel fin-stabilized rockets carry a pre-fragmented proximity-fused warhead, and reloading time is ten minutes. Another version of the Valkiri, the Mk II or Bateleur, mounts a total of 40 127mm (5in) tubes.

<table>
<tr><td>Specifications</td></tr>
<tr><td>Crew: 2</td></tr>
<tr><td>Calibre: 127mm (5in)</td></tr>
<tr><td>Rocket length: 2.68m (8ft 9in)</td></tr>
<tr><td>Rocket weight: 53.5kg (118lb)</td></tr>
<tr><td>System combat weight: 6400kg (14,110lb)</td></tr>
<tr><td>Range: 22,700m (14.1 miles)</td></tr>
<tr><td>Rate of fire: 24-second full salvo</td></tr>
</table>

Chapter 6

Modern Conflicts, 1991–2010

**Firepower, manoeuvrability and accuracy
of fire are as crucial to victory on the modern battlefield as
they were in the conflicts of centuries past, and no other
weapon delivers the tactical or strategic advantage that is
provided by artillery. With the potential to dominate the
modern battlefield, artillery remains a primary component of
combined-arms doctrine. Whether towed, self-propelled or
man-portable, artillery has evolved with technologically
advanced delivery systems and with munitions which may
be guided to distant targets with pinpoint accuracy.
From shoot and scoot to fire and forget, these weapons
deliver devastating fire and increase the survivability
of the operator.**

◀ **Guns across the desert**
A US Marine Corps (USMC) gun crew from Mike Battery, 4th Battalion, 14th Marines, fire an M198 155mm
(6.1in) howitzer at targets near Camp Fallujah, Iraq, 2007.

Introduction

Modern artillery incorporates continuing innovation in the designs of weapons and ammunition with unprecedented precision guidance and stand-off capabilities to destroy targets at long range.

GLOBAL UNREST is a reality in the modern world. Conflicts from the Balkans to Southeast Asia, the Horn of Africa, the Middle East and the Indian subcontinent require a response which is mobile, rapid and decisive. Terrorist and insurgent activity combined with the continuing threat of violence from rogue states such as Iran and North Korea compel other nations to maintain the ability to react swiftly if necessary.

On the move

Lightweight, airmobile guns provide the power behind the deployment of light infantry formations which are capable of rapid movement. In contrast, the movement of tanks and armoured vehicles may be a ponderous task. Therefore, when time is of the essence it is artillery that is adapted to support an armed intervention on the most efficient and mobile basis.

While artillery remains a principal component of combined arms in both offensive and defensive scenarios, it does present the commander with the option of a lone response. Artillery may fire from a distance without the necessity of engaging troops or air support. On the offensive, artillery may be used to blast a gap in an opposing line or to suppress enemy fire against advancing troops, protecting flanks for formations on the move and shifting forward at a pace which is conceivably more rapid than that maintainable by armour, particularly when the latter is required to deploy in difficult terrain or confined space. On the defensive, meanwhile, artillery is a game changer when brought to bear against an enemy counterattack or in the defence of fixed positions. In counterbattery operations, it prevents enemy artillery from hitting marshalling areas or command-and-control centres. Gaining the upper hand on the battlefield allows freedom of movement, and artillery establishes the base from which other ground operations may exploit the enemy's weakness.

▲ **Field howitzer**
British soldiers fire an M777 155mm (6.1in) howitzer at Taliban fighting positions in the Sangin district from an undisclosed forward operating base in the Helmand Province of Afghanistan, April 2007.

▲ **MLRS test-firing**
An MLRS test-fires somewhere near Tikrit, Iraq, 2005. The unitary-guided multiple launch rocket system is the latest addition to the US Army's artillery arsenal and is designed to minimize collateral damage.

Advocates of both rocket and towed artillery point out that each has become lighter and more battlefield-efficient than its predecessors, while even lighter self-propelled artillery is in some cases fit for rapid ground deployment. One component of firepower with favourable mobility involves the introduction of lightweight titanium in the construction of field artillery.

Strong and durable, titanium has replaced heavier materials in the construction of the M777 155mm (6.1in) howitzer. The introduction of the material was a key element of the response of the Global Combat Systems division of defence contractor BAE Systems to the demands of modern ground combat.

Designated originally as an 'ultralight' field howitzer, the M777 is roughly 42 per cent lighter at just over 4000kg (9000lb) than the M198 towed howitzer which it is designated to replace. With an effective striking arc of up to 40km (25 miles) with extended-range ammunition, the M777 entered service in 2005 and has equipped units of the US, Canadian and Australian armed forces.

Its airmobile transport capability has made the M777 an ideal heavy support weapon during the wars in Iraq and Afghanistan, equipping the artillery batteries of many light infantry and airborne units. During one engagement against Taliban forces in Afghanistan, a pair of Canadian M777s inflicted serious casualties on the enemy while firing only a few rounds. Among the sophisticated ammunition used by modern artillery systems are high-explosive fragmentation and improved conventional munitions (ICMs), which are often used for area bombardment; anti-personnel flechette projectiles; HEAT (high-explosive anti-tank) munitions; smoke shells; cluster munitions which scatter smaller bomblets across the battlefield; and ADHPM (artillery-delivered high precision munitions).

The M982 Excalibur artillery shell, developed by US defence contractor Raytheon Missile Systems and the Swedish BAE Systems Bofors, has been battle-tested with outstanding results. Fired from such platforms as the M777 155mm (6.1in) field howitzer and the 155mm (6.1in) M109A6 Paladin self-propelled howitzer during action in Iraq, the Excalibur is an extended-range shell which utilizes folding fins to assist in gliding to its target. Precision is achieved through a GPS system which guides the shell with astonishing accuracy.

Reports from Iraq indicate that the Excalibur shell was utilized in the summer of 2007 and 92 per cent of Excalibur rounds landed within four metres (13ft) of the intended target. The use of Excalibur not only improves the results of the artillery fire and allows it to function in a close-support role but also limits collateral damage in populated areas.

Gulf War
1990–91

Deployed over great distances and in a harsh climate, artillery proved decisive in numerous engagements during the war to liberate Kuwait from Saddam Hussein's Iraqi forces.

WHEN THE IRAQI ARMY invaded tiny Kuwait on 2 August 1990, a multinational coalition was assembled in response, and a tremendous logistical undertaking which lasted several months resulted in the most impressive assemblage of military power in the air and on land and sea in the history of warfare. Following an intense aerial bombardment of several weeks, the Coalition ground forces launched a lightning 100-hour land campaign which led to the rout of the Iraqi forces. Often, artillery took centre stage as the Coalition military commanders executed their battle plan.

During Operation Desert Shield, as the build-up was called, and the following Operation Desert Storm, modern artillery and state-of-the-art military technology were on full display. Along with towed and self-propelled guns and howitzers which are capable of inflicting tremendous damage with concentrated fire, anti-tank missiles, anti-aircraft systems, free-flight rockets and intermediate-range ballistic missiles were utilized during the fighting. In addition, embryonic anti-ballistic-missile technology made its combat debut during Operation Desert Storm, providing a glimpse of the future of missile defence technology.

With the advent of computerized fire direction and lighter, more efficient artillery, the world witnessed a spectacular display of firepower and accuracy during Operation Desert Storm. Half a century after World War II, the ranging of field artillery during a live-fire situation had improved from approximately six minutes to as little as 15 seconds. Even in the harshest of desert climates, with the continuing problems of sand, wind and extreme heat, the barrels of field weapons were known to fire as many as 500 rounds in as little as four hours

▲ **Out of commission**
An Iraqi ZSU-23-4 self-propelled anti-aircraft gun lies damaged by the roadside – probably hit by air attack – following Operation Desert Storm.

without appreciably degrading the efficiency of the barrel or supporting equipment.

Effective deployment

Both the Coalition forces and the Iraqi Army faced significant challenges in terms of the deployment and effective usage of artillery during Desert Storm. For the Iraqis, there is no question that some modern and highly effective weapons systems were available, including the infamous Scud missile, the Soviet-made 122mm (4.8in) 2S1 and 152mm (6in) 2S3 self-propelled howitzers and proven towed artillery such as the 155mm (6.1in) GHN-45 and G5 howitzers. The 122mm (4.8in) D-30 field howitzer had entered service with Soviet forces more than 25 years earlier but remained a viable system. However, the array of weapons acquired by Saddam Hussein, either captured during the 1980–88 war with Iran or purchased through the international arms market, created inconsistencies in training for artillery units as operational instructions were often in foreign languages such as English or Chinese, and compatible ammunition was often difficult to procure.

The challenges inherent in Coalition warfare during Desert Storm contributed to incidents of casualties by friendly fire and confusion among the artillery forces of different nations. Nevertheless, while Iraqi artillery often outranged its Coalition counterpart, the relentless air campaign which preceded the ground phase of the Gulf War, superior fire control and superb training made Coalition artillery deadly and efficient in support of ground action. The Patriot anti-ballistic missile system produced debatable results against the Iraqi Scud but provided analysts with valuable data on the performance of the system during live combat conditions. In the final analysis, there is no rigorous testing programme or research protocol which can totally simulate the conditions of combat. The truest measure of the effectiveness of any artillery system remains combat itself.

The reliance placed on artillery by Coalition forces is readily apparent in the number and types of units engaged. At the height of its deployment for Operation Desert Storm, the Coalition had amassed more than 3800 artillery pieces of 100mm (3.9in) or greater with at least 600 of these self-propelled and the remainder towed. Multiple launch rocket systems such as the US MLRS totalled approximately 800 mobile launchers, and at least 100 tactical surface-to-surface missile launchers were in theatre on the eve of the ground offensive which commenced in January 1991.

Coalition forces
1991

Highly trained and specialized artillery units provided Coalition forces with a decided edge in performance over the Iraqi Army during the Gulf War.

WHEN EGYPTIAN REPORTER Nabila Megalli of the Associated Press telephoned the Khafji Beach Hotel on 30 January 1991, she was seeking confirmation of an Iraqi report that tactical surface-to-surface missiles had set fire to nearby oil refineries. The voice on the other end of the telephone line spoke Arabic, but the accent was distinctive. An Iraqi soldier informed the reporter that the Saudi border town of Khafji had been occupied by Iraqi troops. 'We are with Saddam, with Arabism,' shouted one soldier. A second taunted, 'See you in Jerusalem!'

When it was indeed realized that Iraqi forces had crossed the frontier between Saudi Arabia and Iraq under cover of darkness and executed the lone Iraqi ground offensive of the Gulf War, Saudi and US ground commanders conferred as to the best way to dislodge the invaders. Huey Cobra helicopter gunships, Harrier jump jets and A-10 Warthog ground-attack aircraft destroyed up to 35 Iraqi tanks and scores of armoured personnel carriers with Hellfire anti-tank missiles, while Coalition self-propelled and field artillery units swung into action.

The Iraqi advance had swept past a pair of US Marine reconnaissance teams which managed to remain undetected and called in an artillery fire mission on the occupying Iraqis. Miraculously, all 12 of the trapped Marines survived the battle and managed to avoid being killed by their own artillery.

The heavy gun section of the 3rd Marine Regiment and the artillery of the 1st Battalion, 12th Marines, worked over Iraqi positions for two days. Then, on the third day, Saudi artillery took over. One Marine observer remembered, 'The Saudis insisted that it was their sector and their responsibility, so they wanted to fire their artillery.'

Self-propelled sledgehammer

The Saudis utilized the self-propelled M109A2 155mm (6.1in) howitzer, a variant of the original M109 which had been developed in the early 1950s, deployed in 1963 and continually upgraded for more than 40 years. The M109A2 contained 27 improvements to the early M109 which were designated RAM (Reliability, Availability, Maintainability). These included the introduction of the M185 cannon and the M178 gun mount along with the ability to install the M140 sight-alignment device, plus better ballistic protection for the panoramic telescope. The M109A2 also included increased ammunition storage capacity, improving the load of 155mm (6.1in) ammunition from 28 shells to 36.

OPERATION DESERT STORM: COALITION GROUND FORCES		
Numbers of Artillery	Aug 1990	Dec 1990
Artillery 100mm (3.9in)+	3820	3750
(self-propelled)	620	550
(towed)	3200	3200
Multiple rocket launchers	790	800
SSM launchers	100	100

OPERATION DESERT STORM: US ARTILLERY UNITS	
Corps	Brigade
XVIII Corps	18th FA Bde 212th FA Bde 196th FA Bde
VII Corps	210th FA Bde 42nd FA Bde 75th FA Bde 142nd FA Bde

The earliest version of the M109 was initially utilized in combat with US forces during the Vietnam War and with Israeli mobile formations during the Yom Kippur War of 1973. During Desert Storm, variants of the M109 were fielded by US, British and Saudi forces.

▲ **M109 SP howitzer**

Royal Saudi Land Forces / 17th Mechanized Brigade, 1991

The M109 155mm (6.1in) self-propelled howitzer is one of the longest-lived platforms of its kind in military history. Its development began in the United States in 1952, and its latest variant, the M109A6 Paladin, remains in service although heavily re-engineered. During the 1991 Gulf War, units of the regular Saudi Army and of the Saudi National Guard operated the M109A2, which remains in service with the Royal Saudi Land Forces today.

Specifications

Crew: 6
Weight: 23,723kg (52,192lb)
Length: 6.612m (21ft 8.25in)
Width: 3.295m (10ft 9.75in)
Height: 3.289m (10ft 9.5in)

Engine: 304kW (405hp) Detroit Diesel 8V-71T
Speed: 56km/h (35mph)
Road range: 390km (240 miles)
Armament: 155mm (6.1in) howitzer

▲ **Dug-in launchers**
Saudi Arabian troops man an ASTROS II MLR prior to the start of Operation Desert Storm. The ASTROS II was used by both Saudi and Iraqi forces during the conflict.

The ground game

The towed 155mm (6.1in) M198 and the 105mm (4.1in) M102 field howitzers were workhorses of the Gulf War. Introduced in 1979 as a replacement for the M114, the M198 has a maximum range of more than 29,992m (32,800 yards) with rocket-assisted ammunition, while standard high-explosive rounds reach distances of 17,800m (19,685 yards). With a sustained rate of fire of two rounds per minute and a maximum rate of four rounds per minute, the M198 is served by a crew of nine. Representative of a generation of late Cold War artillery, it is also nuclear-capable. During 14 years of production from 1978 to 1992, more than 1600 were built. Although it is gradually being replaced by the lighter M777 155mm (6.1in) howitzer, the M198 remains in active service with the US Army and US Marine Corps, as well as the armed forces of Australia, Thailand and other countries.

Rocket reaction

Advanced technology in free-flight surface-to-surface rocket systems was demonstrated during the Gulf War by the M270 Multiple Launch Rocket System (MLRS). A fully mobile, self-contained platform, the MLRS displays awesome firepower, with a battery potentially delivering up to 8000 M77 explosive rounds into a target area approximately 550m by 275m (600 yards by 300 yards) in as little as 45 seconds. Its shoot-and-scoot capability allows the MLRS to rapidly displace, reducing the effectiveness of enemy counterbattery fire.

The MLRS was developed as a joint venture by the United States, Germany, France and Great Britain during the 1970s. The US M270 MLRS system entered service in 1983, and its M269 launcher-loader module typically carries a variety of rockets up to 227mm (8.94in) in diameter. A single launcher fires missiles at a rate of 12 per minute or two in 20 seconds. Capable of firing both guided and unguided munitions, the MLRS's effective rocket range is approximately 42km (26.1 miles), while ballistic missiles may reach out to 300km (186 miles). Each M269 pod contains six rockets or a single guided missile such as the US ATACMS (Army Tactical

Missile System), a surface-to-surface missile with a diameter of 610mm (24in) and a length of four metres (13ft), which delivers a high-explosive warhead of up to 227kg (500lb) or cluster munitions. The MGM-140 ATACMS was first used in combat during Operation Desert Storm, when at least 32 were fired by the M270 MLRS.

Patriot parallax

Perhaps the most publicized weapon of the Gulf War was the MIM-104 Patriot surface-to-air missile system, which gained fame in defence of Coalition installations and Israeli cities against attacks by Iraqi Scud missiles. Although originally known as the SAM-D programme and conceived not only as an anti-ballistic missile (ABM) but also as a replacement for the HAWK and Nike Hercules anti-aircraft missiles, the Patriot's continuing development has concentrated on the ABM role. Research on ABM technology began in the United States during the 1960s; however, it was not until 1975 that the forerunner of the modern Patriot underwent testing and field evaluation. In 1976, the SAM-D programme was officially renamed the Patriot Air

▲ M198 155mm howitzer

US Army / 18th Field Artillery Brigade, 1991

Production of the 155mm (6.1in) M198 field howitzer began in 1978, and the weapon was designated to replace the World War II-era M114 weapon. The M198 provided a 155mm (6.1in) medium artillery platform which could be airlifted and could fire at greater range than its predecessor. The M198 remains in service with numerous countries although it is being replaced by the M777 system.

Specifications

Crew: 9	Weight: 7163kg (7.05 tons)
Calibre: 155mm (6.1in)	Range: 18,100m (19,795 yards)
Elevation: - 5 degrees to + 72 degrees	Muzzle velocity: 684m/sec (2244ft/sec)

▲ M270 Multiple Launch Rocket System (MLRS)

US Army / 42nd Field Artillery Brigade / 27th Regiment / 1st Battalion, 1991

The M270 Multiple Launch Rocket System deploys the MLRS rocket, which was developed as a joint venture between the United States, Great Britain, Germany and France. The M270 entered service in 1983, and more than 1300 have been produced. The MLRS proved valuable in preliminary bombardment of fixed Iraqi positions prior to the launching of the ground phase of the 1991 Gulf War. Its chassis is an adapted version of the M2 fighting vehicle.

Specifications

Crew: 3	System combat weight: 25,191kg (55,420lb)
Calibre: 227mm (8.94in)	Range: 42km (26.1 miles)
Rocket length: 3.94m (12ft 11in)	Rate of fire: 12 rounds/min
Rocket weight: 308kg (679lb)	

Defense Missile System. The weapon was not used in live combat until 15 years later during the Gulf War of 1991.

In the late 1980s, the Patriot programme was expanded to include anti-ballistic missile capabilities. Improvements to the system in recent years include computer technology and software upgrades along with improved radar and missile design and guidance. Patriot has appeared in several variants, including the PAC-2, which is powered by a solid-fuel rocket engine and has a range of 160km (100 miles) and a weight of 900kg (1984lb). The missiles are fired from pods mounted atop the M860 trailer which is towed by the M983 HEMTT Dragon Wagon. The Patriot can be prepared to fire from mobile configuration in about 45 minutes.

Scud destroyers?

While controversy still surrounds the quality of the Patriot's performance during the Gulf War, it does appear that some incoming Scud missiles were intercepted. More than 40 documented Scud launches were engaged by Patriots during the course of the war, and the deployment of the system in protection of Israeli cities helped prevent Israel from entering the conflict against Iraq. Repeatedly, the Iraqis launched Scuds against targets in Kuwait, Saudi Arabia and Israel, and some feared that these might deliver chemical or even low-level nuclear warheads. It is known that combat pilots of the Israeli Air Force remained on full alert, sometimes sleeping in their cockpits.

In assessing the impact of the Scud attacks, Major General Ya'acov Lapidot, who directed the Israeli military police, recalled, 'It emerged that the Scud missiles were armed with only conventional warheads. There were 17 launchings in all, with 41 missiles having been fired at primarily urban-civilian targets … About 10,000 homes were damaged … About 40,000 persons were affected by the attacks. In terms of indirect injury, 10 persons died as a result of suffocation, although we had attempted to instruct the population in the proper use of the gas masks. The rate of cardiac failure and premature births rose, as did the level of psychological stress.'

An error in the Patriot system may have prevented its interception of the Scud which struck a barracks housing members of the US Army 14th Quartermaster Detachment at Dhahran, Saudi Arabia, on 25 February 1991, killing 28 soldiers. An

11th Air Defence Artillery (ADA) Brigade, US Army, 1991

Providing theatre ballistic missile defence against Iraqi Scud attacks, the US Army's 11th Air Defence Artillery Brigade deployed a complement of 12 MIM-104 Patriot anti-ballistic missile batteries during the Gulf War of 1991. Development of the Patriot had begun in the 1960s, and the forerunner of the modern system had undergone testing by 1975; however, the technology was still in its relative infancy when Patriot batteries were deployed during Operation Desert Storm. Powered by a solid-fuel rocket motor, the Patriot is guided by radar which homes the missile in on its target, while a proximity fuse detonates the high-explosive fragmentation warhead. The actual rate of successful Patriot-versus-Scud engagements during Desert Storm remains a point of debate.

investigation into the incident determined that the Patriot's internal timekeeping system had lost approximately one-third of a second during 100 hours of deployment on alert status. The result was an incorrect positioning of the incoming Scud. When the speed of the Scud is considered, the miscalculation proves significant – up to 600m (656 yards) – and the subsequently calculated firing solution sent the Patriot on an errant path.

Anti-armour options

During the Gulf War, US and other Coalition troops were armed with several anti-tank guided missiles, some of which had been specifically designed to defeat the armour of the Soviet T-54/55 and T-62 tanks which were fielded by the Iraqi Army.

The M47 Dragon was common among US ground troops, offering a lightweight and mobile medium-range defence with a warhead of 5.4kg (11.9lb) which was capable of penetrating armour up to 500mm (19.6in) thick. The Dragon was a shoulder-fired, wire-guided missile which was in service with the US military from 1975 to 1995 and was later replaced with the FGM-148 Javelin. Its effective range was up to 1000m (3300ft), and the combined missile and launcher weighed only 10.9kg (24lb).

The excellent performance of Coalition artillery during Operation Desert Storm also identified areas for improvement during future cooperative military ventures. Upgraded communications were deemed imperative to improve accuracy and reduce the number of friendly-fire incidents, while continually advancing technology in target acquisition and fire direction was considered a priority.

Additionally, the number of weapons systems encountered in the Iraqi arsenal indicated that the capabilities of systems from many countries, rather than simply those of Soviet origin, had to be recognized and evaluated.

Iraqi Army
1991

By the time his forces invaded Kuwait in 1990, Saddam Hussein had fought a bloody war with Iran, made good his losses and reconstituted one of the largest armies in the world.

O N PAPER THE IRAQI ARMY which fought the multinational coalition during the 1991 Gulf War appeared formidable – and in some aspects of its military prowess that was the case. However, the tactical execution of the strategic decision to seize and occupy Kuwait presented considerable problems for the Iraqi forces, not the least of which were the operational capabilities of the equipment deployed and the quality and extent of the training Iraqi soldiers had undergone prior to the Kuwaiti adventure.

Mismatch

In the event, the Iraqi Air Force was no match for Coalition air assets. Iraqi armour proved inferior on the battlefield, with the majority of its T-54/55, T-62 and T-72 main battle tanks destroyed in armour-versus-armour clashes with the superior M1A1 Abrams main battle tank and other types belonging to the Coalition armies. The fighting spirit and quality of Iraqi infantry proved lacklustre in most cases, although some Republican Guard units put up a spirited resistance. For the most part, Iraqi conscripts were eager to surrender to Coalition ground forces following a sustained aerial bombardment of several weeks.

Likewise, Iraqi artillery performance was adversely affected by the relentless Coalition air campaign, which degraded the artillery's combat-effectiveness. Training was apparently inadequate, and Iraqi artillerymen were also faced with the requirements of operating something of a jumble of field artillery, rocket systems and missiles of Soviet, Chinese, US, Brazilian and other manufacture.

The quality and quantity of appropriate ammunition also proved problematic for the Iraqis, with antiquated types proving inadequate for the ranges and fire-support missions required to slow down the Coalition ground juggernaut.

▶ **Spoils of war**

An Iraqi FROG-7 system lies abandoned following the end of Operation Desert Storm.

Missile capability

Although Coalition commanders maintained a healthy respect for all types of Iraqi artillery capabilities, it was the potential destructive power of missile and rocket systems which caused the greatest angst, and these indeed delivered the heaviest blows dealt by Saddam's forces. Although it had already been in service for decades, the Soviet BM-21 mobile rocket launcher posed a threat to Coalition infantry concentrations. A single truck-mounted BM-21 was capable of firing 18 122mm (4.8in) high-explosive rockets at a rate of two rounds per second, while a typical BM-21 battery could lay 35,560kg (35 tons) of explosives in a target area 27.4km (17 miles) distant in the brief span of only 30 seconds. The Iraqi Army was known to possess numerous BM-21 batteries, as well as the Brazilian ASTROS II MLRS.

In the air defence role, the Iraqis possessed a variety of light machine guns and cannon of Eastern Bloc manufacture. These were seen lighting up the dark sky over the Iraqi capital of Baghdad on the first night of the Gulf War, 17 January 1991. However, the display laid bare a serious defensive weakness. US Tomahawk cruise missiles launched from warships and submarines in the Gulf and the Red Sea hit command-and-control centres in Baghdad, disrupting communications and disabling much of the Iraqi fire-control capacity.

Perhaps the most menacing of Iraqi air defence missiles was the Soviet-designed Isayev S-125, known in NATO circles as the SA-3 Goa. On the third day of the war, an SA-3 shot down a US F-16 fighter-bomber over Baghdad, and its pilot was captured. The SA-3 entered service with Soviet forces in 1963 to engage enemy aircraft at low altitude and had been upgraded on several occasions. The Iraqis also possessed a limited number of SA-9 and SA-13 air defence missiles.

▲ FROG-7

Iraqi Army / 6th Nebuchadnezzar Mechanized Division, 1991

Developed during the mid-1960s as an upgrade to the original FROG-1 mobile tactical missile system, the FROG-7 single-stage, solid-fuel rocket is carried aboard a wheeled 8X8 chassis which mounts a transporter-erector-launcher. Fin-stabilized and unguided, the rocket is capable of carrying high-explosive, chemical or nuclear warheads.

Specifications

Crew: 4	Range: 70km (43.5 miles)
Calibre: 550mm (21.65in)	Road range: 500km (310 miles)
Rocket length: 9.11m (29ft 10in)	Launch preparation time: 15–30 minutes
Rocket weight: 2500kg (5512lb)	
System combat weight: 23,000kg (22.63 tons)	

The mobile FROG-7 missile launcher was expected to resist Coalition ground forces with its free-flight, fin-stabilized rocket which carried a 550kg (1200lb) warhead to a range of 70km (43 miles). The FROG-7 entered service with Red Army forces in 1965 and was initially nuclear-capable. During the Gulf War, Coalition domination of the air resulted in the destruction of numerous FROG-7 launchers prior to the commencement of the ground campaign.

Scud scare

By far the most successful weapon system of the Gulf War for the Iraqi armed forces was the mobile SS-1 Scud B theatre ballistic missile. Designed in the Soviet Union during the early 1960s, the Scud B was exported to the Middle East in large numbers. Iraqi modifications to the original weapon included a longer-range version known as the Al Hussein, which could reach out to 645km (400 miles). During the course of the Gulf War, more than 40 Scuds were fired at Israeli cities, while others targeted civilian and military areas in Kuwait and Saudi Arabia.

The total number of Scud launches neared 200. The early Scud was mounted on an 8X8 wheeled chassis which supported a transporter-erector-launcher system. Its range was roughly 280km (173 miles), and its conventional or nuclear warhead weighed up to 985kg (2172lb).

Attacks by Iraqi Scuds nearly brought Israel in to the Gulf War and troubled the Coalition leadership to the extent that Scud-hunting teams of special forces personnel were deployed deep into the Iraqi desert to find the mobile launchers. Hundreds of sorties by tactical aircraft were also initiated to seek out and destroy the Scud platforms.

Specifications

Configuration: two-stage, solid fuel
Deployment: mobile or fixed
Length: 6.7m (22ft)
Diameter: 450mm (17.7in)

Launch weight: 950kg (2094lb)
Range: 30km (18.5 miles)
Launch preparation time: reload 15 minutes

▲ S-125 (SA-3 Goa)

Iraqi Army / 145th Surface-to-Air Missile Brigade, 1991

The Soviet-designed Isayev S-125 surface-to-air missile, designated the SA-3 Goa by NATO, traced its lineage to the mid-1950s and the early days of air defence missile technology. The SA-3 went into production in 1959 and equipped units of the Red Army by 1963. Powered by a solid-fuel motor, the missile was lifted by a booster rocket which then fell away, and the warhead was guided to its target by a radar beam.

Specifications

Configuration: single-stage, liquid fuel
Deployment: mobile
Length: 11.25m (36ft 11in)
Diameter: 850mm (33.5in)

Launch weight: 6300kg (13,888lb)
Range: 280km (173 miles)
Launch preparation time: 1 hour

▲ SS-1 Scud B

Iraqi Army / Independent Operation, 1991

The Scud B variant of the Soviet SS-1 theatre ballistic missile debuted in the mid-1960s in response to a directive to improve deployment time. Older SS-1 designs required fuelling after the missile had been erected into its firing position. The Scud B was mounted on a wheeled 8X8 chassis, and its mobility challenged Coalition forces during the Gulf War of 1991. The extended-range Al Hussein variant was among several types which had been modified by the Iraqis.

NATO air defence

1991–PRESENT

Focused on countering aircraft and ballistic missiles, NATO air defence capabilities have been tested in numerous regional conflicts around the globe.

DURING AN ERA of supersonic attack aircraft, ballistic missiles capable of speeds greater than Mach 2, heavily armed helicopters and tank-killing planes flying low and slow over the battlefield, NATO air defence capabilities require more versatility today than ever before. At theatre level, the MIM-104 Patriot anti-ballistic missile system continues to be refined, and a new generation of the Patriot and similar weapons is taking shape. From the soldier's perspective, the lightweight, man-portable FIM-92 Stinger missile provides a daunting air defence capability for the individual soldier or squad with boots on the ground.

From either perspective, state-of-the art systems and extensive training have proved their worth. In the case of the Patriot, although theory and conjecture have surrounded its performance during the 1991 Gulf War, its mere presence in theatre reduced the potential for armed intervention by Israel and bolstered the confidence of the civilian populations in areas which had been targeted by Iraqi Scud B missiles. The FIM-92 Stinger, on the other hand, was instrumental in compelling the Soviet Union to withdraw its forces from Afghanistan during the late 1980s and remains a battle-tested weapon.

Intercontinental engagement

The land-based nuclear intercontinental ballistic missile (ICBM) defence of the United States is trusted to the Minuteman III, a three-stage, solid-fuel missile with a range of up to 13,000km (8100 miles), which was developed during the late 1960s and is expected to remain in service, pending upgrades, until at least 2025. The Minuteman is complemented by the submarine-launched Trident missile and other munitions which are delivered by aircraft. Its MIRV (multiple independent re-entry vehicle) capability allows several nuclear warheads to impact targets independently, and its heaviest warhead is the W-87 with an estimated yield of up to 475 kilotons.

The reliance on the Minuteman III came as a result of the START II treaty negotiated between the United States and Russia during the early 1990s. Although START II was never formally enacted, the decision was made to deactivate the LGM-118 Peacekeeper missiles which were then in the US arsenal. Following nearly 15 years of research by defence contractors Boeing, Martin Marietta, Denver Aerospace and TRW, approximately 50 Peacekeepers had been deployed by the mid-1980s in response to an array of MIRV-capable Soviet ICBMs. Popularly known as the MX missile, the Peacekeeper MIRV

▲ **Starstreak**
British Army / 12th Regiment Royal Artillery, 1999
The versatile Starstreak surface-to-air missile is fired from the shoulder, from wheeled Land Rover vehicles, or from a launcher fixed to the roof of the Alvis Stormer armoured fighting vehicle. Introduced in 1997 to replace the Javelin missiles then in service with the British Army, the Starstreak actually fires three submunitions, called darts. These are detonated by a delayed fuse.

Specifications

Configuration: two-stage, solid fuel	Launch weight: 16.82kg (37.08lb)
Deployment: man-portable, mobile or fixed	Range: 7km (4.4 miles)
Length: 1.4m (55in)	
Diameter: 127mm (5in)	

carried up to ten re-entry vehicles bearing the W-87 nuclear warhead, which was originally a weapon of 300 kilotons and was later increased.

While the reasons for the deactivation of the Peacekeeper were numerous, among the most compelling were its somewhat disappointing range of 9600km (6000 miles) and its per-unit cost of roughly $70 million. The last of the LGM-118 missiles was dismantled during the autumn of 2005, and as many as 500 W-87 warheads originally intended for Peacekeeper missiles may, in fact, be transferred to the longer-range Minuteman III.

Mobile air defence

While the HAWK system has been a mainstay of NATO air defence for decades, mounted at fixed sites or towed on trailers, the shoulder-fired, wheeled or tracked Starstreak surface-to-air missile provides a close-in additional deterrent to air attack. Deployed by the British Army in 1997, the Starstreak was developed by Thales Air Defence Limited, and the missile is guided to the target by a triangular laser pattern emitted from the launch unit. The weapon actually fires three warheads powered by a two-stage, solid-fuel rocket booster, and the trio of submunitions is detonated by a delayed fuse when the projectile reaches the target. Each submunition, referred to as a dart, weighs 900g (1.98lb). Intended to replace the Javelin missile, the Starstreak weighs 16.82kg (37.08lb).

The tracked version of the Starstreak consists of the Alvis Stormer armoured fighting vehicle chassis with a launcher carrying eight missiles fixed to the roof and internal storage of 12 additional rounds. The Stormer has an operational range of 640km (800 miles), and the Starstreak missile itself is effective at a range of up to seven kilometres (4.4 miles).

Since its introduction in 1971, the Rapier missile has been a mainstay of British air defence and serves as the primary weapon of its kind today, replacing

▲ **Tracked Rapier**

British Army / 22 Air Defence Regiment / 11 Air Defence Battery, 1993

The tracked Rapier surface-to-air missile system was developed in response to a request from the government of the Shah of Iran in the late 1970s. However, with the overthrow of the Shah's regime the vehicles were subsequently purchased by the British Army. The tracked Rapier mounts the missile launcher atop the modified M548 cargo carrier version of the M113 armoured personnel carrier. The Rapier reaches a speed of Mach 2.2 and carries a high-explosive armour-piercing warhead.

Specifications

Configuration: two-stage, solid fuel
Deployment: fixed or mobile
Length: 2.24m (88.2in)
Diameter: 133mm (5.25in)
Launch weight: 42kg (94lb)
Range: 7250m (4.5 miles)
Launch preparation time: 30 seconds

other gun and missile systems in their entirety. In the region of 25,000 Rapier missiles have been manufactured, as well as some 600 launchers, and the system is expected to remain in place until 2020.

Rapier is fired from fixed sites and mobile tracked launchers. Its two-stage rocket powers a semi-armour-piercing warhead at a speed of Mach 2.2, and an all-weather version of the Rapier includes the Blindfire radar guidance system. The tracked Rapier incorporates the launcher atop the modified M548 cargo carrier version of the M113 armoured personnel carrier.

Specifications

Configuration: solid-fueled rocket
Deployment: fixed or mobile
Length: 5.31m (17ft 5in)
Diameter: 41cm (16in)
Launch weight: 900kg (2000lb)
Range: 160km (100 miles)
Time of flight: 9 seconds – 3.5 minutes

▲ MIM-104 (GE) Patriot

US Army / 35th Air Defense Brigade / 1st Battalion, 1991

The MIM-104 Patriot anti-ballistic missile entered service with the US military in 1981 following extensive research and development which dated to the 1960s. The Patriot achieved notoriety during the 1991 Gulf War and was originally intended to defend against enemy aircraft as well as missiles. Powered by a solid-fuel rocket motor, the missile has an effective range of 160km (100 miles). Its high-explosive fragmentation warhead weighs 73kg (160lb) and is detonated by a proximity fuse.

▲ LGM-118 Peacekeeper

US Air Force / 400th Missile Squadron, 2003

Popularly known as the MX missile, the LGM-118 Peacekeeper ICBM was deployed in limited numbers by the mid-1980s in response to the Soviet Union's fielding of multiple MIRV-capable ICBMs. Following the negotiations which resulted in the START II treaty, the US began dismantling its Peacekeepers even though the treaty was not enacted. Today, US land-based ICBM missile defence rests with the Minuteman III system.

Specifications

Configuration: four-stage, solid and liquid fuel
Deployment: silo
Length: 21.6m (70ft 10in)
Diameter: 2.34m (7ft 8in)
Launch weight: 88,450kg (87 tons)
Range: 9600km (6000 miles)
Launch preparation time: under 30 minutes est.

Balkans conflicts
1991–95

Fuelled by nationalistic fervour, war raged in the Balkans, a region torn by ethnic strife, during the early 1990s, and artillery took a heavy toll in military and civilian lives.

WHEN THE FORCES OF CROATIA AND BOSNIA and Herzegovina opposed the Serbian Army in the summer of 1995, each side was able to muster nearly 600 artillery pieces of various types, including field guns, self-propelled howitzers, air defence weapons and rocket launchers. The LVRS M-77 Oganj MLRS was one of a relative few weapons deployed during the Balkan unrest of the early 1990s which were actually designed and manufactured in the former Yugoslavia. The development of the weapon, which included a 6X6 FAP 2026 wheeled flatbed truck and a launcher which held 32 128mm (5in) rockets, was undertaken by a Yugoslav mechanical engineer who also served as the chief operating officer of the artillery department of the country's military technical institute.

First seen in public in 1975, the rocket launcher was also produced in a later variant, the Oganj 2000 ER, which was capable of firing the Soviet-designed BM-21 Grad rocket from a bank of 50 122mm (4.8in) tubes. Croatian forces also modified the Oganj to fire the 122mm (4.8in) rocket and named the weapon the M-91 Vulkan.

Another Eastern European weapon produced outside the Soviet Union, the M53/59 Praga self-propelled anti-aircraft gun was deployed by the Yugoslav People's Army and appeared to be something of a battlefield anachronism in the 1990s. A Czech design of the late 1950s, the weapon mounted a pair of 30mm (1.2in) autocannon atop the chassis of the Praga V3S 6X6 truck. Mounted at the back of the truck bed, the cannon were fed by 50-round belts, and the vehicle usually carried up to 900 rounds of ammunition.

The M53/59 possessed no radar, and the guns were aimed visually, limiting their use to daylight and favourable weather conditions. Although the weapon is functionally obsolete as an anti-aircraft platform, it may still play a role in the armed forces of underdeveloped nations, since the penetrating power of the 30mm (1.2in) round is effective against light armoured vehicles and infantry. When the Czech military brought in the Soviet self-propelled ZSU-57-2 57mm (2.2in) anti-aircraft gun for testing against the M53/59, they actually preferred the

▲ LVRS M-77 Oganj MLRS

Serbian Army / 2nd Land Force Brigade

Mounting 32 tubes for launching 128mm (5in) rockets, the LVRS M-77 Oganj proved a devastating weapon system during the Yugoslav Wars. Introduced in 1975 following several years of development in Yugoslavia, it is still in use today with the Serbian armed forces.

Specifications

Crew: 5	Engine: 191kW (256hp) 8-cylinder diesel
Weight: 22,400kg (49,400lb)	Speed: 80km/h (50mph)
Length: 11.5m (37ft 7in)	Road range: 600km (370 miles)
Width: 2.49m (8ft 2in)	Armament: 32 + 32 x M-77 or M-91 rockets, plus
Height: 3.1m (10ft 2in)	1 x 12.7mm (0.5in) HMG

performance of their own weapon and declined further Soviet deliveries.

Both Serbian and Croatian forces maintained substantial inventories of Soviet-made surface-to-air missiles, and among the most readily available was the Lavochkin OKB S-75, commonly referred to in NATO circles as the SA-2 Guideline. By the 1990s, the SA-2 was getting on in years. Its development began in the early 1950s, and it had reached Red Army artillery units by 1957. It gained notoriety for its shooting-down of an American U-2 spy plane piloted by Francis Gary Powers in 1960, an event which spawned a major dispute between the superpowers. The SA-2 was later supplied to North Vietnam to provide some protection against devastating raids by US bombers against the North Vietnamese capital of Hanoi and the major port city of Haiphong. China also produced the missile, designating it the HQ-1 and HQ-2.

In the hands of the Serbian and Yugoslav armies, the SA-2 posed a serious threat to NATO aircraft flying combat or patrol missions in the Balkans. Its operational range was up to 45km (29 miles), and its radar guidance delivered a 200kg (441lb) high-explosive fragmentation warhead.

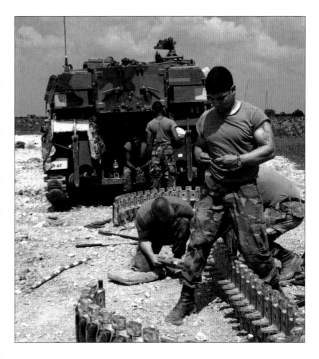

▲ **Running repairs**
US Army soldiers of Alpha Battery, 1st Battalion, 6th Field Artillery, 1st Infantry Division (Mechanized), attached to Camp McGovern, Bosnia and Herzegovina, replace worn-out track pads on an M109 SP howitzer during Operation Joint Guard, July 1997.

▲ **Lavochkin OKB S-75 (SA-2 Guideline)**
Serbian Army / 21st Kordun Corps Artillery Battalion, 1995
The Soviet-designed Lavochkin OKB S-75 surface-to-air missile was known to NATO as the SA-2 Guideline. An early Soviet air defence missile, the SA-2 remains in operation with upgrades after half a century and equipped units of several armies during the Balkan conflicts of the 1990s. Mounted on a trailer, the rail-launched missile was towed into firing position and guided to its target by radar.

Specifications	
Configuration: two-stage, solid and liquid fuel	Launch weight: 2300kg (5071lb)
Deployment: mobile	Range: 45km (29 miles)
Length: 10.6m (34ft 9in)	Launch preparation time: 8-hour radar set-up
Diameter: 700mm (27.6in)	

In the mid-1990s, when elements of the British Army deployed with NATO forces they were equipped with the 155mm (6.1in) AS-90 self-propelled gun, which was designed and manufactured by Vickers Shipbuilding and Engineering as a replacement for the army's aging complement of 155mm (6.1in) M109 and 105mm (4.1in) Abbot self-propelled howitzers. Following the failed SP70 gun programme of the 1980s, the development of the AS-90 accelerated, and the weapon was introduced in 1993. Mounting the NATO-compatible 155mm (6.1in) L31 gun, it is capable of firing three rounds in a ten-second burst, six rounds per minute for up to three minutes or two rounds per minute for the duration of one hour.

A Turret Controlled Computer (TCC) provides the technology which facilitates the rapid-fire burst.

The AS-90 (Artillery System for the 90s) equips two regiments of the Royal Horse Artillery and three regiments of the Royal Artillery. Its operational range is 420km (261 miles), and its autonomous navigation and gun-laying systems allow it to fight without external visual aids. Nearly 200 examples of the AS-90 were produced between 1992 and 1995, and in 2002 approximately half of these were upgraded from a 39-calibre barrel to a longer 52-calibre barrel.

▲ M53/59 Praga SP anti-aircraft gun

Yugoslav People's Army / 51st Mechanized Brigade

Dating to the 1950s, the M53/59 Praga self-propelled anti-aircraft gun fielded twin 30mm (1.2in) cannon atop the Praga six-wheeled truck chassis. The gun could also be removed from the truck and operated independently. The gun crew of four was protected during relocation by an armoured compartment.

Specifications

Crew: 2 + 4	Engine: 82kW (110hp) Tatra T912-2
Weight: 10,300kg (22,660lb)	6-cylinder diesel
Length: 6.92m (22ft 8in)	Speed: 60km/h (37mph)
Width: 2.35m (7ft 9in)	Road range: 500km (311 miles)
Height: 2.585m (8ft 6in)	Armament: 2 x 30mm (1.2in) guns

▲ AS-90 SP gun

British Army / 3rd Regiment Royal Horse Artillery, 1995

Developed during the mid-1980s and built by the Vickers company, the AS-90 self-propelled gun mounts the 155mm (6.1in) L31 gun atop its tracked chassis. Entering service in 1993, the AS-90 replaced the 105mm (4.1in) Abbot and 155mm (6.1in) M109 self-propelled weapons then in service.

Specifications

Crew: 5	Engine: 492kW (660hp) Cummins V8 diesel
Weight: 45,000kg (99,225lb)	Speed: 55km/h (34mph)
Length: 7.2m (23ft 8in)	Road range: 240km (150 miles)
Width: 3.4m (11ft 2in)	Armament: 1 x 155mm (6.1in) howitzer, plus
Height: 3m (9ft 10in)	1 x 12.7mm (0.5in) MG

War in the Caucasus

1992–PRESENT

Unrest in the Caucasus erupted with the collapse of the Soviet Union and continues today with territorial and ethnic disputes which remain unresolved.

THE TERRIBLE CIVIL WARS and ethnic cleansing which have wracked the region of the Caucasus since the fall of the Soviet Union have been characterized by political turmoil as well as military clashes. Several of these episodes have involved the former Soviet republic of Georgia and the breakaway provinces of South Ossetia and Abkhazia, which have sought independent governments, while forces of the Russian Federation have battled Islamic separatists and Chechen nationalists for years. Throughout these hostilities, civilian, paramilitary and military casualties have been high, particularly due to the use of artillery in shelling both targets of military importance and civilian population centres. Mercenary forces have been hired on several occasions, and the use of landmines has led to the maiming and crippling of thousands.

The South Ossetia War of 1991–92 ended with a tenuous cease-fire in place; however, tensions continued to smoulder. Neither side could muster well-trained and experienced troops, with the Georgian National Guard forming only days before the war began in early 1991. As the fighting wore on, it often degenerated into a contest of armed militia factions vying for control of the region, and the government of Georgia accused the Russian Federation of intervening on behalf of the rebel forces. Georgian government troops deployed Soviet-era equipment, including towed and self-propelled howitzers along with truck-mounted multiple launch rocket systems, and implemented Soviet-style counterinsurgency tactics, with the artillery playing a key role in neutralizing guerrilla activities.

Following the seizure of the Black Sea coastal resort town of Gagra in the autumn of 1992, one of the bloodiest battles between Georgian government troops and Abkhaz militia took place, the latter supported by the militant Confederation of

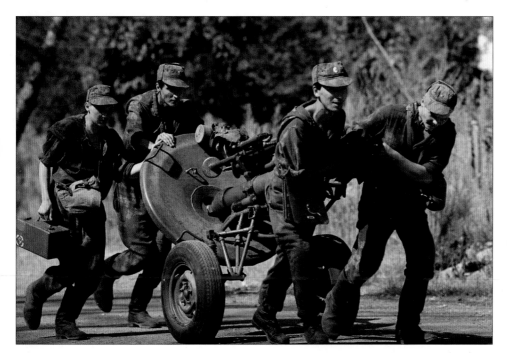

◀ **Man-handled mortar**
Russian Army infantry man-handle an 120mm (4.72in) mortar along a road somewhere in Abkhazia as part of a peacekeeping force in 1994, following the end of the Abkhazia War of 1992–93. The pro-Russian region of Abkhazia attempted to break away from Georgia following Georgia's declaration of independence from the old Soviet Union.

Mountain Peoples of the Caucasus (CMPC). The fighting at Gagra left hundreds dead and caused relations between Georgia and the Russian Federation to deteriorate rapidly.

One major bone of contention between the Russians and the Georgians was the apparent willingness of the Russians to funnel military hardware and supplies to the Abkhaz forces, including T-72 main battle tanks and BM-21 Grad multiple launch rocket systems. The truck-borne BM-21 is a devastating weapon which the Abkhaz militia had not possessed prior to its Gagra offensive, and much of the weaponry was apparently funnelled to the rebels through the town of Gudauta on the Black Sea, where Russian forces, including an air defence regiment and a supply unit, were known to be operating.

The mistrust which these early civil wars engendered sowed the seeds of more than a decade of conflict between the Russian Federation and Georgia, culminating in a brief but bitter invasion of Georgia by Russian forces in 2008.

Chechnya

1994–PRESENT

Declaring full independence from Russia, the breakaway province of Chechnya became a battleground in the mid-1990s and again at the end of the twentieth century when Chechen and allied forces invaded the neighbouring republic of Dagestan.

FACTIONAL INFIGHTING erupted in civil war in Chechnya in 1994 as vigorous debate raged over independence from the Russian Federation and threatened regional stability. On the premise of restoring constitutional order, the Russian Army entered Chechnya and embarked on an arduous campaign to subdue separatists under the leadership of former Soviet Air Force general Dzhokhar Dudayev. From the outset, the war was unpopular with the Russian populace, and despite early successes, including the capture of the Chechen capital of Grozny, the Russians found themselves embroiled in a battle with a tenacious insurgency reminiscent of the Afghan debacle of the 1980s.

Conscript confusion

Many of the Russian troops sent to Chechnya were draftees who had little military training. Casualties were high due to landmines, booby traps and the hit-and-run tactics of the Chechens. Predictably, Russian commanders fell back on their superior firepower in the hope of demoralizing the rebels and degrading their ability to fight. Although they exerted control over extensive areas in the valleys and flatlands of Chechnya, the Russians faced serious problems in their effort to clear the rebels from the surrounding mountains. Ambushes were highly effective, actually destroying heavy Russian armoured columns while they transited the narrow roads and mountain passes. Before a cease-fire ended the fighting in 1996, more than 5000 Russian troops were estimated to have been killed and at least 20,000 wounded, although these numbers are unverified. Meanwhile, casualties among Chechen rebels and civilians may have exceeded 100,000.

The Russians undertook a second invasion of Chechnya in the summer of 1999 following the invasion of neighbouring Dagestan by guerrillas of the Chechen-sponsored Islamic International Peacekeeping Brigade (IIPB). The IIPB consisted of veteran Chechen fighters and Islamic guerrillas from numerous Middle Eastern countries. By the spring of 2000, the Russians had taken control of the Chechen capital at Grozny and re-established direct control over Chechnya. Although large-scale military operations have ceased, a persistent insurgency has remained active in the region for nearly a decade and even expanded into neighbouring areas of Russian territory. Chechen fighters have perpetrated numerous acts of terrorism inside Russia.

Breakaway firepower

On both occasions during which Russian forces have fought Chechen rebels in recent years, they have done so with overwhelming firepower at their disposal. Applying the difficult lessons of Afghanistan and the First Chechen War, Russian commanders often refused to send troops into confined areas where manoeuvre was limited or into urban areas where guerrillas were known to be holed up. Rather, they ranged their artillery on surrounding high ground and called in massive air strikes which obliterated targets but caused widespread collateral damage and killed thousands of Chechen civilians.

Field artillery deployed by the Russian Army included the long-serving 122mm (4.8in) D-30 howitzer and older towed weapons generally of 100mm (3.9in) or 152mm (6in). The D-30 has remained the towed workhorse of the Soviet and subsequently the Russian armed forces for more than 40 years. Based on a World War II-era Czech design for the German Army, the D-30 is capable of firing a high-explosive shell of nearly 22kg (48lb) to a maximum range of 15,400m (16,840 yards).

SP guns

Although the terrain was often a challenge for the Russians, particularly in marshy or rugged areas, the 2S1 M1974 self-propelled howitzer proved adept at fighting across the Chechen landscape in direct support of Russian troops. The amphibious 2S1 mounts the 122mm (4.8in) 2A18 howitzer, the same weapon as the D-30 field howitzer, atop the MT-LB chassis. Although the boatlike bow of the MT-LB resembles that of the light amphibious PT-76 tank, it is a completely separate design. The 2S1 equipped the armoured divisions and motorized rifle regiments of the Russian Army, and its relatively light weight of 15,700kg (34,540lb) resulted in a favourable ground pressure and greater mobility.

Designated the M1974 by Western sources since it was first seen in a Polish military parade during that year, the 2S1 is known to the Russians as the Gvozdika, or Carnation. Several variants were produced in the Soviet Union, Poland and Bulgaria, with more than 500 of the weapons deployed by the two Soviet client states at one time. Although the 2S1 exhibits excellent road speed at 60km/h (37mph), its light armour makes it susceptible to rocket-propelled grenades and anti-tank weapons.

Rocket systems

The Russian Army deployed two notable rocket systems to Chechnya, the 300mm (11.8in) BM-30 Smerch and 220mm (8.7in) TOS-1 multiple launchers. The largest weapon of its kind in the world, the Smerch, or Tornado, mounts 12 tubes atop the 8X8 wheeled 9A52 vehicle. The Smerch was responsible for much of the heavy bombardment endured by the Chechens, and a full salvo can be released in 38 seconds to saturate an area of 67 hectares (166 acres). The system may be readied to fire in as little as three minutes, while reloading is a 36-minute process.

▲ BM-30 Smerch heavy multiple rocket launcher

Russian Ground Forces / 136th Motor Rifle Brigade, 1997

The BM-30 Smerch multiple rocket launcher is capable of placing massive firepower over a considerable area. Its bank of 12 300mm (11.8in) rocket tubes is mounted atop the 8X8 9A52 wheeled vehicle, and a full salvo could be fired in as little as 38 seconds. The Smerch was designed in the early 1980s and entered service with the Soviet Army in 1989. A typical battery consists of six launch vehicles and six reloading vehicles carrying an additional 12 rockets each.

Specifications

Crew: 4

Calibre: 300mm (11.8in)

Rocket length: 7.6m (24ft 11in)

Rocket weight: 243kg (536lb)

System combat weight: 44,401kg (43.7 tons)

Range: 70km (43.5 miles)

Rate of fire: 12 rounds in 38 seconds

The short-range TOS-1 launcher was suspected of having fired thermobaric ammunition against fixed fortifications and in some urban areas during the Chechen wars (TOS is an abbreviation for 'heavy flamethrower system'). The thermobaric warhead contains flammable liquid which is released in a cloud and ignites when in contact with oxygen. The resulting explosion creates a devastating swirl of flame and extreme pressure. Loosing up to 30 rounds in a span of 15 seconds, the weapon consists of a launcher mounted atop the chassis of the T-72 main battle tank. With an effective range of up to 3500m (3828 yards), the TOS-1 was first used in combat in Afghanistan in the early 1980s.

▲ 2S1 M1974 SP howitzer

Russian Ground Forces / 5th Guards Tank Division, 1996

Mounting a 122mm (4.8in) main gun, the 2S1 Gvozdika (Carnation) self-propelled howitzer has been known in the West as the M1974, referencing the year in which it was first observed in public. Several former Soviet republics maintain the M1974 in their inventories today.

Specifications

Crew: 4	Engine: 179kW (240hp) YaMZ-238V V8
Weight: 15,700kg (34,540lb)	water-cooled diesel
Length: 7.3m (23ft 11.5in)	Speed: 60km/h (37mph)
Width: 2.85m (9ft 4in)	Road range: 500km (310 miles)
Height: 2.4m (7ft 10.5in)	Armament: 1 x 122mm (4.8in) howitzer, plus
	1 x 7.62mm (0.3in) anti-aircraft MG

▲ TOS-1 multiple rocket launcher

Russian Ground Forces / 860th Independent Flamethrower Battalion, 1999

Highly effective against fixed fortifications, the TOS-1 30-barrel 220mm (8.7in) rocket launcher is capable of firing devastating thermobaric ammunition which bursts into flame when its warhead disperses combustible liquid. The TOS-1 was most likely involved in the clearing of landmines during the Chechen wars as well. The system first appeared in combat in Afghanistan during the late 1980s. Its maximum rate of fire is 30 rounds in 15 seconds.

Specifications

Crew: 3	System combat weight: 46,738kg (46 tons)
Calibre: 220mm (8.7in)	Range: 3500m (3828 yards)
Rocket length: unknown	Rate of fire: 30 rounds in 15 seconds
Rocket weight: 175kg (385.8lb)	

South Ossetian conflict
2008

During less than two weeks of fighting, the former Soviet republic of Georgia lost control of its remaining territory in South Ossetia, defeated by the firepower and mobility of the Russian Army.

IN AUGUST 2008, war broke out for at least the third time in the troubled region of South Ossetia as Georgia sought to assert control over the area. In response to Georgia's offensive, Russian forces were deployed within hours. A four-day battle raged around the city of Tskhinvali as Georgian forces moved forward under a steady artillery barrage from 152mm (6in) field howitzers and 122mm (4.8in) BM-21 Grad multiple launch rocket systems. According to some sources, a Georgian rocket or shell was falling on the city every 15 to 20 seconds.

Russian response

The Russians counterattacked the following day and reportedly fired at least one SS-21 short-range ballistic missile against the Georgian city of Borzhomi, while attack aircraft pounded the Georgian infantry and artillery around Tskhinvali, forcing the Georgians out of the city in the largest battle of the brief conflict. As the tide turned in favour of the Russians, the Georgian forces suffered

not only from the effective fire of Russian artillery and air support but also from flagging morale. Eventually, the Georgians were turned back in disarray, and Russian troops rolled into four cities across the Georgian frontier. Within days, a French-sponsored peace agreement had been reached.

During the course of the short but sharp South Ossetia War, much of Georgia's heavy equipment was disabled. The single Georgian artillery brigade had deployed more than 100 weapons, including 122mm (4.8in) D-30 towed howitzers and the self-propelled 152mm (6in) SpGH DANA, 152mm (6in) 2S3 Akatsiya and 203mm (8in) 2S7 Pion. The Georgians also fired Soviet-made BM-21 and Czech-built R-70 122mm (4.8in) rocket launchers. Russian artillery included the self-propelled 152mm (6in) 2S19 MSTA and the 2S3 along with the BM-21 and the 300mm (11.8in) BM-30 Smerch rocket launchers.

The 2S3 Akatsiya, or Acacia, was designated the SO-152 by its Soviet manufacturers. It is easily distinguishable from the lighter 2S1 because its 152mm

▲ **DANA SP guns**
Two DANA SP howitzers stand at the roadside following the end of hostilities in South Ossetia in 2008.

(6in) howitzer extends well beyond the forward edge of the hull while the shorter 122mm (4.8in) gun of the 2S1 is flush with the edge. The 2S3 was developed in the late 1960s to counter the American 155mm (6.1in) M109 self-propelled howitzer, and it entered service with the Red Army in 1971. Since that time, it has continued to outfit armoured formations of the forces of former Soviet republics while it has been exported to at least a dozen countries.

By the end of the 1980s, Soviet armoured and motorized rifle divisions each contained up to three battalions of the 2S3, totalling as many as 54 weapons. The 2S3 mounts an adapted version of the D-20 towed field howitzer, and the chassis is the modified Objekt 123 tracked vehicle which also powers the 2K11 Krug air defence missile system.

The 152mm (6in) 2S19 MSTA self-propelled howitzer ushered in a new generation of mobile

▲ **2S3 Akatsiya M1973 SP howitzer**

Russian Ground Forces / 20th Guards Motor Rifle Division, 2008

The 2S3 Akatsiya provided direct fire support to Soviet and Russian armoured and motorized rifle divisions. Its heavy gun is fitted atop the shortened chassis of the SA-4 air defence missile system. Equipped with nuclear, biological and chemical defences, improved armour, and night vision equipment, it was usually serviced by a crew of six, two of whom stood behind the vehicle to handle ammunition.

Specifications

Crew: 6	Engine: 390kW (520hp) V12 diesel
Weight: 24,945kg (54,880lb)	Speed: 55km/h (34mph)
Length: 8.4m (27ft 6.7in)	Road range: 300km (186 miles)
Width: 3.2m (10ft 6in)	Armament: 1 x 152mm (6in) howitzer
Height: 2.8m (9ft 2.25in)	

▲ **2S19 MSTA SP howitzer**

Russian Ground Forces / 131st Motor Rifle Brigade, 2008

Development of the 2S19 as a replacement for the aging 2S3 self-propelled howitzer began in 1985, and the weapon entered service with the Soviet armed forces in 1989. Its 152mm (6in) main armament was modified from the 2A65 towed howitzer, and in 2008 the Russians introduced an improved version which incorporated an automatic fire-control system.

Specifications

Crew: 5	Engine: 630kW (840hp) V-84A diesel
Weight: 42,000kg (92,593lb)	Speed: 60km/h (37mph)
Length: 7.15m (23ft 5in)	Road range: 500km (311 miles)
Width: 3.38m (11ft)	Armament: 1 x 152mm (6in) howitzer
Height: 2.99m (9ft 9in)	

armour for the Soviet Union and later the forces of the Russian Federation. Mounting a modified version of the 2A65 152mm (6in) towed howitzer, the 2S19 is capable of firing up to eight rounds per minute. The weapon incorporates the chassis of the modern T-80 main battle tank and the reliable engine of the T-72. Intended as a replacement for the 2S3, it is equipped with an automatic loader, protection against nuclear, biological and chemical weapons, night vision equipment and improved armour

protection. The weapon fires high-explosive fragmentation rounds as well as smoke and chemical shells, and the laser-guided Krasnopol munition. It is also nuclear-capable.

Based on the 8X8 Tatra 813 truck, the 152mm (6in) DANA self-propelled howitzer was introduced by Czech designers in the 1970s and remains active with the armies of Georgia, the Czech Republic, Libya, Poland and Slovakia. During the South Ossetia War, four DANAs of the Georgian forces were

▲ DANA SP howitzer

Georgian Army / Joint Artillery Brigade, 2008

Developed in Czechoslovakia as a wheeled alternative to the expense of the Soviet 2S3 self-propelled 152mm (6in) howitzer, the DANA incorporated the chassis of the Tatra 813 truck and an enclosed turret mount for the main weapon. The DANA was one of the first artillery systems to introduce an autoloader which could load a shell with the barrel at any elevation.

Specifications	
Crew: 4/5	Engine: 257kW (345hp) V12 diesel
Weight: 23,000kg (50,600lb)	Speed: 80km/h (49.71mph)
Length: 10.5m (34ft 5in)	Road range: 600km (375 miles)
Width: 2.8m (9ft 2in)	Armament: 1 x 152mm (6in) gun, plus
Height: 2.6m (8ft 6in)	1 x 12.7mm (0.5in) HMG

▲ 2S7 Pion SP gun

Georgian Army / Joint Artillery Brigade, 2008

The 203mm (8in) 2S7 Pion self-propelled gun entered service in the mid-1970s with the main armament situated atop the chassis of the T-80 main battle tank and mounted externally. The 2S7 is capable of firing conventional and rocket-assisted ammunition. During the South Ossetia War, the Georgian Army deployed several of these weapons which had been acquired from Ukraine.

Specifications	
Crew: 7	Engine: 630kW (840hp) V-46-I V12 diesel
Weight: 47,246kg (46.5 tons)	Speed: 50km/h (31mph)
Length: 10.5m (34ft 5in)	Road range: 650km (404 miles)
Width: 3.38m (11ft)	Armament: 1 x 203mm (8in) howitzer
Height: 3m (9ft 10in)	

reported destroyed by Russian ground-attack aircraft while three were captured. The weapon was meant to supply the direct fire support needed for infantry operations without the expense of purchasing the 2S3 from the Soviets, and through more than 30 years of service over 750 DANAs have been manufactured.

The heaviest gun deployed to South Ossetia, the 203mm (8in) 2S7 Pion, or Peony, was first seen in the West in 1975 and consists of the hull of the T-80 main battle tank and an externally mounted gun. Its crew of seven can ready the gun to fire within five minutes and prepare the tracked chassis for displacement with as little as three minutes' notice. Four 203mm (8in) shells are carried aboard the 2S7, while a support vehicle is usually close by with additional rounds. To date, more than 1000 2S7s have been built, and the system has been operated by several former Soviet republics and Eastern Bloc nations.

▲ 9K22 Tunguska

Russian Ground Forces / 67th Separate Anti-Aircraft Brigade, 2008

The 9K22 Tunguska air defence weapon incorporates twin 30mm (1.2in) autocannon and the 9M311 air defence missile. Developed in the 1970s as a counter to low-flying tank-destroyer aircraft, the Tunguska entered service with the Red Army in 1982. Its 30mm (1.2in) guns generate a combined rate of fire of up to 5000 rounds per minute, while the semi-automatic command to line of sight (SACLOS), two-stage, solid-fuel missile is detonated by a radio fuse.

Specifications

Configuration: two-stage, solid fuel	Launch weight: 57kg (126lb)
Deployment: mobile	Range: 3500m (11,000ft)
Length: 2.56m (8ft 5in)	Secondary armament: twin 30mm (1.2in) cannon

▲ BM-21 rocket launcher

Russian Ground Forces / 9th Motor Rifle Division, 2008

Developed in the early 1960s as a successor to the original Katyusha multiple rocket launcher of World War II fame, the BM-21 Grad, or Hail, has been in service around the world for nearly 50 years. It mounts a bank of up to 40 122mm (4.8in) rocket tubes, which may be fired at a rate of two rounds per second, atop the Ural 375D 6X6 truck. The weapons carry high-explosive fragmentation, cluster or incendiary warheads.

Specifications

Crew: 4	System combat weight: 13,700kg (13.48 tons)
Calibre: 122mm (4.8in)	Range: 20.37km (12.66 miles)
Rocket length: 3.226m (10ft 7in)	Rate of fire: 2 rounds per second
Rocket weight: 77.5kg (171lb)	

Russian air defence

1992–PRESENT

During the last decade of its existence, the Soviet Union significantly upgraded its short-range air defence missile capabilities, and these types proved their usefulness in later conflicts.

DURING THE 2008 SOUTH OSSETIA WAR, the Russian Air Force was reported to have lost several aircraft. Three of these were Sukhoi Su-25 close-support attack aircraft, while a fourth was a Tupolev Tu-22 strategic bomber. Although it may not be unusual for an air force to sustain losses in combat, the irony of the Ossetia shooting-downs stems from the fact that these planes were most likely lost to air defence missiles initially deployed during the last years of the Soviet Union and fielded by the small Georgian armed forces against the Russians in South Ossetia. Therefore, it must be concluded that the Russians had failed at least in part to develop or maintain countermeasures against the missiles they had inherited.

Gadfly and Gopher

Although these losses in no way threatened Russian air supremacy, they indicated a pronounced gap in the effectiveness of Russian aerial countermeasures and jamming equipment in relation to the improvements which had been incorporated in two air defence missile systems during the late 1970s. These were the 9K37M1 Buk-1M medium-range missile system, identified by NATO as the SA-11 Gadfly, and the 9K35 Strela-10 short-range missile system, known to NATO observers as the SA-13 Gopher. Intended to replace the SA-6 Gainful and SA-9 Gaskin air defence missiles which had been in service since the 1960s, the Gadfly and Gopher missiles entered service with the Soviet armed forces in 1979 at roughly the same time that the tracked 9K22 Tunguska combined missile and 30mm (1.2in) cannon air defence system was entering service as well. This was due in part to a cost-saving initiative.

The sophisticated radar, nicknamed Snow Drift, of the 9K37M1 Buk, or Beech, is capable of tracking up to six individual targets at the same time and engages fixed-wing aircraft, helicopters and cruise missiles. Thought to be effective up to 90 per cent of the time,

Specifications

Configuration: single-stage, solid fuel
Deployment: mobile
Length: 5.55m (18ft 2in)
Diameter: 860mm (33.86in)
Launch weight: 690kg (1521lb)
Range: 30km (19 miles)
Launch preparation time: 5 minutes

▲ **9K37M1 Buk-1M (SA-11 Gadfly)**
Russian Ground Forces / 66th Guards Motor Rifle Regiment, 1994
The SA-11 Gadfly, officially known as the 9K37M1 Buk-1M to the Soviets and then the armed forces of the Russian Federation, entered service with the Red Army in 1979 as an eventual replacement for the medium-range SA-6 Gainful air defence missile system. Incorporating numerous improvements, such as advanced radar and guidance systems, the SA-11 is capable of tracking up to six separate targets simultaneously and is effective against fixed-wing aircraft, helicopters and cruise missiles.

the system is capable of rapid movement, displacing in as little as five minutes. Along with the Snow Drift radar, the system consists of the TELAR (transporter-erector-launcher and radar) vehicle which is a variant of the GM-569 tracked chassis. A standard battalion consists of a command vehicle, six TELAR vehicles, and support vehicles which carry missile reloads. The missile itself is typically a variant of the 9M38 with a high-explosive fragmentation warhead which is detonated by a proximity fuse.

The SA-13 Gopher, known as the 9K35 Strela-10 (Arrow) to the Russians, consists of a modified MT-LB tracked chassis and is capable of firing either the 9M37 missile or the earlier 9K31 mounted by the SA-9 Gaskin air defence system. The missiles are visually aimed and utilize infrared guidance against low-flying targets. Known as Hat Box, the SA-13 radar is situated between two missile pods and provides the range to the target. Four radar antennae are positioned at each corner of the rear deck of the chassis. The 9M37 missile is typically capable of a speed approaching Mach 2. It weighs approximately 40kg (88lb), and it is 2.2m (7ft 3in) in length.

During Operation Desert Storm in 1991, the SA-13 was reportedly responsible for shooting down at least two US low-flying A-10 Thunderbolt 'Warthog' ground-attack aircraft, and it is likely that the system damaged several others. In Kosovo, Serbian forces deployed the SA-13 and were known to have damaged a pair of A-10s.

Great Grumble

The long reach of Soviet air defence missiles was extended in the late 1970s with the introduction of the SA-10 Grumble, officially known as the S-300 missile. The S-300 also spawned subsequent variants, the SA-12 Giant/Gladiator and the SA-20 Gargoyle. The S-300 entered service with Soviet forces in 1978, and the system has undergone a series of upgrades over the last 30 years. It consists of the 5P85-1 vehicle – which is a combined truck and trailer – surveillance and low-altitude radar, and the sophisticated 30N6 fire-control system. A variety of missiles are available depending on the range to the target and each delivers a high-explosive fragmentation warhead weighing up to 150kg (330lb). In 2007, the Russian Federation agreed to sell numerous S-300 systems to the Islamic Republic of Iran; however, the governments of the United States and Israel objected and the sale has not been concluded.

The basic SA-10 was intended to defend major Soviet cities against cruise-missile attack, and during the mid-1980s at least 80 examples of the system were deployed, with many of these forming a defensive cordon around Moscow. Although there is no official record of the SA-10 in combat, it is considered by Western analysts to be a highly capable system. It is fielded by several former Soviet republics and client states today.

Specifications

Configuration: single-stage, solid fuel

Deployment: mobile

Length: 2.19m (7ft 3in)

Diameter: 120mm (4.72in)

Launch weight: 41kg (90lb)

Range: 5km (3.1 miles)

Launch preparation time: 3 minutes

▲ **ZRK-BD 9K35 Strela-10 (SA-13 Gopher)**

Russian Ground Forces / 28th Guards Tank Regiment, 1996

The ZRK-BD Strela-10 air defence missile, designated the SA-13 Gopher by NATO, entered service with the Soviet Red Army in 1979 as a short-range, optically aimed and infrared-guided system which was intended to replace the SA-9 Gaskin. The SA-13 was capable of firing both the 9M37 missile which was its primary armament and the 9K31 which originally was fielded with the Gaskin. The SA-13 is mounted atop the modified chassis of the tracked MT-LB vehicle and its operational range is 500km (311 miles). The SA-13 system vehicle is known as a TELAR (transporter-erector-launcher and radar).

▲ **S-300 (SA-10 Grumble)**
Russian Ground Forces / 5th Air Defence Brigade, 2003
The S-300 air defence missile, known in NATO nomenclature as the SA-10 Grumble, entered service with Soviet forces in 1978, initially as a defence against cruise missiles although later versions were adapted for use against incoming ballistic missiles. By the mid-1980s, at least 80 of these transporter-erector-launcher vehicles, which include a truck-and-trailer combination designated the 5P85-1, were reportedly in service protecting major Soviet cities. An improved version, the S-400 (NATO SA-21) entered service with Russian forces in 2004.

Specifications	
Configuration: single-stage, solid fuel	
Deployment: mobile	
Length: 7.5m (24ft 7in)	
Diameter: 500mm (19.69in)	
Launch weight: 1800kg (3968lb)	
Range: 200km (124 miles)	
Launch preparation time: 5 minutes	

War in Iraq and Afghanistan

2001–PRESENT

A decade on from the end of the Gulf War, the world was a very different place. Saddam Hussein threatened the use of weapons of mass destruction, and the arduous War on Terror had begun.

THE WAR ON TERROR and the looming threat of weapons of mass destruction compelled an armed coalition, including NATO countries, to commit troops and military hardware to preserve security in the Middle East and elsewhere. Since his army had been defeated decisively during the Gulf War of 1991, Saddam Hussein had rebuilt the Iraqi war machine into an apparent threat to peace in the Middle East once again. Using chemical weapons against the separatist Kurds in northern Iraq and brutally suppressing an uprising in the south around the major port city of Basra, the Iraqi strongman caused growing concern in the West regarding his willingness to plunge the Middle East into another destabilizing war of conquest.

Simultaneously, the horrific events of 11 September 2001 confronted the United States, Great Britain and other nations with the stark reality that Islamic fundamentalism and its accompanying philosophy of Jihad, or holy war, against the West constituted a very real threat to the safety and security of the world.

In response to these dual threats, the armed forces of numerous nations were mobilized in a coalition which moved to quell the menace. From bases in Saudi Arabia, Kuwait, Bahrain, the United Arab Emirates and other locations, logistical planning began in earnest in 2002 as the deadline for Iraq to comply with United Nations resolution 1441 approached. The resolution had set a deadline for Iraq to disclose any and all of its weapons of mass destruction capabilities and allow UN inspectors on the ground inside the country to verify these disclosures. US President George W. Bush had promised to authorize military intervention in Iraq in the event of non-compliance, asserting that Saddam Hussein's unwillingness to comply would trigger the provisions of earlier UN resolutions which were enacted during the Gulf War period.

Beyond Babylon

Although Secretary of State Colin Powell had addressed a plenary session of the UN Security

Council in February 2003 and outlined US concerns and 'evidence' of Iraqi weapons of mass destruction, the discovery of such weapons proved elusive during the actual invasion which followed, calling into question the legitimacy of the invasion. Nevertheless, the record amassed by Saddam Hussein during the years of authoritarian rule by his Baath Party had contributed greatly to his own demise.

Aside from chemical and biological weapons, his nuclear programme was considered a clear threat to Israel, and as early as 1981 the Israelis had bombed a nuclear reactor which was under construction in Iraq and could have potentially produced fuel for a nuclear weapon. During the Iran–Iraq War of the 1980s, Saddam Hussein had enlisted the services of Canadian astrophysicist Gerald Bull, who was widely known for his research into 'super guns', artillery pieces capable of firing shells tipped with nuclear warheads. During the Gulf War, components of such weapons were discovered by Coalition troops and intercepted in transit from various countries.

Two big guns, known as Baby Babylon and Big Babylon, had been under construction in Iraq, with Baby Babylon actually placed in an excavated position

for testing in the summer of 1989. Baby Babylon was impressive enough with a bore of 350mm (13.8in) and a barrel of roughly 52m (170ft) in length. The weapon was installed 145km (90 miles) north of Baghdad at Jabal Hamrayn, and its range was estimated at approximately 668km (415 miles). Big Babylon was conceptualized on a truly gargantuan scale, with a barrel which was 152m (500ft) in length and 1500 tonnes (1476 tons) in weight, and with a bore of one metre (3.3ft). Had Big Babylon become operational, it would have provided further data for Bull's development of an even bigger weapon under his HARP (High Altitude Research Project) programme. One HARP design consisted of a 91m (300ft) barrel weighing 1905 tonnes (1875 tons).

Super guns aside, Coalition and NATO planners respected even the conventional artillery capabilities of the Iraqi Army and acknowledged the difficulty of tracking the rocket launchers, heavy mortars and shoulder-fired weapons of the Al Qaeda and Taliban forces. They were also well aware of the need for air-transportable field artillery and self-propelled guns which could keep pace with advancing infantry during sustained ground campaigns.

▲ **Fire support**

US Army artillerymen calibrate their 105mm (4.1in) howitzer to provide fire support at a forward operating base near Kalsu, Iraq, 2007. The artillerymen are with Alpha Battery, 2nd Battalion, 377th Parachute Field Artillery Regiment.

Iraq
2003

Rapid Coalition movement, supported by field artillery and self-propelled guns, resulted in the reduction of the Iraqi Army and the capture of Baghdad and Basra.

WITH HIS COUNTRY on the brink of invasion, Saddam Hussein's Iraqi Army consisted in part of at least three armoured divisions, three mechanized infantry divisions and 11 infantry divisions. While these formations have been estimated at actually 70 to 80 per cent of their official strength, they still constituted a potent fighting force. Along with more than 2500 assorted field artillery pieces, self-propelled guns, multiple launch rocket systems and surface-to-surface missiles, the Iraqis also possessed substantial man-portable anti-tank weapons and surface-to-air missiles of Soviet origin.

Iraqi air defence

In addition to the Soviet-era ZSU-23-4, ZSU-57-2, M1939 twin 37mm (1.5in) and assorted guns of 85mm (3.3in), 100mm (3.9in) and 130mm (5.1in) calibre, the Iraqis fielded a variety of air defence missiles, including the SA-2, SA-6, SA-9, SA-13 and SA-16. While several of these were carried atop tracked or wheeled transporter-erector-launcher

IRAQI ARMY ARTILLERY, 2003		
Type	**Weapon**	**Strength**
Towed Artillery	105mm (M-56 pack) 122mm (D-74; D-30; M1938) 130mm (M-46; Type 59-1) 155mm (G-5; GHN-45; M114)	1900
Self-propelled Artillery	122mm (2SI) 152mm (2S3) 155mm (M109A1/A2; AUF-1 (GCT))	200
Multiple Rocket Launchers	107mm 122mm (BM-21) 127mm (ASTROS II) 132mm (BM-13/16) 262mm ('Ababeel-100')	200
Mortars	81mm 120mm 160mm (M1943) 240mm	–
Surface-to-Surface Missiles	FROG (Free Rocket Over Ground)	50
	Scud	6

▲ **BM-21 rocket launcher**

Iraqi Republican Guard / Hammurabi Armoured Division / 8th Mechanized Brigade, 2003

The Soviet-era BM-21 multiple launch rocket system was prominent among the weapons deployed by Iraqi Republican Guard and regular army divisions during Operation Iraqi Freedom. Although it was highly mobile, the BM-21 proved susceptible to Coalition air power and its performance was average at best when compared with more modern MLRS platforms such as the 127mm (5in) ASTROS II.

Specifications

Crew: 4

Calibre: 122mm (4.8in)

Rocket length: 3.226m (10ft 7in)

Rocket weight: 77.5kg (171lb)

System combat weight: 13,700kg (13.48 tons)

Range: 20.37km (12 miles)

Rate of fire: 2 rounds per second

Specifications

Crew: 4

Weight: 29,750kg (29.28 tons)

Length: 6.19m (20ft 3in)

Width: 3.15m (10ft 3in)

Height: 3.24m (10ft 7in)

Engine: 302kW (405hp) Detroit Diesel

Speed: 56km/h (35mph)

Road range: 405km (252 miles)

Armament: 1 x M126 155mm (6.1in) howitzer

▲ M109A6 Paladin SP gun

US Marine Corps / 1st Marine Expeditionary Force / 11th Marine Regiment, 2003

The standard self-propelled howitzer of the US Army and Marine Corps, the 155mm (6.1in) M109A6 Paladin was the latest of a series of improvements to the M109 design which had entered service more than 40 years earlier. The M109A6 was used exclusively by the US forces and has not been exported to other countries. The Paladin has been described as an all-new system in comparison to earlier M109 variants and incorporates the latest in explosive reactive armour and an internal navigation system.

SP Artillery Battalion, US Army, 2007

The self-propelled artillery battalion of the US Army during Operation Iraqi Freedom incorporated a headquarters and service battery and three firing batteries equipped with a complement of at least 18 M109A6 Paladin 155mm (6.1in) self-propelled howitzers, which were assigned to heavy brigade combat teams and fire brigades. Each Paladin battery consists of a battery headquarters, two firing platoons of three sections and a support platoon. The support platoon includes two ammunition sections; maintenance, supply and food service sections; and platoon headquarters. A battery operations centre provides fire-direction control.

ORGANIZATION

US SP Artillery Battalion

HQ

1 Firing Battery — HQ — 1 2 Sup

2 Firing Battery — HQ — 1 2 Sup

3 Firing Battery — HQ — 1 2 Sup

HHS Battery — HQ

Battery 1 (6 x M109A6 Paladin SP guns)

Battery 2 (6 x M109A6 Paladin SP guns)

Battery 3 (6 x M109A6 Paladin SP guns)

vehicles, the SA-16 Gimlet, as it was designated by NATO, was a man-portable weapon which was known to have shot down a Coalition Panavia Tornado fighter-bomber during the Gulf War. Its light weight of 10.8kg (24lb) allowed for rapid deployment and target acquisition.

Officially known to the Soviets and later the Russian ground forces as the 9K38 Igla, or Needle, the SA-16 entered service in 1981 and was later upgraded to the SA-18 Grouse. Its infrared guidance system, IFF (Identification Friend or Foe) capability and countermeasure resistance combine in a formidable short-range weapon.

Howitzer hammer

Operation Iraqi Freedom was a tour de force for Coalition artillery. One defence analyst observed that it 'proved to be the deciding factor in many of the conflicts – although the enemy artillery outnumbered and outranged the coalition force FA [field artillery]. The FA in Operation Iraqi Freedom was the lowest ratio of artillery pieces to troops in war since before World War I. Artillery fires came at a premium with lines of communication stretched from the Kuwait border to Baghdad ... The magnificent soldier and Marine field artilleryman adapted to changes while rapidly moving great distances, made critical decisions independently in decentralized operations with little or no sleep and executed fire missions with extraordinary precision in constant movements to contact, meeting

engagements and urban operations as part of the most effective joint fires team in history....'

Along with the 155mm (6.1in) M198 towed field howitzer, the 155mm (6.1in) M109A6 Paladin served as the workhorse of US artillery during Operation Iraqi Freedom. Although the M109 had been in service for more than 40 years and undergone numerous upgrades, the Paladin was virtually a new system. Its M126 main weapon could produce a rate of fire of up to four rounds per minute, while the vehicle's extended operational range of 405km (252 miles) allowed it to work closely with front-line troops during offensive operations. Its sophisticated target-acquisition and gun-stabilization equipment allow the Paladin to operate in varied climates and weather conditions, while its crew of four is protected by advanced explosive reactive armour and nuclear, biological and chemical defences.

The M198 equipped units of the US Army and Marine Corps, with one American infantry division's supporting artillery firing nearly 14,000 rounds during the ground campaign. A number of these were precision-guided M898 SADARM submunition sense-and-destroy rounds, which home in on enemy targets, particularly light armoured vehicles and tanks, within a radius of the 155mm (6.1in) shell which bursts above the target. As Marines cleared the insurgent stronghold of Fallujah, one

Specifications

Crew: 5

Weight: 45,000kg (99,225lb)

Length: 7.2m (23ft 8in)

Width: 3.4m (11ft 2in)

Height: 3m (9ft 10in)

Engine: 492kW (660hp) Cummins V8 diesel

Speed: 55km/h (34mph)

Road range: 240km (150 miles)

Armament: 1 x 155mm (6.1in) howitzer, plus

1 x 12.7mm (0.5in) MG

▲ **AS-90 SP gun**

British Army / 1st Armoured Division / 7th Armoured Brigade / 3rd Royal Horse Artillery, 2003

Dubbed the AS-90 (Artillery System for the 90s), this 155mm (6.1in) self-propelled gun was developed during the 1980s and entered service in 1993 as a replacement for the aging British complement of M109 weapons. Its crew of five is capable of firing three rounds in a ten-second burst, six rounds per minute for up to three minutes or two rounds per minute for a period of one hour. Manufactured by Vickers Shipbuilding and Engineering, it initially equipped five regiments of the Royal Artillery and the Royal Horse Artillery.

soldier reported that the M198 had made 'everybody get out of town'.

Fighting alongside the US 1st Marine Expeditionary Force, the British 1st Armoured Division was augmented by the attachment of the 3rd Royal Horse Artillery. For the action, the regiment had increased its complement of AS-90 155mm (6.1in) self-propelled guns to 32. In the event, it provided tactical fire support to four battle groups within the 7th Armoured Brigade and constituted one of the largest formations of artillery assembled by the British Army since World War II.

Along with the US 11th Marine Regiment – an artillery unit – elements of the 3rd Royal Horse Artillery and the 7th Royal Horse Artillery became an effective fighting unit despite inherent challenges such as incompatible communications equipment. As the Coalition forces fought their way through the strategic town of Naseriyah, British guns fired more than 9000 rounds of 155mm (6.1in) ammunition and 13,000 105mm (4.1in) rounds.

Artillery officer Brigadier Andrew R. Gregory praised the performance of the AS-90 and the towed 105mm (4.1in) L118 Light Gun. 'The AS-90 howitzer proved to be robust, versatile and provided the range, accuracy and, when required, significant weight of fire to degrade almost all enemy actions … The L118 light gun also proved its worth, particularly when it was lifted along with sufficient ammunition onto the Al Faw peninsula early in the operation.'

▲ **M1045 HMMWV TOW missile carrier**

US Army / 3rd Infantry Division / 2nd Brigade, 2003

The M1045 HMMWV is one of several variants of the ubiquitous M998 'Humvee' family of light military vehicles. This HMMWV (High-Mobility Multi-purpose Wheeled Vehicle) mounts the wire-guided TOW anti-tank missile and is equipped with supplemental armour for the protection of its crew. The TOW firing platform is capable of 360-degree traverse to engage enemy armour. Another variant, the M1046, includes the TOW missile launcher and a powered towing winch.

Specifications

Crew: 4	Engine: 112.5kW (150hp) 6.2-litre V8 fuel-
Weight: 2359kg (5200lb)	injected diesel
Length: 4.57m (15ft)	Speed: 89km/h (55mph)
Width: 2.16m (7ft 1in)	Road range: 563km (350 miles)
Height: 1.83m (6ft)	Armament: TOW anti-tank missile

Specifications

Configuration: two-stage, solid fuel
Deployment: fixed or mobile
Length: 2.4m (94.5in)
Diameter: 160mm (6.3in)
Launch weight: 63kg (139lb)
Range: 6.2km (3.9 miles)
Launch preparation time: 8 seconds

▲ **Roland surface-to-air missile**

Iraqi Army / 5th Mechanized Division / 20th Mechanized Brigade, 2003

The Roland air defence missile was a joint development by France and Germany during the 1960s and has remained in service for decades. The system was also purchased by the US Army and equipped several Iraqi air defence units during both Operation Desert Storm and Operation Iraqi Freedom. Credited with shooting down a US A-10 Thunderbolt ground-attack aircraft during Iraqi Freedom, the Roland was deployed by the Iraqis mounted on the bed of an 8X8 truck or as a self-propelled weapon atop the modified chassis of the AMX-30 main battle tank.

Afghanistan

2001–PRESENT

The War on Terror has focused attention on light, air-transportable artillery systems which maintain critical firepower superiority in rugged terrain.

ALMOST A DECADE OF FIGHTING in Afghanistan has emphasized the need for durable, lightweight artillery which may be airlifted to critical areas and recovered quickly for maintenance and upkeep. The vast mountainous regions of the country often restrict the movement of self-propelled artillery; therefore, towed weapons have retained a signicant role in the fight against the Taliban and Al Qaeda strongholds.

During the war in Afghanistan, US and British forces, as well as contingents of troops from other NATO countries, have deployed the M777 155mm (6.1in) ultralight field howitzer, the GIAT LG-1 and L118 Light Gun 105mm (4.1in) towed howitzers, and self-propelled weapons including the M109A6 Paladin and AS-90 155mm (6.1in) howitzers. Artillery units of the Afghan Army have brought the Soviet-era D-30 122mm (4.8in) towed howitzer into action following extensive training by British forces.

'I'm extremely pleased with what I've seen …' reported one British officer. 'The ANA [Afghan National Army] are progressing extremely quickly, and you can really see the progress that is being made. This is just an example of how much better the ANA is getting as a fighting force. The advantage of having extra D-30 guns is that we can augment our already existing guns within Afghanistan and particularly in Helmand in the fight against the insurgency in southern Afghanistan.'

A versatile field artillery weapon, the British L118 Light Gun has been in service since the 1970s and widely exported. It was developed by the Royal Armament Research and Development Establishment (RARDE), and production was undertaken in 1975 by the Royal Ordnance Factory, Nottingham. The weapon traces its lineage to the World War II-era QF 25-pounder and replaced the Italian OTO Melara Mod 56 105mm (4.1in) pack howitzer and several small mortars in service with the British Army. A modified version of the L118, the L119A, has been placed in service with the US Army.

British gun crews serving in Afghanistan have nicknamed the L118 the Dragon due to its excellent results in action against the Taliban. The weapon can acquire and engage a target at a distance of three kilometres (1.86 miles) within five seconds. An

7TH PARACHUTE REGIMENT, ROYAL HORSE ARTILLERY, 2007	
Unit	Strength
F (Sphinx) Parachute Battery	4
G Parachute Battery (Mercer's Troop)	4
H Parachute Battery (Ramsay's Troop)	4
I Parachute Battery (Bull's Troop)	4
Aviation Tactical Group	–
LAD REME	–

7th Parachute Regiment, Royal Horse Artillery, 16th Air Assault Brigade, British Army, 2007

The only parachute artillery regiment of the British Army, the 7th is equipped with the L118 Light Gun. It consists of six batteries and has actively participated in several modern conflicts, including the wars in Afghanistan, Iraq and Kosovo. The 105mm (4.1in) L118 has proved an effective and highly mobile field artillery weapon, particularly when deployed in support of light infantry and airborne units. Serving with the 16th Air Assault Brigade, elements of the 7th Parachute Regiment have deployed the L118 by air and with light ground-transport vehicles. The weapon's maximum rate of fire is up to eight rounds per minute.

Battery (4 x L118 Light Guns)

automatic pointing system (APS) allows the gun to be unlimbered and in action within 30 seconds. At 1158kg (4100lb), the L118 is often towed by medium-weight vehicles such as the Land Rover or Humvee or airlifted by Chinook or Wessex helicopter. Its rate of fire is up to eight rounds per minute.

The more powerful M777 155mm (6.1in) howitzer incorporates titanium in its construction which accounts for a considerable reduction in weight compared with predecessors such as the M198 155mm (6.1in) howitzer. The M777 is light enough to be transported by the V-22 Osprey aircraft or the CH-47 Chinook helicopter. On several occasions the M777 has worked in cooperation with tanks and self-propelled artillery, firing at a maximum rate of up to five rounds per minute.

As in Iraq, the M982 Excalibur extended-range guided artillery shell has been used with success in Afghanistan. Fired from the M777, the Excalibur has been quite effective against caves and remote Taliban command or training centres. Sergeant Henry Selzer of the US Army's 173rd Airborne Brigade Combat Team noted that the M777 and Excalibur combination was fired for the first time at Camp Blessing in the Kunar Province of northeast Afghanistan. 'The M777 is designed to be a digitally programmed weapon,' he said. 'The fuse setting was performed by the Enhanced Portable Inductive Artillery Fuse Setter, placed on the tip of the round, sending a digital message containing the coordinate for the round to find.' Captain Ryan Berdiner of C Battery, 3rd Battalion, 321st Field Artillery

▲ M777 155mm Ultralight Field Howitzer

US Army / 173rd Airborne Brigade Combat Team / 321st Field Artillery Regiment / 3rd Battalion, 2009

Specifications

Crew: 5

Calibre: 155mm (6.1in)

Elevation: - 5 degrees to + 70 degrees

Weight: 4182kg (9200lb)

Range: 40km (25 miles)

Muzzle velocity: 827m/sec (2713ft/sec)

The M777 Ultralight Field Howitzer enhances the capabilities of heavy field artillery by providing a lighter and more mobile alternative to the M198 towed howitzer which remains in service with the armed forces of numerous countries. The M777 was developed by BAE Systems' Global Combat Systems Division and entered service with the US Army and Marine Corps in 2005. It has also been deployed by Canadian and Australian artillery units.

The M777 utilizes a digital fire-control system similar to that which equips the M109A6 Paladin self-propelled howitzer and is transported by aircraft, helicopter or medium truck.

▲ GIAT LG-1 towed howitzer

Canadian Army / Royal Horse Artillery / 5th Heavy Artillery Regiment, 2006

The French GIAT LG-1 towed howitzer entered service with the Canadian armed forces in 1996 and provides a lightweight, airmobile weapon which is particularly suited to supporting fire in difficult terrain such as NATO troops have encountered in Afghanistan. The LG-1 is capable of an impressive rate of fire of 12 rounds per minute and weighs only 1520kg (3400lb). In mid-2005, the Canadian armed forces embarked on a programme to upgrade their LG-1 complement with an improved muzzle brake and larger carriage tyres.

Specifications

Crew: 5

Calibre: 105mm (4.1in)

Elevation: - 3 degrees to + 70 degrees

Weight: 1520kg (3400lb)

Range: 19.5km (12.1 miles)

Muzzle velocity: 490m/sec (1608ft/sec)

Regiment, added, 'By using the Excalibur we are mitigating a lot of collateral damage that other rounds may cause. The main purpose of the M777 is that it is more able to help the units in the Korengal Valley by providing more timely and accurate fire.'

The French 105mm (4.1in) LG-1 entered service in the mid-1990s and was specifically designed for rapid deployment. Its light weight of 1520kg (3400lb) reduces the useful life of the barrel; however, the weapon is capable of firing an impressive maximum of 12 rounds per minute. In addition to service in Afghanistan, the LG-1 has been deployed to the Balkans. The gun may be towed by light vehicles such as the Land Rover or Humvee and is also airmobile via parachute drop or delivery. Four guns may be transported in the cargo space of the C-130 transport aircraft. Firing the standard NATO 105mm (4.1in) round, the LG-1 may be taken in and out of service in less than 30 seconds.

Precision rocket

Having initially developed it to improve the accuracy of the M26 rocket, the US military continues to refine the GMLRS (Guided Multiple Launch Rocket System), which is compatible with the existing M270 or HIMARS launchers. Potential vulnerability to a new generation of accurate long-range rocket and artillery ammunition prompted research on the GMLRS, which extends the range of the older M26 to 60km (37.28 miles). The GMLRS currently includes two types of ammunition, the dual-purpose improved cluster munition (DPICM), which carries 404 bomblets, and the M31A1 rocket, with a single 91kg (200lb) high-explosive warhead. Each is guided by a global positioning system with internal measurement unit guidance.

The stated objective of the GMLRS is to provide greater range, more accurate fire and therefore better results with fewer rockets. It also enhances the shoot-and-scoot capabilities of the HIMARS and M270 launchers, which have seen action in both Iraq and Afghanistan. More than 150 GMLRS rockets were fired during Operation Iraqi Freedom, and reports indicate that the system has been in use against the Taliban as well, since its extended range and pinpoint accuracy are capable of striking enemy positions which would be difficult for ground troops to reach in force.

Fire and forget

The ability to displace quickly is a key to the survival of individual soldiers and small operating units which field portable missiles for use against armoured vehicles and hardened targets. In Afghanistan, the

Specifications

Crew: 3
Calibre: 227mm (8.94in)
Rocket length: 3.94m (12ft 11in)
Rocket weight: 360kg (675lb)
System combat weight: 10,886kg (24,000lb)
Range: 32km (20 miles)
Rate of fire: 6 rounds in 45 seconds

▲ **HIMARS MLRS**

US Army / 3rd Field Artillery Regiment / 5th Battalion, 2007

The HIMARS (High Mobility Artillery Rocket System) was deployed for the first time by the US Army in 2005 following a decade of development led by Lockheed Martin Missiles and Fire Control. The system was adopted by the US Marine Corps in 2002. Situated atop a 6X6 truck which is one of the latest in the army's FMTV (Family of Military Tactical Vehicles), the HIMARS carries six high-explosive rockets or a single ATACMS.

Taliban have been on the receiving end of the FGM-148 Javelin missile, which has been fielded by troops from several NATO countries. Intended as a replacement for the Dragon anti-tank missile, the Javelin was developed by divisions of Raytheon and Lockheed Martin beginning in the late 1980s and entered service in 1996.

During Operation Iraqi Freedom, the Javelin proved deadly against the T-54/55, T-62 and T-72 main battle tanks of the Republican Guard and the Iraqi Army. In Afghanistan, it has performed well against Taliban concentrations in buildings or urban settings as well as caves and mountainous strongholds. The Javelin's fire-and-forget technology allows the operator to immediately displace rather than linger in position to guide the weapon with wire or other means. In soft-launch mode, the missile is fired when ready; however, the rocket propulsion system does not fully engage until the missile reaches some distance from the launch site, minimizing backblast and any tell-tale exhaust signature. Its shaped high-explosive anti-tank (HEAT) warhead weighs 8.4kg (18.5lb) and is detonated by contact.

Specifications

Crew: 3

Calibre: 227mm (8.94in)

Rocket length: 3.94m (12ft 11in)

Rocket weight: 90kg (200lb)

System combat weight: 24,756kg (54,578lb)

Range: 60km (37 miles)

Rate of fire: 12 rounds in 60 seconds

▲ **Guided Multiple Launch Rocket System (GMLRS)**

US Army / 3rd Field Artillery Regiment / 5th Battalion, 2007

The GMLRS system provides the US Army and Marine Corps with additional defence against a new generation of precision-guided missiles and artillery shells, while also offering an improved strike capability over the older M26 rocket. The GMLRS includes improved range and economy of force, with fewer rockets required to accomplish a fire mission, while also minimizing collateral damage. Two types of GMLRS ammunition are currently in use, the M31A1 high-explosive projectile and the DPICM (dual-purpose improved cluster munition) which carries more than 400 bomblets.

▲ **FGM-148 Javelin**

US Army / 75th Ranger Regiment, 2005

The Javelin anti-tank missile was widely used during Operation Iraqi Freedom and recorded numerous successes against the Soviet-era main battle tanks deployed by the Iraqi forces. The weapon has also been deployed to Afghanistan and utilized against hardened Taliban targets. Its fire-and-forget technology allows the operator to displace quickly and minimizes the exhaust signature of the missile due to its soft launch, which also reduces backblast.

Specifications

Configuration: two-stage, solid fuel	Launch weight: 22.3kg (59lb)
Deployment: man-portable	Range: 2500m (2734 yards)
Length: 1.1m (43in)	Rate of fire: 3 rounds in 2 minutes
Diameter: 127mm (5in)	

▲ Raytheon Griffin

US Special Operations Command (SOCOM), Afghanistan, 2009

First developed in 2006 and deployed from around 2008, the Griffin is a precision-guided miniature missile designed to support US Special Forces in combat operations. Two versions of the missile have been produced: Griffin A is designed to be launched from aircraft such as the MC-130W Combat Spear Hercules; Griffin B is a tube-launched, forward-firing missile that can be carried by helicopters, unmanned aerial vehicles (UAVs) and ground vehicles such as the Humvee or a light truck. Targets are designated by a controller using a graphic interface with GPS/INS coordinates or direct laser guidance.

Specifications

Configuration: single missile, solid fuel

Deployment: aircraft, UAVs and ground vehicles

Length: 1092mm (43in)

Diameter: 140mm (5.5in)

Launch weight: 15kg (33lb)

Warhead weight: 5.9kg (13lb)

Guidance system: GPS/INS with laser terminal homing

Range: unknown

Recent developments
2000–PRESENT

Rapidly advancing technology continues to push the proverbial envelope in terms of the research and development of new artillery systems, while the modern battlefield serves as a proving ground for such weapons.

COOPERATION AMONG NATIONS in the development of new arms and related technology is nothing new. However, with increasing costs and complexity and limited resources such activities may well continue on an unprecedented scale. Although some cooperative ventures have failed in the past, others have been extraordinarily successful. One such endeavour in the sphere of field artillery is the M777 155mm (6.1in) howitzer. Its manufacturer is the British firm BAE Systems, while more than 70 per cent of its components are produced by US contractors and the weapon was tested in the United States at Camp Shelby, Mississippi, with final assembly taking place in the US.

The M777 has become a model of efficiency and was slated to eventually replace the 155mm (6.1in) M198 towed howitzer with the US Army and Marine Corps as well as the 105mm (4.1in) L118 Light Gun in use by British forces, thus providing a viable alternative to a 105mm (4.1in) weapon in terms of mobility while also packing a stronger punch.

Research on the M777 was begun by Vickers in the 1990s, and by 2010 as many as 650 examples of the weapon were expected to be in service with the US armed forces.

Russian response

One of the most advanced and versatile Russian field artillery weapons is the 120mm (4.7in) Nona-K 2B16 towed cannon. Research on the Nona-K was begun in the late 1980s following the Soviet military experience in Afghanistan, and the weapon was eventually produced in a towed and self-propelled version. Firing at a maximum rate of up to five rounds per minute, the Nona-K is capable of sufficient elevation to operate as an anti-tank gun, howitzer or mortar. The towed version is serviced by a crew of five and transported by the UAZ-469 or GAZ-66 4X4 trucks. With a range of 12km (7.46 miles), it weighs 1200kg (2646lb) and fires a variety of ammunition suitable for the varied targets being engaged. The towed Nona-K and its offspring were the product of cooperation between several design bureaux within the former Soviet Union, including the Precision Mechanical Engineering Central Research Institute. To facilitate rapid firing, the gun is equipped with a compressed-air system which clears the barrel and places a new round in the breech.

The self-propelled Nona-K has been produced in both an amphibious wheeled version designated the 2S23 and a tracked variant known as the 2S9. The tracked 2S9 is airmobile and deployed with Russian airborne artillery units. It consists of the 120mm (4.7in) gun in an enclosed turret atop the chassis of the BMD fighting vehicle. Its modern systems include nuclear, biological and chemical weapons safeguards and night-vision equipment.

▲ ADATS

Canadian Army / 4 Air Defence Regiment, 1995

The ADATS (Air Defence Anti-Tank System) entered service with the Canadian Army in 1989 as a combination air-and-armoured-vehicle-defence system mounted atop the modified chassis of the M113 armoured personnel carrier. The Swiss Oerlikon firm developed the system during the early 1980s, and it includes a bank of eight missiles with high-explosive fragmentation warheads which are tracked by electro-optical equipment following target surveillance and acquisition by radar. The missile's effective range is ten kilometres (6.2 miles).

Specifications

Configuration: single-stage, solid fuel
Deployment: mobile
Length: 2.08m (6ft 10in)
Diameter: 152mm (6in)
Launch weight: 51kg (112.5lb)
Range: 10km (6.2 miles)
Launch preparation time: 5 seconds

▲ 76mm Otomatic Air Defence Tank

Italian Army / never entered service

Developed primarily to defend ground troops from attack by helicopter and fixed-wing aircraft, the 76mm (3in) Otomatic Air Defence Tank entered trials during the late 1980s but was never accepted into service as the Italian Army maintains 20mm (0.79in) to 40mm (1.57in) weapons as primary air defence guns. Capable of operating in adverse weather conditions, the system's radar tracked targets to a distance of 15km (9.32 miles).

Specifications

Crew: 4	Engine: 562.5kW (750hp) MTU V10 multifuel
Weight: 47,000kg (46.26 tons)	Speed: 60km/h (37mph)
Length: 7.08m (23ft 3in)	Road range: 500km (310 miles)
Width: 3.25m (10ft 8in)	Armament: 1 x 76mm (3in) gun
Height: 3.07m (10ft 1in)	

Self-propelled successors

In 2002, the United States government cancelled the $11 billion XM2001 Crusader project, which had been intended to produce a replacement for the venerable M109 self-propelled howitzer, particularly its latest incarnation, the M109A6 Paladin. However, the Paladin was deemed sufficient for a time, while research continued under the auspices of the army's Future Combat Systems (FCS) programme. Meanwhile, British designers also abandoned an upgrade of the AS-90 howitzer known as the Braveheart. That project ended due to complications with propelling charges for several rounds which were to be compatible with the long, 52-calibre 155mm (6.1in) main weapon.

Following the failure of the SP70 project – a combined effort between Germany, the United Kingdom and Italy to produce a self-propelled 155mm (6.1in) howitzer during the 1970s – German designers embarked on their own project and produced the highly successful Panzerhaubitze 2000. A joint venture between Krauss-Maffei Wegmann and Rheinmetall, the PzH 2000 (Armoured Howitzer 2000) has been utilized in combat in the Balkans and in Afghanistan.

A Rheinmetall product which has been adopted by several other countries, the 155mm (6.1in) L52 howitzer main gun of the PzH 2000 is well known for an outstanding rate of fire of up to three rounds in nine seconds in burst situations, ten rounds in as little as 56 seconds and a sustained rate of up to 13 rounds per minute. Its chassis is supplied by Krauss-

▲ **SBAT 70 multiple rocket launcher**

Brazilian Army / 1st Artillery Battalion, 1995

Developed by the Brazilian firm Avibrás, the SBAT 70 is designed to fire multiple ordnance against varied targets such as armoured vehicles and troop concentrations. Its bank of 36 tubes is transported by a two-wheeled trailer. Originally conceived as an aircraft rocket, the SBAT 70 was reconfigured as a ground weapon and is operated by a crew of four. It has been offered for export.

Specifications

Crew: 4

Calibre: 70mm (2.75in)

Rocket length: 1.41m (55.5in)

Rocket weight: 11.7kg (29.8lb)

System combat weight: 1000kg (2204lb)

Range: 8500m (9295 yards)

Rate of fire: unknown

Specifications

Crew: 5	Engine: 745.7kW (1000hp) MTU 881 V12 diesel
Weight: 55,000kg (121,275lb)	Speed: 60km/h (27mph)
Length: 7.87m (25ft 10in)	Road range: 420km (260 miles)
Width: 3.37m (11ft)	Armament: 1 x 155mm (6.1in) L52 gun, plus
Height: 3.4m (11ft 2in)	1 x 7.62mm (0.3in) MG
	Radio: n/k

▲ **Panzerhaubitze 2000**

German Army / 1st Armoured Division

The self-propelled Panzerhaubitze 2000 provides heavy fire support to NATO troops in Afghanistan with its Rheinmetall 155mm (6.1in) L52 gun. The system has been selected by several nations to replace the aging M109 gun. It is operated by the armed forces of Germany, Italy, the Netherlands and Greece.

Maffei Wegmann and incorporates numerous components of the Leopard 1 main battle tank chassis. Wegmann also designed the turret.

Anti-tank tech

In response to a generation of improved main battle tanks, including the Russian T-90, Israeli Merkava, German Leopard 2 and US M1A1 Abrams, sophisticated anti-tank missiles are under development. The Russian 9M133 Kornet was reported in the hands of Hezbollah militants during the Israeli invasion of southern Lebanon in 2006, and its shaped HEAT charge is capable of penetrating up to 1190mm (47in) of armour protection. During one reported engagement, 11 Merkava tanks were damaged by Hezbollah fighters armed with the Kornet, which is usually carried by a two-man crew. The missile is also effective against low-flying aircraft, and has a range of 5000m (5468 yards).

In 2004, the Russian Ground Forces also deployed the AT-15 Springer anti-tank missile, which is officially known as the 9M123. Mounted atop the 9P157-2 tank-destroyer chassis, which is adapted from that of the BMP-3 fighting vehicle, the AT-15 tracks targets with radar and locks on with an onboard laser.

Although the United States cancelled its LOSAT (Line of Sight Anti-Tank) programme, the Compact Kinetic Energy Missile (CKEM) has been tested extensively, including a live-fire event which occurred in 2006 against a stationary T-72 tank. The CKEM delivers a kinetic energy penetrator warhead at a speed of up to Mach 6.5. The missile weighs 45kg (99lb) and has an estimated range of 10,000m (10,936 yards).

Future fire

In the coming years, more complex and capable artillery systems will emerge. Among those in research and development today, the BAE Systems NLOS (Non-Line-Of-Sight) cannon shows promise. Leveraging technology from the abandoned XM2001 Crusader project, the NLOS will combine the ultimate in shoot-and-scoot capability with light weight and a fully automated target-acquisition, gun-laying and firing system.

British engineers are also currently working on a new generation of artillery ordnance dubbed the ERO/MCS (Extended Range Ordnance/Modular Charge System). The project also includes upfitting the AS-90 self-propelled howitzer with the longer 155mm (6.1in) 52-calibre barrel from the 39-calibre version installed on many of the vehicles, thus extending the howitzer's range from nearly 25,000m (27,000 yards) to 30,000m (33,000 yards). In essence, the project is designed to

▼ 2S9 (A-222) Bereg SP gun

Russian Ground Forces / 1592nd Separate Self-Propelled Artillery Battalion, 2004

The 2S9 Bereg 130mm (5.1in) self-propelled gun was developed as a coastal artillery system and is mounted on a wheeled MAZ-543 8X8 transporter-erector. The transporter contains sophisticated radar tracking equipment and command structure. The weapon is intended to engage surface ships, fast attack boats and ground targets and is able to function in environments involving extreme countermeasures while taking on targets travelling as rapidly as 37km/h (23mph) within two minutes.

Specifications

Crew: 8
Weight: 43,700kg (96,340lb)
Length: 12.95m (42ft 6in)
Width: 3.1m (10ft 2in)
Height: 3.93m (12ft 10in)
Engine: 394kW (525hp) diesel
Speed: 63km/h (39mph)
Road range: 650km (404 miles)
Armament 1 x 130mm (5.1in) gun

also lengthen the service life of the entire AS-90 weapon system.

Although some military analysts are predicting the demise of artillery as it is known in the traditional sense, the future appears set to contradict that opinion. Considering the nature of modern warfare, it can also be asserted with confidence that the need for firepower delivered in a timely manner and with

pinpoint accuracy is greater today than ever before. Although other weapons such as futuristic aircraft will undoubtedly play an important role in armed conflicts of the twenty-first century, there remains no other force which can dominate a battlefield so thoroughly and on such a sustained basis as artillery.

▲ **Caesar 155mm self-propelled artillery system**
French Army / 40th Armoured Artillery Regiment, 2008
The French-designed Caesar 155mm (6.1in) self-propelled howitzer is mounted atop a Renault 6X6 truck. Developed by GIAT, the weapon is operated by a crew of five which can be reduced to three if necessary. It is air-transportable by heavy aircraft such as the C-130 or by CH-53 helicopter. The Caesar is also deployed by the Royal Thai Army and entered service in 2003. Saudi Arabia has also purchased a large number of the systems.

Specifications

Crew: 5	Engine: 180kW (240hp) 6-cylinder diesel
Weight: 17,700kg (17.4 tons)	Speed: 100km/h (62mph)
Length: 10m (32ft 10in)	Road range: 600km (373 miles)
Width: 2.55m (8ft 4in)	Armament: 1 x 155mm (6.1in) cannon
Height: 3.7m (12ft 2in)	

Specifications
Crew: 4
Weight: 33,500kg (73,855lb)
Length: 14.1m (46ft 3in)
Width: 3m (9ft 10in)
Height: 3.3m (10ft 10in)
Engine: 255kW (340hp) diesel
Speed: 70km/h (43.5mph)
Road range: 500km (311 miles)
Armament 1 x 155mm (6.1in) cannon

▲ **Archer FH77 BW L52 self-propelled howitzer**
Swedish Army / to be deployed 2011
BAE Systems Bofors of Sweden developed the Archer FH77 L52, which mounts a 155mm (6.1in) howitzer atop a wheeled 6X6 Volvo A30D chassis. The weapon is served by a crew of up to four. Its burst rate of fire is three rounds in 15 seconds, while its sustained rate is 75 rounds per hour and its intense rate is 20 rounds in two and a half minutes. The Archer is complete with onboard computerized fire-control and gun-laying systems. It is scheduled to enter service in 2011.

Bibliography

Bidwell, Shelford. *Artillery of the World*. Brassey's, London, 1977.

Crismon, Fred W. *U.S. Military Tracked Vehicles*. Motorbooks International, Osceola, Wisconsin, 1992.

Crismon, Fred W. *U.S. Military Wheeled Vehicles*. Motorbooks International, 1994.

Department of the Army, United States Army Intelligence and Security Command, United States Army Intelligence and Threat Analysis Center. *Soviet Army Operations*. U.S. Army, Arlington, Virginia, 1978.

Haskew, Michael E. *Artillery from the Civil War to the Present Day*. Metro Books, New York, 2008.

Hogg, Ian. *Tank Killing: Anti-Tank Warfare by Men and Machines*. Sarpedon, New York, 1996.

Hogg, Ian. *Twentieth Century Artillery*. Freidman/Fairfax Publishers, New York, 2000.

Jackson, Robert. *Tanks and Armoured Fighting Vehicles Visual Encyclopedia*. Amber Books Ltd., London, 2009.

Leyden, Andrew. *An After Action Report: Gulf War Debriefing Book*. Hellgate Press, Grants Pass, Oregon, 1997.

Mossman, Billy C. *United States Army in the Korean War: Ebb and Flow November 1950–July 1951*. Center of Military History United States Army, Washington, D.C., 1990.

Useful Websites

armchairgeneral.com
army-technology.com
defenseindustrydaily.com
eliteforces.info
enemyforces.net
fas.org
globalsecurity.org

history.army.mil
historyofwar.org
israelnewsagency.com
janes.com
militaryfactory.com
militaryhistoryonline.com
militaryphotos.net

military-today.com
o5m6.de
olive-drab.com
orbat.com
sinodefence.com
turretsandtracks.co.uk

Index

Page numbers in *italics* refer to illustrations.